LOWE'S
Let's Build Something Together™

complete home
decorating

complete home
decorating

STAFF FOR THIS BOOK

Text and Research: *Christine E. Barnes*

Senior Editor: *Sally W. Smith*

Associate Editor: *Linda J. Selden*

Design Consultants: *Annette M. Starkey,*
CKD, CBD, Living Environment Design;
Juliana Edlund, ASID

Art Director and Page Production:
Alice Rogers

Copy Editor: *Phyllis Elving*

Photo Director/Stylist:
JoAnn Masaoka Van Atta

Photo Researcher/Editor: *Cynthia Del Fava*

Illustrator: *Beverley Bozarth Colgan*

Color Palettes: *Christine E. Barnes*

Production Coordinator: *Eligio Hernandez*

Proofreader: *Alicia Eckley*

Indexer: *IRIS Indexing*

The talents and energies of many people went into
making this book. Special thanks to Ann Maguire
of Beehive Studios for her input on the color palettes
and to Sherry Snodgrass for the creation of the
presentation board on page 237.

ON THE COVER

Top: photo by *Mark Rutherford;* styling by
JoAnn Masaoka Van Atta

Bottom: photo by *Jean Allsopp and Harry*
Taylor; design by *Lovelace Interiors*

Cover design by *Vasken Guiragossian*

LOWE'S COMPANIES, INC.

Robert Niblock, CEO and Chairman of the Board

Larry D. Stone, President and Chief Operating Officer

Nick Canter, Executive VP, Marketing and Merchandising

Bob Gfeller, Senior VP, Marketing

Theresa Anderson, Senior VP, General Merchandise Manager

Melissa S. Birdsong, VP, Trend and Design

Karena Bailey, VP, Merchandising

Sarah Wagner, Merchandising Director

Lowe's and the gable design are registered trademarks of LF, LLC.

10 9 8 7 6 5 4 3 2 1

First printing August 2008

Copyright © 2008, Sunset Publishing Corporation, Menlo Park, CA 94025. Second edition. All rights reserved, including the right of reproduction in whole or in part in any form.

ISBN-13: 978-0-376-00924-1
ISBN-10: 0-376-00924-1
Library of Congress Control Number: 2007940188
Printed in the United States of America

preface

WE'RE PROUD TO BRING YOU AN ALL-NEW EDITION OF THIS BOOK, ORIGINALLY published in 2001. The first edition of *Lowe's Complete Home Decorating* was welcomed by Lowe's customers as a beautiful, practical guide to creating the easy-to-live-with, good-looking interiors they wanted for their homes. Building on that success, we've updated the book with hundreds of new photos, the latest information on decorating materials, fresh color palettes, and an expanded chapter of do-it-yourself projects. Still gorgeous and practical, this book will be a wonderful resource as you plan a new home interior— or just dream about one.

This and the other Lowe's books are part of our commitment to helping our customers with all their home improvement projects. You'll find inspiration, ideas, and how-to information in *Complete Home Improvement and Repair, Complete Landscaping, Decorating with Paint & Color, Complete Patio & Deck, Complete Tile & Flooring,* and *Complete Home Wiring,* along with the Lowe's Creative Ideas series that includes *Organizing Your Home, Kids' Spaces, Makeovers,* and *Color.*

The sales associates at Lowe's are ready with all sorts of decorating help, from mixing the perfect shade of paint to estimating wall-paper needs, from choosing great kitchen appliances to finding the ideal lighting fixture. Remember that Lowe's also offers extensive assistance via Lowes.com and the in-store clinics conducted throughout the year, plus a range of installation services.

Founded 62 years ago, Lowe's has been actively improving homes from day one. Let us help you realize your decorating dreams.

contents

about this book

"IT'S GREAT TO BE HOME!" WHO HASN'T SAID THAT—AFTER A LONG DAY AT WORK, perhaps, or on returning from a trip? Think how good it feels to be at home curled up on the sofa with a cup of coffee, the family cat, and the Sunday paper.

Home is where we spend a large part of our time, where we experience many of life's joys and escape its hassles. No wonder making our home a great place to be is a high priority for most of us, whether we own a spacious house or rent the tiniest apartment.

Decorating your home to make it attractive, comfortable, and efficient is a straightforward goal, but the project may never get off the ground if it seems too complicated, or too time-consuming. Where to begin? And who has time to spare?

Lowe's Complete Home Decorating is all about demystifying the process and helping you proceed step by step. Here you'll find guidance for making your home beautiful by using practical approaches that really work, no matter what the scope of your plan. You may have in mind a small project or a single

A study in sleek and soothing design, the dining area in this contemporary home derives much of its drama from the lighting plan. Blown-glass pendants cast an intriguing pattern onto the metal surface of the dining table, which was designed to be a desk. An up/down sconce washes the wall with accent light. (Turn to pages 154–157 for more photos of this home.)

ABOVE: The foyer of the home pictured on these pages features a built-in cabinet with receptacles for charging cell phones, organizers for keys and other small items, and a deep bottom drawer for satchels and handbags. The cabinet is curly maple; doors to the interior rooms are plain maple with white laminated glass.

RIGHT: In the compact powder room (just visible at the end of the hallway in the photo above), limestone subway tiles and 1-inch glass-mosaic tiles contrast in value and scale; toasty hues unite them. The white bronze vessel sink, a mirror mounted away from the wall, and a stylish uplight add to the modern appeal.

purchase—a fresh coat of paint for your child's bedroom or new wood flooring to replace aging carpet. You can dip into this book at any point for help with dozens of projects and choices. But if you're planning something more involved—redoing your master bedroom and bath, for example, or taking the plunge with a whole-house makeover—you'll want to read the chapters in sequence to get the most out of them. Throughout the book, "Lowe's Quick Tips" provide bite-size pieces of decorating wisdom on everything from selecting a countertop material to setting tile.

No matter what your project or plan, keep in mind that decorating is more than choosing a color, buying a chair, or laying new flooring. It's also about discovering who you are, what you love, and how you want to live. Think of decorating as a process and a journey— the destination reveals itself in a more beautiful, functional home.

Eco-friendly materials make this open-plan urban home a study in sustainable, stylish design. In the living room, the plum sofa and neutral chairs are anchored by a pale wool rug atop concrete flooring stained dark mocha. Beyond the two-sided steel shelf opposite the sofa is the media area; the "picture frame" on the far wall is fixed, but the art rolls up and back (much like a window shade) to reveal a flat-panel TV.

Ready to embark on your own decorating adventure? Lowe's can show you the way, chapter by chapter.

room-by-room design To get the creative process going, this gallery of more than 200 photos is packed with decorating ideas for every part of the house. Its room-by-room organization makes it easy to zero in on the areas that interest you most. A recurring special feature, "A Closer Look," offers in-depth, illustrated analysis of the decorating decisions behind four outstanding rooms. The last section in the chapter, "Open House," takes you on a tour to show how designers carry a color-and-design theme through different rooms in a home. Ideas—lots of them—are what this chapter

provides, whether you find a whole-house look you'd like to interpret in your own home or a single furnishing that would be just right for one of your rooms.

all about color "What color shall we paint the walls?" is often the first question homeowners ask when thinking about changing their decor. It's fun to focus on what's "hot" at the moment, but the most satisfying schemes come from an understanding of how to balance warm and cool colors, light and dark colors, and bright and dull colors to create a sense of harmony and ease in a room. This chapter explains these concepts and opens your eyes to the possibilities of color through-

continues on page 12 >

RIGHT: A brilliant island is the focal-point feature in the minimalist kitchen. Yellow-green lacquered cabinetry supports a thick countertop made of concrete mixed with recycled rice hulls for texture; a stainless-steel planter blocks the view of kitchen clutter. Glass tile makes up the back-splash on the far wall.

BELOW: Eames molded-plastic dining chairs with chrome bases surround a locally built teak table. Wood decking on the ceiling warms up this spacious, open room.

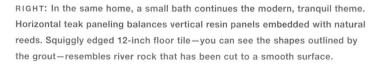

RIGHT: In the same home, a small bath continues the modern, tranquil theme. Horizontal teak paneling balances vertical resin panels embedded with natural reeds. Squiggly edged 12-inch floor tile—you can see the shapes outlined by the grout—resembles river rock that has been cut to a smooth surface.

out the home—in flooring, furniture, window treatments, fabrics, and more. Included in the chapter is a simplified, user-friendly version of the classic color wheel—a versatile tool for creating an entire palette or for adding a bit of depth and drama to colors you've already chosen. The "Color Encyclopedia" shows at a glance different applications of each color, with palettes keyed to room settings. Here you can revisit your favorite colors—and discover new ones. Sixteen ready-made color palettes from Lowe's present harmonious combinations you can work with as is, or use as a jumping-off point for your own selections.

practical design What *is* design? Simply put, good design is both appropriate and pleasing. A well-designed room has appropriate furnishings and color, as well as pleasing proportions and an atmosphere of well-being. If something is "off" in a room's design, you can usually sense it, no matter what your decorating experience. Taking you beyond that intuition and teaching you how to consciously use the principles of design to create a successful scheme—or to remedy a room's problem—is the objective of this chapter. It's easier than you think, and visual examples bring the design concepts to life.

elements of a room The materials and furnishings that go into a home are the building blocks of decorating, and choosing them can be both delightful and difficult. Half the battle is knowing what you're looking for and what's available. Use this chapter as a resource guide to everything from paint to furniture, flooring, and light fixtures. You'll see many of the furnishings and materials in room settings, providing you with yet more decorating ideas. One "Case Study" explores various wall treatments in a single home; another focuses on lighting design.

BELOW: A bedroom in the same home demonstrates the effective use of a single color throughout a room. The strawberry red of the chairs repeats in the toile throw and spotted pillows and also accents the bed linens and curtain panels. Art with a blue background cools the warm hues.

techniques and projects When you can take a decorating idea and implement it in your home—with your own hands—you gain an immeasurable sense of pride and satisfaction. In this chapter, you'll find a host of decorating projects ranging from wallpapering a room or installing crown moulding to building a console table or sewing curtain panels. Presented in easy-to-follow, fully illustrated steps, each project details all the materials and techniques you need to create something that will add function and style to your home.

room-by-room design

LOOKING AT PHOTOS OF BEAUTIFUL INTERIORS, DO YOU WONDER HOW SUCH

rooms come together so successfully? How is it that every element just seems to "belong,"

and everything works together so harmoniously?
Well, you may think, it's easy enough for interior
designers—they can draw on years of training and
experience to work their magic. Many of the rest
of us, though, could use a little help.

That help is here, presented in this chapter in
the form of more than 200 photos of rooms—from
entries to great rooms, children's rooms to outdoor
living spaces. Accompanying captions point out the
decorating elements and the decisions behind the
designs. Use these examples to find a look you like,
to spark your own decorating plan, or simply to get
acquainted with the range of contemporary and traditional style possibilities. Look, read, and take it all
in as this chapter makes its way through the entire
house, room by room.

a warm welcome

IF ROOMS COULD SPEAK, THE ENTRY WOULD SAY "WELCOME!" THE SPACE JUST inside the front door is usually what visitors see first, setting the tone for everything that lies beyond. To get off to a good start, choose a single piece of furniture or accessory for your entry and build on that.

For a sense of visual flow, hint at what's to come by using colors that work with the hues in adjoining rooms.

An entry has a functional role to play as well: it aids in the transition between indoors and outside. A console table makes a handy drop-off for mail and keys, and a mirror on the wall lets you—and your guests—make a quick appearance check. Stain-resistant flooring holds up to outdoor elements brought inside, and an umbrella stand or coat rack simplifies comings and goings. At the back entrance, a mudroom with a storage unit for outdoor gear is a big plus.

Whether your entry is a separate room or just a place to pause, let it greet your guests and family with style, in a manner that invites everyone to come in.

Linked to the entry on the facing page by the same wall color, the living room is delineated by a change from practical terra-cotta flooring to deep, dark hardwood.

An ornate door is the star of the entrance to a home designed in Spanish-Moorish style. Dark-stained case goods and neutral upholstery continue the light-and-dark contrast of the door and walls.

RIGHT: In a spare, contemporary home, the entry's earth-toned concrete floor tiles abut dark hardwood in the adjoining room. This shift in flooring places an easy-care material in the more highly trafficked area.

FACING PAGE: A pared-down approach can have the greatest impact, as this simple entry illustrates. Dark furnishings and accessories punctuate pale walls and flooring; the suspended fixture is a playful touch (see pages 44–45 for more photos of this home).

LEFT: Natural materials and Asian elements set the style for this modern entry area. Venetian plaster walls radiate warmth and reflect light; curvilinear accessories, including a column lamp with papyrus shade, repeat motifs in the art.

Because both family and guests use it, this foyer needed to blend practicality with formality. Matching 48-inch-high partitions separate the open space into dining room, entry, and living room.

RIGHT: A mirrored antique hall tree with marble tabletop makes a charming focal-point furnishing in a cottage-style entry. Old-fashioned accessories complete the picture.

LEFT: Viewed from a long hallway lined with French doors, the entry to this elegantly rustic home looks warm and welcoming. A wall of local stone forms a natural backdrop for a bold painting and a distinctive chest.

RIGHT: A mudroom entry at the back door includes a handsome built-in bench. With kids coming and going during wet weather, the tough, easy-to-clean linoleum flooring was a practical choice.

LEFT: Accessed from the garage, a mudroom with slate flooring serves as the family's casual entrance to this lodge-style home. A wall of manufactured stone veneer is lighter in weight than natural stone, yet it captures the nuances of the real thing. (See pages 140–143 for more photos of this home.)

Warm-toned wood, translucent etched-glass panels, and heated concrete flooring create a sleek, hardworking entry. The 8- by 20-foot space features maple cabinetry (including a coat closet) and a 4-foot bench above shoe-storage space.

serene spaces

DESCENDANT OF THE OLD-FASHIONED PARLOR, THE LIVING ROOM WAS FOR decades the place in the home where everyone came together. People actually *lived* in their living rooms.

With the advent of the family room in the early 1960s, living rooms assumed a more ceremonial function: they became spaces for formal entertaining, separated from the casual clutter of daily life. That pattern continues in homes with both living and family rooms—the two coexist, each with its own purpose. But today's living room is more than a showplace for company; it is a refuge from a hectic life, a space where family members can pursue quiet activities. As such, it merits a careful decorating plan.

Whether the living room is traditional or modern, its palette can be carried with variation throughout the house, ensuring continuity and simplifying color and design decisions. Is it any wonder that when we decide to decorate we often start with this primary room?

An occasional chair continues the neutral palette established by the sofa and curtains shown on the facing page.

In an expansive living room with soaring windows, the designer created several intimately scaled seating areas. Here, a neutral rug and upholstery are balanced by dark wood trim and case goods. Simple curtain panels keep the distinctive windows clearly visible.

In a century-old California Craftsman home, understated materials imbue the living room with a sense of calm and grace. A solid-surface slab surrounds the fireplace opening; above the mantel, the canvas wall covering has a crackle finish resembling antique porcelain. Etched-glass doors flanking the fireplace and an antique mirrored screen behind the piano are in smooth contrast to a host of plush fabrics.

BELOW: Befitting the room's elegance, crystals sparkle against a lightweight linen curtain opposite the fireplace. To create subtle gathers, shirring tape was sewn to the underside of the curtain heading; crystal drops hanging from narrow ties catch the light.

RIGHT: Side-by-side floral arrangements in pavé style (see page 261) inject intense natural color into the living room's quiet palette.

BELOW: Once compartmentalized into several spaces, the top floor of this hillside home is now wide open. Bare windows and unfussy furnishings keep the focus on the outdoors, and palm fronds sweeping the windows make this airy room feel like a treehouse.

FACING PAGE, TOP: Layers of wallpaper and bright blue paint formerly overpowered the elegant proportions of this Victorian home, so the new owners literally peeled away the years. Warm undertones in the new white paint keep the room from feeling stark.

FACING PAGE, BOTTOM: Tall glass doors glide into wall pockets, facilitating the connection between this contemporary living room and the garden. A slipcovered sofa set back from the doors forms one boundary of an inner room.

a closer look

Decorative painter Peggy Del Rosario "aged" the surface of the carved-wood fireplace surround, custom built for the room, with umber glazes applied over a creamy base coat.

In this spacious living room, interior designer Tres McKinney saw an opportunity to create two seating areas directed toward the focal-point fireplace. For the first, a pair of gold sofas dotted in plum form an inner room anchored by a generous area rug.

a closer look
continues >

FACING PAGE, BOTTOM: In a nod to the homeowners' preference for contemporary art, McKinney designed the secondary seating area to reflect a more modern aesthetic. In a modest departure from the symmetry of the primary seating area, the designer chose two very different chairs to flank this sofa.

a closer look

A pair of lacquer-topped tables and an open-backed chair lighten a scheme that features numerous upholstered pieces.

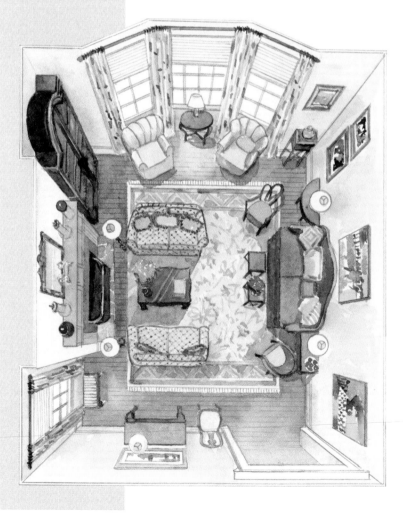

a bird's-eye view

This elegant, eclectic living room conveys an atmosphere of layered beauty through the use of exquisite patterned fabrics and painted finishes. Noteworthy case goods and varied accessories chronicle the homeowners' travels and love of antiques. Furniture arrangement was a top priority in planning the space: sofas, chairs, and tables create three inner rooms, each with its own identity and ambience. The primary seating area, established by matching sofas, is decidedly traditional and tranquil, while a secondary space, with its plush camelback sofa and contemporary art, has a vibrant, lighthearted feel. For a fresh but sophisticated effect, the designer chose a palette of low-intensity plum, gold, and robin's-egg blue.

DESIGN DETAILS

1 Buttercream walls bathe the room in flattering warmth; off-white paint accentuates the lines of the coffered ceiling and extensive crown moulding.

2 To bring out the wood detailing in the painted fireplace mantel, raised areas were gilded. A dark chocolate-brown marble surround echoes the rich tones of wood pieces throughout the room.

3 The wood-and-gilt mirror over the mantel is carved in the French Colonial style; accessories and wall sconces illustrate the principle of symmetrical balance, with touches of asymmetry to soften the formality.

4 Where there was once a built-in unit, an antique bibliothèque now stands, balancing the scale of the window on the other side of the fireplace.

5 A carved wood coffee table reflects Spanish and Italian design elements and visually anchors the primary seating area.

6 In the bay window, a pair of channelback club chairs and an occasional table offer a third seating area, one that makes the most of the natural light. (See page 232 for a photo of this space.)

7 The soft blue in the rug repeats in upholstery, pillows, and embellishments.

8 A blue barrelback chair adjacent to the plum sofa completes the seating area and gives it a soothing a sense of enclosure.

9 Furniture and pillows are finished with tassel, bead, and looped-ribbon fringe and other sumptuous trimmings.

dining in

MORE THAN ANY OTHER ROOM IN THE HOUSE, THE DINING ROOM HAS ASSUMED new roles in recent years. Traditionally reserved for family suppers and formal dinners, it now often doubles as a bill-paying station, a sewing studio, or homework headquarters. For some busy families, just clearing off the dining room table is a project in itself!

If you are fortunate enough to have a dedicated dining room, by all means play it up. Link it to the adjoining room (usually the living room) with related colors and patterns—a deeper version of the living room's wall color, for example. When the dining area has fuzzier boundaries—perhaps it's simply a space for a small table in the kitchen—emphasize the "room" by using a freestanding piece of furniture like a hutch as a divider, or define it with a distinctive area rug. A built-in banquette can be the coziest of all places, for eating or simply reading the morning paper.

No matter where your family and guests gather to eat, make it a special spot. After all, many of life's important conversations take place around the dinner table.

A study in symmetry, the buffet arrangement is at the same time elegant and nonchalant.

An oval dining table and buffet made of cherry with a deep walnut stain illustrate "transitional" style, a melding of traditional and contemporary elements. Modern fabrics and art blend beautifully with the old-world ambience of a gilt-and-crystal chandelier.

ABOVE: The paneling in this formal dining room was hand painted to mimic traditional scenic wallpaper. Subtly patterned upholstery is in keeping with the naturalistic wall motifs; a delicate chandelier adds a bit of glamour.

BELOW: Carrying the same warm wall color from the dining room into the adjoining living room makes for a smooth transition between spaces. Rich brown tones in the highboy, dining table, and dining chairs are a pleasing contrast to the walls.

FACING PAGE, BOTTOM: At first glance this open dining room appears traditional, yet it incorporates a number of contemporary elements, including a minimalist chandelier and unadorned curtain panels. Round-backed chairs upholstered in a large-scale plaid are a modern take on 18th-century Hepplewhite chairs.

ABOVE: A suspended fixture wrapped in a nutmeg-colored linen shade is the focus of attention in this ultramodern dining room.

ABOVE: Warm walls set off the white cabinetry of this contemporary dining room. The chandelier, while new, is a nod to the past, but fluted ceramics and streamlined chairs are strictly modern touches.

ABOVE: Muted blue and silvery gray on the walls of this casual dining room were inspired by the colors of the sky. A pedestal table, a banquette, and rattan chairs painted red contribute to a Swedish-farmhouse flavor.

LEFT: In an open room designed for entertaining, architectural features—a narrow wall near the entry, a framed-in beam, and a tray ceiling in the dining area—define two distinct spaces.

LEFT: A table, benches, and banquette of unfinished teak introduce natural tones and texture to a small eating area off the kitchen, created as part of a remodel. New windows provide lots of natural light, and a contemporary chandelier makes the space feel cozier.

FACING PAGE: In a cozy dining nook, an hourglass-shaped table leg, birch benches, and beadboard paneling have a retro feel. The black granite tabletop, which aligns with the kitchen counters, is both modern and practical. Built-in benches contain storage bins.

RIGHT: A banquette and its companion table combine rich wood and white painted surfaces to create a cheerful eating area adjoining the kitchen. Matching styles and colors for the banquette and the window trim strengthen the architectural significance of the space.

open living

TODAY'S CASUAL LIFESTYLES AND PREFERENCE FOR OPEN FLOOR PLANS MAKE the great room—that combination kitchen, dining, living, family, and media space—an ongoing favorite with designers and homeowners alike. Its more modest forerunner, the family room, often combines a kitchen and living area. Great room or family room, such a space might be described as "the place everyone likes to be, and nobody wants to leave."

With its multiple functions and nonstop use, a great room or a family room presents a decorating challenge: how do you unify the different areas within the room? Painting the walls a single color does the job nicely. To imply inner rooms, arrange furniture to create distinct seating areas.

Continuing the same flooring throughout unites the spaces. If you prefer a change underfoot—limestone in the kitchen and carpet in the living area, for instance—choose materials of a similar color value to avoid a jarring contrast.

A room where the whole family lives during their waking hours? Now that's a "great" idea.

In the kitchen of the great room pictured opposite, open shelves let guests help themselves to dishes, contributing to the sense of informality.

The great room in this coastal getaway takes its color cues from the ocean and dunes outside its windows. The design emphasizes simplicity and durability: the sofa and window seat cushions are covered in washable denim, and the floor is easy-care linoleum laid in two patterns of pale yellow and deep amber.

FACING PAGE, TOP: The curved countertop at the end of the kitchen island provides a spot where the kids can do homework or just hang out. A trio of hand-blown glass pendants, made by the home-owner's brother, adds a dash of color and informal design.

BELOW: A blend of vibrant materials and finishes, this great room was designed to be used and enjoyed by the family, yet still be formal enough for entertaining. Sturdy materials—stone, leather, chenille, and wood—stand up to daily use. The concrete-and-steel fireplace extension is front and center; console seating wraps around the leather sectional and separates the living area from the dining and kitchen space (see facing page).

BELOW: Cherry cabinetry, a ceiling-high glass-tile backsplash, and granite countertops give the kitchen area an air of casual elegance. At the island's far end, an extra-tall base cabinet with glass panels shields the prep area from the view of seated diners.

Unobstructed windows and glass doors in an L-shaped great room take advantage of sweeping beach views. In the seating area (above), comfy furnishings carry out a warm-and-cool color scheme; a mix of patterns and textures keeps it casual. In the dining area behind the sofa (right), stylish chairs combine rich wood and breezy cotton fabric for a chic, relaxed look.

The kitchen faces the dining area across a counter and bar. Pearlescent quartz composite countertops and a brilliant blue tile backsplash reflect the surf-and-sand environment.

BELOW: This open room with walls of glass on two sides was built as a bridge between the original bungalow and a new wing; it's now the heart of the home. When all the doors are open, it becomes a breezeway. Neutral concrete flooring makes a smooth visual transition from the original house to the new wing.

ABOVE: To emphasize the fine pattern of the amber-toned wood veneer, the media center (top photo) was designed with clean and simple lines; the suspended open "box" in the foreground hides a recessed light fixture. A teak coffee table and a contemporary area rug (above and facing page) unify the seating area.

ABOVE: The homeowners call this enclosed patio an "outdoor retreat" because the space feels like an extension of their garden. It functions as a family room, with a table for games and plenty of seating for family and guests.

RIGHT: Cherry cabinetry stained espresso brown flanks the fireplace, contributing vivid contrast and visual weight to a light-filled family room; a coffee table and end table stained a similar color balance the built-ins. The geometric-patterned area rug links the neutral upholstery and dark case goods.

ABOVE: The placement of the loveseat and sofa serves two focal points—the fireplace and the media cabinetry—in this traditional family room.

ABOVE: To disguise a necessary steel support, the architect enclosed it in a column that coordinates with other columns in the home. Light-toned kitchen cabinetry and tile surfaces enhance the open feeling of this great room, while a dark-stained cherry island and generous upholstered stools ease the visual transition from kitchen to seating area.

FACING PAGE, BOTTOM: The column serves to visually separate the kitchen from the seating area, where a versatile furniture arrangement orients the sofa and leather club chairs toward the family TV as well as the fireplace.

LEFT: Added to the house during the remodel, the breakfast bay off the kitchen is a comfortable spot for family dining. A dropped soffit (shown on the facing page) sets the space apart from the rest of the room.

a closer look

RIGHT: The great room in a Bauhaus-style house built in the early 1960s boasts floor-to-ceiling windows, a real plus for its light-loving owners. The designer, David Ramey, warmed to the space as soon as he saw it. "The house was strong architecturally, in a style I could appreciate," he says. "I wanted to create a design that was in keeping with the distinctive architecture, but bring it into this century." Take a look at what he did.

ABOVE: Set apart from the rest of the great room, the dining area takes advantage of a view of mature oaks and native plants. The earthy colors of the painting are repeated in the furniture, with textures that range from nubby to smooth. The futuristic light fixture overhead, reminiscent of a mobile, is one of three in this great room.

ABOVE: Multicolored glass tile applied to the curved bar and the kitchen backsplash reiterates hues in other parts of the room, including the ocher-colored media center on the opposite wall (seen in photo at left). Light coming through clerestory windows gives the tile its luminous look.

a closer look continues >

a closer look

Hand-dyed, handwoven chenille in shades of moss, terra-cotta, and ocher covers the chairs and chaise. The cube ottomans are upholstered in leather of similar hues. Glass tile plays a key role in the warm palette.

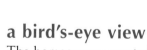

a bird's-eye view

The homeowners wanted a room that was comfortable for them yet could easily accommodate family gatherings and casual parties. "A great room is just an enormous space unless you break it down into areas according to function," the designer says. He loosely divided the large room into inner rooms for eating (at the table and the bar), watching television, and lounging by the fire. The area rug delineates the main inner room. Traffic flows easily past the bar, around the chairs, or into the dining area.

DESIGN DETAILS

1 It all began with the "painting" (see the photo on page 54), a digitally enhanced image taken from an acrylic painting on canvas. Blown up to twice its original size, it evokes the stippled brushwork of pointillism and suggests a palette of nature's colors.

2 In keeping with this home's modern design and materials, the dining table is stainless steel topped with glass. Leather chairs the color of bark show the influence of the outdoors.

3 Ceramic pieces created by the owners' son are showcased in stained shelving surrounding the focal-point media center.

4 Smooth leather ottomans provide contrast with the irregular textures elsewhere—and increase the seating possibilities.

5 A Tibetan wool rug sets the stage for the rich, earth-colored furnishings. Warm, analogous colors ranging from yellow through red border the rug's cool teal interior (see page 55 for a closer view).

6 The stainless-steel fireplace is original to the home. Three layers of green glaze finish the adjoining wall, creating a cozy nook for the chaise.

7 Glass tiles for the bar and backsplash were fabricated in three colors (lemon, tangerine, and earth) and two finishes (gloss and matte, or "sanded"). These variations in color and finish give the surface a pleasingly mottled look.

8 To minimize contrast and strengthen the color statement, the legs on the bar stools were stained to match their leather seats.

the heart of the home

IT SEEMS NO ONE CAN STAY OUT OF THE KITCHEN. MUCH MORE THAN A PLACE TO prepare meals, the kitchen is the heart of the home, where parents share the day's news, kids eat around the clock (or so it seems), and guests congregate to chat with the cook. Everyone ends up in the kitchen, so you might as well make it look great.

If you're in true remodel mode—and the kitchen is the room most often remodeled—you'll have plenty to ponder, from structural changes to the latest in cabinetry, flooring, and countertops. Happily, you'll find a mind-boggling array of innovative components and materials from which to choose.

If your goal is more modest—a new look without a major investment—you can choose manageable projects like replacing cabinet doors with glass-fronted ones, tiling a backsplash, or installing a vinyl-tile floor. Even a change as small as new cabinetry hardware can have a big impact. Whether you're going all out or working with what you have, what's cookin' in the kitchen is creativity!

In the kitchen, natural accent colors seem, well, natural.

Unmistakably traditional in character, this kitchen combines polished granite countertops with face-frame cherry cabinets. Limestone tile set "on point" blends well with the wood and stone.

With its warm wood, cool quartz composite countertops, and neutral slate tile backsplash (shown below), this new kitchen feels as though it has had time to evolve. The designers opted for varied finishes to break up the expanse of cabinetry and lighten the atmosphere. At left, a tall, glass-fronted counter cabinet visually balances the bank of windows and provides maximum storage for the space.

ABOVE: The bold marble on the backsplash and counter-tops was the design catalyst for this classic kitchen; white cabinetry, pewter hardware, and nickel faucets and sinks were chosen to play supporting roles. A mantle-style hood, itself a dramatic feature, showcases the distinctive veining of the stone.

RIGHT: The prep sink, refrigerator, and microwave drawer make up an efficient secondary work triangle—a helpful arrangement when two cooks work together in the kitchen. The homeowner chose a below-counter microwave to allow room for glass-fronted cabinets above.

ABOVE: Where a wall once separated this kitchen from the dining room, open shelving is now suspended from the ceiling by threaded steel rods in aluminum sleeves. Stainless-steel countertops and slate floor tile—cut from salvaged chalkboards—are no-nonsense surfaces.

RIGHT: Ebony-stained maple cabinets and honed granite atop the island define this simple kitchen's main storage and prep zones. To lighten the look, natural maple was used for the island base; the computer niche sports green paint.

RIGHT: A statuary-vein marble countertop and tall backsplash are framed by dark-stained white oak cabinetry in this contemporary kitchen; reflective hardware and appliances provide contrast with the honed stone. For warmth, the island is topped with butcher block and the walls are painted a bright yellow hue.

LEFT: To make way for a long solid-surface countertop in this kitchen, the homeowners replaced the existing windows with new ones installed higher on the wall. Slender trim pieces accent the subway-tile backsplash.

ABOVE: Loaded with charm and punctuated with bright color, this white kitchen is anything but blah. Open shelves showcase colorful tableware; butcher block on the island and a rustic table contribute natural color to the mix.

RIGHT: A combination of cabinetry gives this Victorian farmhouse–style kitchen a sense of period charm. Cherry base cabinets feature decorative corbels and a granite countertop. The cabinets flanking the range hood have glass fronts and windows in back, admitting natural light.

ABOVE: Filled with smart storage and stylish touches, this kitchen delivers a compact, efficient cooking and eating area. White granite tile on the countertop and porcelain tile on the floor are durable, relatively inexpensive choices compared to solid surfaces.

LEFT: A narrow pullout shelf unit fits conveniently between the range and below-counter microwave. The red laminate table (curved and built in to maximize the limited space) seats the whole family.

Vintage leaded glass, light fixtures, and hardware reflect the homeowner's love of antiques. New components—the cherry-and-granite island, enameled hood, and face-frame cabinets—have period styling.

LEFT: The warm tones and handsome proportions of the owners' antique walnut cupboard were copied in the built-to-spec island (far left).

BELOW: Painted cabinets with flush-inset doors are a blend of beauty and practicality; dishwasher drawers below the countertop are up-to-the-minute yet look traditional.

a closer look

RIGHT: Three cramped rooms became a natural—in every sense of the word—family hangout when the homeowners remodeled this 1907 cottage. A desire to "go green" guided their selection of two eco-friendly materials: prefinished cork flooring and cabinets made of wheatboard. Neither product outgases VOCs (volatile organic compounds), a major component of indoor air pollution.

BELOW: Removing two interior walls brought in lots of light and made room for a small table and four chairs painted—naturally—green.

a closer look continues >

The need for more storage was part of the driving force behind the extensive remodel. This floor-to-ceiling built-in cabinet accommodates the washer and dryer at one end.

a closer look

A white farmhouse sink coordinates with the kitchen's refurbished 1940s O'Keefe & Merritt range (shown on page 69); the bridge-style faucet features a gooseneck spout.

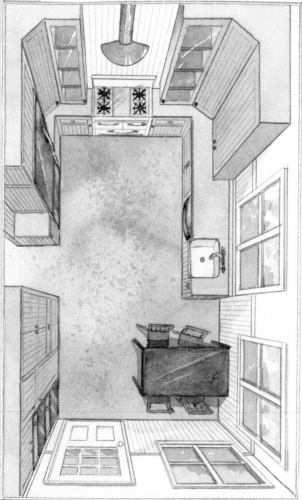

a bird's-eye view

Maintaining the turn-of-the-century aesthetic of this home was key to the renovation plan. "We wanted to keep the style of the house yet add modern touches where it made the most sense," the homeowners explain. The refurbished range and new refrigerator, sink, and dishwasher form an efficient work triangle. Angling the upper corner cabinets maximizes storage and softens the lines of the small space. A favorite with the whole family is the eating area, with its garden views: "I wanted to enjoy my garden and see the kids playing in the yard," the owner says.

DESIGN DETAILS

1 Cabinets are made of wheatboard, a type of fiberboard created by binding straw waste particles with formaldehyde-free resin and then heat-pressing the material into sheets.

2 In addition to housing the laundry appliances, the built-in cabinetry includes a broom closet, a pull-out clothes hamper, linen storage, and office files. The narrow drawer holds household odds and ends.

3 Prefinished cork flooring is easy on legs yet withstands the inevitable foot traffic in a kitchen. The natural-color Edipo cork used here is distinguished by its linear pattern.

4 The stainless-steel hood was a lucky Internet auction find.

5 The homeowners chose pebbly glass for some upper cabinet doors because it lightens the look and echoes the visual texture of the cork floor.

6 For durability, red oak butcher-block countertops are finished with polyurethane.

7 Beadboard cabinets with knobs on the doors and bin pulls on the drawers keep to the vintage cottage theme.

8 Four-foot-high beadboard encircling the room replicates paneling original to the house.

9 An inexpensive pendant fixture from an import-furniture store lights the eating area and gives it a sense of coziness.

rest and renewal

THE MOST PERSONAL LIVING SPACE IN THE HOUSE, THE BEDROOM IS OFTEN THE most neglected—no doubt because it's not routinely seen by guests. Considering its multipurpose nature—sleep space, sanctuary, dressing area—doesn't your bedroom merit more attention?

Though we might not admit it, many of us do a lot of living in this room that once contained only a bed and a chest of drawers. Today's typical bedroom may be outfitted with chairs for reading, a chaise for relaxing, a small desk for paperwork, exercise equipment for working out, and a TV for late-night viewing. Up-to-date task and ambient lighting for all of these activities is a must.

An antique secretary provides display space and gives overnight guests a place to write a quick note or jot in a journal.

Practical functions aside, the bedroom is one place where you (and whoever shares the room with you) can—and should— freely indulge your decorating whims. Choose a palette based on your favorite colors; combine fabric patterns and textures that express your personal style, be it bright and lively or quiet and contemplative. This is your oasis of privacy and serenity, and you have only yourself to please.

A guest bedroom—the retreat we create for others—should be as comfortable and convenient as it is good looking. In this shipshape guest room, storage towers double as nightstands; inside-mount blinds ensure visitors' privacy and, when lowered and tilted shut, let them sleep in.

A lofty master bedroom painted an airy blue-gray is grounded by the upholstered bed and unexpected dashes of orange—in the striped fabric covering the bed frame and headboard, and on the wingback chair. Mismatched lamps break up the symmetry of identical bedside tables. A bank of windows gets treated to tailored Roman shades with contrast banding; the same taupe color repeats in the cushion for the wide window seat.

To achieve an ethereal effect, the designer of this guest room chose a pale palette, with soft green walls and a tufted headboard in a slightly deeper hue. On the curtains and coverlet, a stylized naturalistic design supplies pattern. The étagère between the two windows adds a bit of visual weight to the decor. At the foot of the bed, a settee and diminutive tables give guests a private sitting area.

LEFT: In this ultra-contemporary home, three built-in shelves pierce the wall between the bedroom and the entry. The top and bottom shelves are open to the bedroom, flanked by light-admitting textured resin panels containing recycled materials; the middle shelf and its resin panels face the entry.

RIGHT: Contrast and bright color are the formula for success in this cheerful guest bedroom. The dark leather-upholstered bed frame anchors the scheme, while a channel-quilted bedspread, yellow leather pillows, and a coral accent pillow pick up hues in the whimsical art. Wingback chairs covered in large-scale cotton gingham fabric are perfect for reading or relaxing in the sunny bay.

RIGHT: This master bedroom packs a lot of style into a not-so-big space. The headboard and bed skirt are made of a subtly striped indoor-outdoor fabric. (Many such fabrics are soft enough to use for decorating.) Simple Roman shades dress the windows—and do not interfere with the desk or bedside table.

An upholstered room divider in a studio space wraps around a sleeper sofa; on the other side is a shallow settee paired with a demilune table. To enhance the sense of separation, the designer suspended a wide light fixture above the divider.

ABOVE: In a Zen-influenced master bedroom, a floating partition separates the sleeping area from the dressing room; a wide niche with recessed lighting breaks up the expanse of integrally colored plaster.

LEFT: Taupe walls and a gray bed frame set off linens in a sophisticated combination of intense persimmon, deep chocolate brown, and crisp white. A storage ottoman tucked under the bedside table helps control the inevitable clutter.

The homeowner's love of pattern and detail inspired the decorating plan for this sophisticated, sumptuous master bedroom. Including the pillows, nearly a dozen different fabrics—among them silk taffetas and cottons—adorn the room. The walls get their delicate mottled look from a darker glaze applied over a light base coat and manipulated with a cheesecloth pom-pom.

Styled like a wingback chair, this velvet-upholstered headboard creates a sense of soothing enclosure. Chocolate brown fabrics are cooled by accents of azure blue; the simple chest was inspired by Swedish design.

bathing

A SPLASH OF STYLE, AN EMPHASIS ON EFFICIENCY—THE FORMULA FOR A SUCCESSFUL bathroom is surprisingly simple. Of all the rooms in the house, the bathroom has undergone the greatest transformation over the years. What was once a small, no-nonsense room is now called upon to provide comfort in, and refuge from, a busy world. New bathrooms are often compartmentalized for multiple uses. Many are designed for relaxation as well as practicality, with spa tubs and steam-shower fixtures.

But upgrading your bathroom within its existing layout can be just as rewarding as new construction or a room-expanding remodel. When space is scarce, consider indulging in luxurious materials (after all, you won't need as much in a small area) and the latest hard-working fixtures. For the illusion of a more spacious room, install a pedestal sink or a console sink with vanity legs to reveal more of the walls and floor. Two trends worth noting are furniture feet, which make built-in cabinets feel more like freestanding units, and vintage pieces converted to working sinks—proving that, even in the bathroom, what's old is new again.

The frosted-glass shower surround stays in step with the wall color, while the translucency of the glass allows light into the shower and adds to the open feel.

Soothing hues and clean lines transform a small bath into a calm, restorative space. Chrome towel rings, faucets, and cabinet hardware gleam in the presence of gentle blue-green walls, off-white subway tile, and a Carrara marble countertop.

LEFT: In this clean-and-simple bath, white subway tile sets off a blue-and-red tile border that's just the right height to catch a child's eye. Rounded corners make the sink safer for kids.

RIGHT: Tub-shower fittings include a bar-mounted, hand-held sprayer with an extended hose, a practical fixture for bathing small children.

Glass tile in the shower, a solid-surface countertop, and 20- by 20-inch composite floor tile add up to an easy-care bath for kids. Narrowing the vanity near the entrance and laying the tile on the diagonal are devices to make the room feel wider.

ABOVE: Walls painted a soft cinnamon hue flatter everyone who enters this guest bath. Beadboard door panels on the base cabinets and a widespread nickel faucet are traditional touches, while the solid-surface countertop and undermount sink are more modern.

LEFT: Outfitted with an undermount sink and a marble top, a mahogany table takes on a new purpose as a free-standing vanity. Tumbled limestone tile covers the walls and floor of the bathroom.

BELOW: Light-and-dark contrast gives this traditional master bath its sense of drama. A pale quartz composite countertop with integral sink rests on dark cherry cabinetry; the mirror frame and leather seating cube repeat the dark tones. Limestone tile on the floor contributes natural color and texture.

LEFT: The shower combines glossy porcelain tile on the walls, slab marble on the bench, and basketweave marble on the floor. An awning window with obscuring glass opens for natural ventilation; for safety (and to conform to the local code), the shower includes a ceiling light fixture.

BELOW: As it closes, the bathroom's pocket door reveals a beadboard panel that echoes the curve of the door casing. The wide mirror in the bath reflects matching detailing on the back of the door.

FACING PAGE: An elegant arch frames the entrance to this graceful guest bath; a skylight bathes the space in natural light. Carrara marble tops an espresso brown vanity that has beadboard doors and furniture-style feet. The heated floor is Carrara marble tile with a basketweave inlay pattern. To accommodate a bend in the hallway adjacent to the bath, the vanity and mirror are set at an angle, altering the perception of space.

Slate tiles in varying sizes and grid patterns flow from the floor of this master bath into the shower. A vaulted ceiling repeats the gentle curve of the bow vanity. Opposite the vanity, a compact built-in laundry center (below) efficiently houses the washer and dryer.

BELOW: The natural palette continues, with face-frame cabinets of warm-hued fir and a vanity countertop of green granite. The wide-spread faucet is copper, as are the shower fixtures.

a closer look continues >

a closer look

Safety goes hand in hand with beauty in this shower, where an inward sloping bench makes it easier to rise from a seated position.

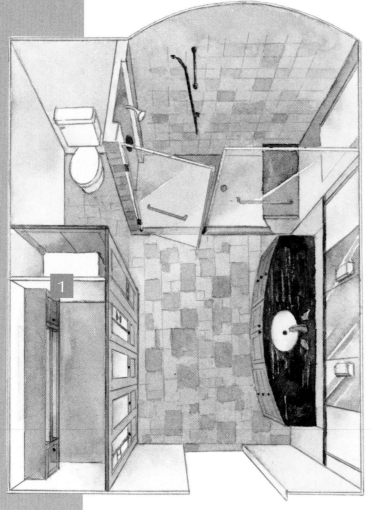

1

a bird's-eye view

To create a restful and restorative space, the architect of this master bath used a palette of natural wood, stone, and copper. Slate on multiple surfaces anchors the scheme. "I'm a big fan of slate," says the architect, "in part because it's such a great deal. In this bath it struck the perfect balance between the toothy texture of a natural material and a smooth, uniform surface that's comfortable to stand and sit on." Perimeter cabinetry is in warm contrast to the cool stone.

DESIGN DETAILS

1 The 7-foot-high cupboard next to the laundry center has a slim footprint but packs plenty of storage. A tankless water heater fits compactly behind its lower doors (illustration on facing page). Water is heated only as it flows though the unit, in contrast to the way a conventional water heater works.

2 When closed, the laundry center's wood-and-glass bifold doors hide the appliances but not the upper cabinetry.

3 In the shower, an adjustable hand-held sprayer mounted on a bar augments the traditional showerhead and makes bathing small children (and pets) a breeze.

4 A skylight over the shower and windows on the exterior wall bathe the room in natural light.

5 Capping the shower dam with the dark green granite rather than the lighter slate gives a visual clue that a threshold, although low, is there to be stepped across.

6 The medicine cabinet is recessed behind a section of the vanity mirror; within are electrical receptacles that keep the countertop uncluttered.

7 An undermount sink leaves the granite countertop largely uninterrupted, showing off its handsome serpentine grain.

8 Above the sink, mirror-mounted sconces on either side of the medicine cabinet provide task and ambient lighting.

9 Flush-inset cabinetry doors and drawers emphasize the smooth, sleek lines of the vanity.

just for kids

"GO TO YOUR ROOM!" IS NOT NECESSARILY A PUNISHMENT WHEN KIDS' QUARTERS are decorated in a fresh, fun way. Sleeping is the least of what happens in these rooms: they are personal environments with multiple purposes—play space, computer workstation, entertainment hub, study hall, and storage locker, to name a few. Flexibility is the name of the game in planning a child's room.

These days, though, it's not enough to create a functional space. Kids are more style conscious than ever, about everything from clothes to electronic gear. They want their rooms to look great, and that means gutsy colors and cool furnishings. Fortunately for parents, high-quality furniture that appeals to kids is plentiful and varied—let your child pick the colors and major pieces. Resist the urge to overfurnish the room; kids need lots of space to exercise their imaginations.

As you'll see on the following pages, some rooms are designed for a specific, limited time in a child's life, whereas others are geared for growth. Whatever your approach, make your child's room a memorable part of his or her young life.

Hidden behind a removable bedskirt is a trundle bed for sleepovers.

This compact room serves its occupant well—he can sleep, study, play, and entertain his pals here. The daybed is not just for slumber—it's also a comfortable spot for hanging out during the day. Unifying the scheme is yellow-and-gold wallpaper on the ceiling as well as the walls.

RIGHT: When it comes to boys' bedrooms, simple is often the best design strategy. A sturdy wooden bed, primary-colored bed linens, and a diamond-patterned wood floor suit the young occupant of this attic bedroom. His beloved dog is there, too, softly painted on the wall.

BELOW: This teen's "X-treme" room is bursting with surf, ski, and skateboard images. A cork valance over the blinds functions as a keepsake bulletin board.

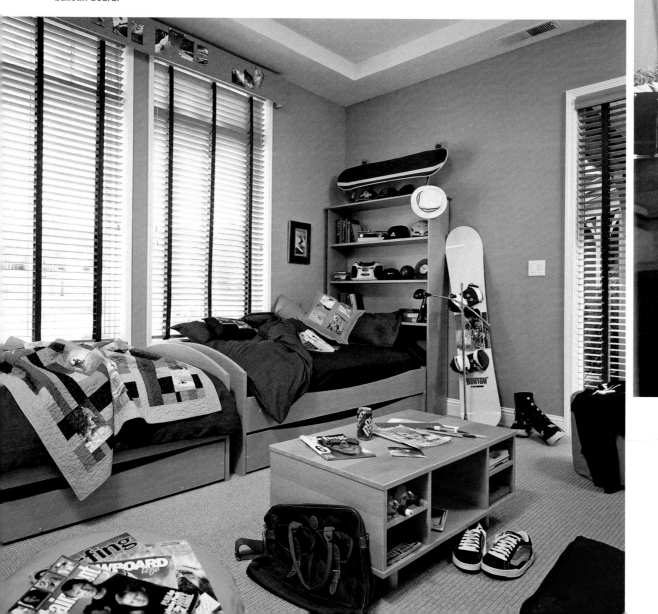

Wallpaper patterned after palm fronds is a sophisticated surprise in this avid surfer's bedroom. (There's even a surfboard suspended from the ceiling.) A bamboo shade, bed linens with a flip-flop motif, and funky furniture are casual touches in the laid-back scheme.

This girl's room is decorated in a riot of patterns and colors, many of them pink—even the floor is a glossy pink. A bright yellow pedestal table and nightstand add spunk to a sweet scheme that includes ruffles, beads, and bows.

LEFT: Old-fashioned yet sophisticated colors create a magical mood for a girls' room, with soft blue walls serving as a quiet backdrop for many gentle shades of green. Antique shutters fold and unfold to control light.

RIGHT: "Going down!" is fast and fun when your elevated bed comes with its own slide. Below the bed, there's plenty of room to stow books, toys, and general gear.

Young boys share a room that boasts two bunk beds, providing plenty of space for friends to stay over. Drawers beneath the bottom bunks store toys, games, clothes, and the "stuff" every kid acquires. At one end of the room, a round table and chairs move easily to accommodate the activity of the moment. Adhesive-backed cork squares allow for changeable art displays.

This variation of a trundle bed works well for the two older kids who share the room, helping to maximize a small space. When more floor space is desired, the lower bed can be rolled under the raised one.

ABOVE: Offbeat colors and lighthearted patterns give this bedroom a boost of energy and a sense of sophistication. Green complements the cardinal red of the four-poster bed and harmonizes with the blue-green of the curtains.

RIGHT: Painting a tall chest the same minty green as the walls makes it all but disappear, a decorating trick for visually expanding a room.

LEFT: Against the wall, this violet floor-to-ceiling storage unit is a standout. The lower cubbies offer easy access for a young child, while house rules dictate that parents retrieve stuff from higher up. The piece is bolted to the wall for stability.

BELOW: A splash of ruby red and lipstick pink on the two chairs balances the room's cool colors and pumps up the volume.

recaptured spaces

THE PHRASE ALONE—RECAPTURED SPACE—HAS A POSITIVE RING. YOUR OWN
"recapture" may be as involved as a spare bedroom undergoing reinvention or as simple
as a closet being transformed into a compact office. From banquettes and window seats
to over-the-garage bonus rooms, there are
all sorts of pleasing and practical ways to
reclaim wasted space and put it to good use.

If you don't think you have any space
to recapture, think—and look—again.
A large laundry room with a sink could do
double duty as a potting "shed"; that extra
bedroom might be turned into a dedicated
play area and craft room. Small recaptured
spaces are just as satisfying: a captain's bed
nestled between bookcases is the perfect
place to catch a nap or read a few more
pages of a favorite book.

By its very nature, such a space feels
like a "prize," so invest the creativity,
energy, and materials needed to make it
special. Soon you'll wonder what you
ever did without it.

Pillows and soft
toys make this
special space even
more inviting.

In this home, "found space" in a high-ceilinged stairwell is a favorite spot for reading and daydreaming—
doubly appealing because you climb a ladder to get there. Paneling below the window bed and recessed
bookshelves at either end add architectural interest; soffit downlights illuminate the alcove at night.

LEFT: Tucked under the stairway, this wine cellar "reclaimed" what had been a 2-foot-deep closet; the space continues into the sloping area beneath the stairs. A glass door (open in photo) reveals the redwood interior and brick flooring.

RIGHT: A built-in bench with bead-board surround affords seating and storage adjacent to the shower in a spacious master bath. Furniture feet appear to raise the bench off the floor.

Literally carved out of the hillside, this hardworking garden room sits below
a deck, which was removed for the construction and then rebuilt once the room
was completed. Reminiscent of a European street lamp, a light fixture designed
for exterior use casts task light onto the sink and countertop.

LEFT: Nestled into the space created by a bend in the stairway, a small desk and armless upholstered chair provide an out-of-the-way spot for doing light paperwork.

BELOW: When the homeowners remodeled the existing stairway in their home, they decided to turn the lost space beneath the stairs into a playroom. The new little room is "paneled" with whiteboard, permitting the kids to draw to their hearts' content.

LEFT: A clever use of closet space in a chic attic sitting room produced cozy recessed seating, complete with world-map "wallpaper," curtains on rings, and stylish pillows.

working quarters

EVERY MORNING, MILLIONS OF PEOPLE GRAB A CUP OF COFFEE AND "COMMUTE" across the room, down the hall, or upstairs to a home office. The benefits of a home office for a full- or part-time worker are clear and enticing—reduced stress, less time in the car, and a better balance between work and family life.

The need for a quiet, organized, and comfortable space in which to work is obvious even if all you're doing is paying bills or e-mailing friends. Interestingly, an inverse relationship exists between the increase in office electronics and our desire to create a more individualized workspace: the more technology we accumulate, the more we want our home offices to look like, well, home. An efficient and attractive work area need not be large, though; with computers getting ever smaller and more portable, a home office can be as simple as an out-of-the-way spot for a desk and a chair.

Whatever your job or your household-management tasks demand, start thinking of your work environment as an extension of your home, and "going to work" will become one of life's pleasures.

Sliding doors on the upper shelf keep less attractive office items out of view.

In a small home that didn't have room for a separate office, the owner converted a living room closet into a compact, streamlined workstation. Removing the closet rod allowed for enclosed storage, an intermediate shelf, and a work surface with an almost-invisible drawer.

ABOVE: In this spacious office used by both homeowners, frameless cabinets with full-overlay doors and slab drawers have elements of fine furniture—recessed panels, a decorative valance above each workstation, and applied mouldings on the sides. Pendant fixtures serve as task lighting for the conference table; the bay at the end of the room has its own set of downlights.

FACING PAGE, TOP: A handy workstation built into a great room permits parents to be at the center of family activities while they manage their own schedules and tasks.

FACING PAGE, BOTTOM: The plan for this simple office arrangement revolved around the conference table, which was custom made for the homeowners several houses ago. Placing the table perpendicular to the window allows for a desk on either side. Different woods—for furniture, flooring, and window trim—add up to a varied yet naturally cohesive materials palette.

An addition above the garage created space for this home office, where a glass-topped table accommodates craft projects. An angled desk directs traffic into the room, toward French doors that open onto
a narrow balcony. Soft green walls and dark wood flooring make the white cabinetry and trim pop.

ABOVE: Where there used to be a full wall separating a spare room from the stairwell, a pony wall has opened up the space and turned a ho-hum area into a family-oriented office where everyone wants to be—for at-home work, craft projects, or just relaxing. A retro tuxedo sofa and whimsical ottoman set against the new wall got the decorating plan rolling, suggesting the cool palette for the walls, cabinets, and area rug.

FACING PAGE: When space is at a premium, versatile storage is essential. A combination of cabinets, shelves, and cubbies in this cozy home office makes the most of the square footage. A warm wood countertop goes beyond utilitarian; undercabinet lighting dispels shadows on the work surface.

RIGHT: In a mixed-purpose room alongside the kitchen (visible beyond the stained-glass window), a wall-mounted TV keeps the homeowners company while they do paperwork and other chores. Cabinets match those in the kitchen for a cohesive look.

LEFT: Smart home-office design combines the best technology with versatile components. Here, a stainless-steel desk on casters adds sleek, professional style while providing the flexibility to reconfigure the space as needed.

utility spaces

EVERY SPACE IN WHICH YOU SPEND TIME DESERVES TO BE AS ATTRACTIVE AS IT is useful, and that includes the room where you do the laundry. These days, the utility room is not only good looking, it's also a multitasking nerve center for the home.

To stand up to the demands made on this space, hardworking surfaces and components are a must. Easy-clean countertops and flooring that's impervious to water are ideal. For cabinetry, open and closed shelving, a broom closet for cleaning tools, and cubbies for the inevitable odds and ends afford maximum storage—and keep the area organized and calm.

Don't forget the fun stuff, the touches that make it a pleasure to walk into your utility room every day. Choose beautiful tile for the backsplash, or indulge your desire for natural-stone flooring. And there's no reason you can't have a *red* countertop, if that's what you want. Not only will your home function better, but chores will feel less like work when you've got a beautiful room in which to do them.

Miscellaneous items are easy to spot when they are stowed in pull-out baskets; open storage like this is a great way to visually lighten base cabinetry.

Solid and woven cabinet doors, a glass-tile backsplash, and a limestone floor with decorative glass-tile inlay add up to a handsome yet practical utility room. A center island provides plenty of room to fold clothes or spread out projects.

A state-of-the-art washer and dryer, ample counter space, and a farmhouse sink make this a dream of a laundry room. Bar stools supply counter seating for projects. Opposite the peninsula is a custom modular storage unit (right) that holds art supplies, scrap-booking paraphernalia, and wrapping materials.

BELOW: In a no-nonsense laundry room at the back of the house, open shelving keeps such mundane items as paper towels and cleaning supplies handy. A generous, old-fashioned porcelain sink with dual wall-mounted faucets is a striking alternative to a standard utility sink.

FACING PAGE: Just outside the guest bath in a contemporary home is this laundry center. Sliding doors fitted with laminated glass hide the washer and dryer when they are not in use; concrete flooring with radiant heat is a practical, comfortable choice for a hallway.

The homeowner and architect got everything they wanted into this compact utility room—"with just enough room for a person to turn around." A traditional tone is set by the granite countertop, white beadboard cabinetry, and deep, self-rimming laundry sink. On the opposite wall (right), the washer and dryer sit on pedestals above storage drawers. To the left is the broom closet.

living al fresco

TO ALMOST EVERYONE, "THE GOOD LIFE" INCLUDES RELAXING ON A PATIO, PORCH, or other outdoor space. As the trend toward outdoor entertaining has grown over the years, we've come a long way from the days of a few lawn chairs on a concrete slab patio. Today's carefully planned outdoor environments incorporate the best of interior design principles.

Decorating an outdoor living area is really no different from decorating any room within your home—except that there are fewer walls. You begin with your givens and your goals, formulate a plan that utilizes color and design concepts, and choose furnishings and accessories that suit your style. Every bit as important outdoors as indoors are furniture-arranging guidelines, for a significant portion of the time most of us spend on a patio, porch, or deck is in entertaining.

Proceed with a plan and a purpose, and your outdoor living space will serve you well—as both a revitalizing retreat and an al fresco living/dining room. In fact, the most versatile room in your house may not be inside at all.

Decorative plates displayed on the shingled wall make the open-air porch feel more like an inside room.

An open sleeping porch off an upstairs bedroom—a traditional feature of Craftsman design—is treated here as a sitting room in exemplary outdoor style. Wrought iron and glass are rugged enough to stand up to the weather, but so are the plush cushions and tailored curtains, thanks to improvements in indoor-outdoor fabrics.

LEFT: A focal-point fireplace makes relaxing on the patio a year-round lifestyle for the owners of this home. The prefab firebox is framed in wood and capped with stone veneer, which is lighter in weight than natural stone yet just as durable and appealing as the real thing.

RIGHT: A high retaining wall carved out the square footage for this leafy patio; recycled timbers form the trellis overhead. A wall fountain and antique wood corbels add touches of romance and old-world charm.

A study in outdoor design, this urban oasis intersperses vertical plantings with the horizontal planes of the deck, pools, and walls. Neutral colors in paving and decking make a calm backdrop for the palette of greens and blues displayed in the plants, tile, and ultramodern lounge chair.

FACING PAGE, TOP: Spanning the front of a two-story home, this balcony hosts multiple seating arrangements—some for lounging, others for dining. Roll-up fabric shades can be lowered against the sun.

BELOW: This tranquil outdoor family room lies between the living-dining and bedroom wings of a contemporary home. To facilitate the visual transition from indoor to outdoor spaces, the owners chose glass doors and neutral-toned composite wood decking.

A wide wraparound porch is home to a table and chairs for outdoor dining,
as well as deep wicker chairs with colorful cushions. The gas fireplace, cozy
on cool evenings, backs up to the fireplace in the family room.

RIGHT: Classic white wicker furniture invites sitting back and sipping lemonade on this vine-shaded porch. Lace curtains hung on the outside of the windows are part of the old-fashioned ambience.

LEFT: In a setting with strong architectural features, simple furniture is often most appropriate. Here, arched arbors frame the brick path to a front-yard patio just beyond swinging teak doors.

BELOW: On a terrace with far-reaching views of the city, chic indoor-outdoor fabric dresses up teak furniture. White welting on the cushions and pillows accentuates crisp pink and white stripes.

open house

FOR THOSE OF US WHO LOVE HOUSES AND DECORATING, A HOUSE TOUR IS AN irresistible event, opening doors to beautifully designed, architecturally significant homes. That's what this special section offers—a guided house tour via photos and words.

These homes illustrate a variety of decorating styles—from new traditional to contemporary casual, cottage charm to city chic. You won't see every room in each house, but you'll get a strong sense of the decor and perhaps see ways to interpret its palette or adapt the overall scheme to your own home.

Generous room shots illustrate how the pros arrange furniture and combine patterns and textures; close-ups focus on decorating details. A number of the homes belong to artists and designers—as you will see, they have applied their signature styles to their own living spaces. All the homes presented on these pages exemplify sound principles of color and design.

But why read when you can look? To "take the tour," you need not get in your car or even put on your walking shoes— simply turn the page.

Neutral surfaces— on walls, furnishings, and floors—intensify color in accessories and plants.

Living and dining areas flow seamlessly together in a remodel that renews the contemporary feel of this 1970s home. Vaulted ceilings embrace the space, making it feel cohesive; simple furnishings and a palette of warm, earthen hues reflect the natural surroundings. You'll see more photos of this home on the following pages.

FACING PAGE, TOP: The view across the dining table and into the kitchen gains dynamism from the striking work of art. Above the table, pendant fixtures lighted by halogen bulbs are fitted with frosted-glass cylinders inside clear ones.

BELOW: An integral-color plaster fireplace replaced the original brick surround, blending beautifully with other neutral materials in the room. For simplicity's sake, the homeowners opted not to include a mantel. Slate lines the firebox and covers the hearth.

LEFT: A towering lamp with scrunched-paper shade is both a light fixture and a decorative accessory, its verticality balancing the room's strong horizontal lines. Next to the lamp, a rounded wood table contrasts in color, texture, and visual weight.

house tour continues >

BELOW: In the house also shown on the previous pages, bamboo flooring unifies the kitchen and family room and harmonizes with maple cabinetry at the perimeter. The island cabinets are mahogany stained a light reddish brown.

RIGHT: In the seating area, a custom wall unit "steps down" with the vaulted ceiling. Open shelving holds books and mementos from the owners' travels; sliding doors below and closed cabinetry at one end hide less decorative items. Convenient to the comfy leather chairs, a tiered glass-and-metal side table keeps the space feeling open.

ABOVE: Countertops made of *pietra grigia*—a natural stone with properties of both limestone and slate— are the centerpiece of the kitchen design; wrapping the material over the ends of the island highlights its smooth surface and natural grain. On the backsplash, glass subway tile picks up the color of the walls, while a rich terra-cotta red behind the hood accentuates the room's height.

house tour ends

FACING PAGE: A folk-style Victorian farmhouse is the perfect canvas for a gutsy modern palette. In the dining room, crisp white beadboard and mouldings set off crimson walls, while historical photos and tabletop accessories stand out against the intense color.

RIGHT: In the bathroom, muted green bead-board and a deeper-hued vanity showcase the tub's elegant lines.

BELOW: Awash in creamy white and cool blue-green, the kitchen has a freshness and charm in keeping with the home's simple architecture. Carrara marble tiles make up the backsplash; the integral drainboard surrounding the sink is also marble. Mahogany countertops add a darker element (and visual weight) to the light-and-airy space.

house tour ends

ABOVE: An artfully organized open space and a blend of earthy materials give this mountain retreat its contemporary-cabin feel. A crushed-marble and stainless-steel chandelier over the dining table supplies a touch of glamour; a band of picture windows over the sink wall in the kitchen creates a space-enhancing, transparent backsplash.

LEFT: Opposite the kitchen, a built-in banquette is tucked behind a partial wall that separates it from the entry.

LEFT: A modern spin on a classic style, the farmhouse sink contrasts with textured steel-mesh cabinet inserts.

BELOW: Rough, board-formed concrete walls echo the look of wood used throughout the home and make an organic backdrop for the sleek, spare furnishings.

house tour continues >

Colors inspired by the ever-changing surrounding landscape make up the rich palette for the master bedroom. Behind the bed, an accent wall finished in suedelike plaster is an effective counterpoint to the redwood and concrete in the ceiling and on the other walls. A comfortable lounge chair (pictured above) beckons from a light-filled corner, where the deep windowsills double as display space.

The design cues in the soothing guest bedroom also come from the environs. Stylized botanical patterns covering the pillows, walls the color of native plants, and art inspired by the home's breathtaking setting make this space a natural getaway. A concrete vanity embedded with river rock carries the organic theme into the guest bath.

house tour ends 🏠

Though this home is new, the many elements of Craftsman design in the great room give it a traditional feeling. Mission-style chairs flank a fireplace made of black and gray granite with handpainted tiles; the black-granite hearth matches the kitchen countertops (see facing page, top photo). Integral-color plaster walls and knotty-alder cabinetry wrap the room in warmth.

ABOVE: The cabinets continue into the kitchen, but the real star is the distinctive island, painted with blue-green milk paint and finished with a charcoal glaze. Limestone tile on the floor and backsplash and a plaster-covered hood lighten the space. Tile and wood inlays duplicate the curve of the flooring as it transitions from the kitchen to the living area.

RIGHT: A stained-glass pendant in period style supplies ambient light over the antique trestle table, which is situated between the living area and the kitchen.

house tour ends 🏠

Function and flair come together in this lighthearted, kid-oriented home. Apple green cabinetry, yellow walls, and mustard countertops made of precast concrete set an upbeat mood in the open kitchen. In a departure from the usual rectangular shape, the island is curved at one end, easily accommodating three stools and accentuating the butcher-block top.

The homeowner wanted a centrally located desk, just around the corner from the kitchen, so the architect carved space from a pantry in the adjacent laundry room.

Close to the kitchen, this strategically located blackboard encourages the kids to draw—but not on the walls.

house tour
continues >

LEFT: In the living room of the home pictured on the previous pages, narrow moulding at plate-rail height allows the owners to hang (and move) art as they please.

BELOW: Since the house has no spare room, this charming hideaway does double duty as guest quarters and a den for watching TV. Curtains give the daybed a sense of enclosure; pocket doors fitted with antique-style glass provide privacy for guests. Drawers under the bed maximize storage.

ABOVE: In the dining room, directly opposite the kitchen (see page 146), the architect designed built-in cabinetry to replace a seldom-used window seat. "Ribbon" windows are at eye level when diners are seated, affording a view of the garden; a small window at either end cranks open.

LEFT: A fanciful sconce, complete with "insect life," delights all who see it.

house tour ends 🏠

The homeowners desired a single open space for the living room, dining room, and kitchen of their 1970s home, so walls were removed and replaced with slender, bronze-patina columns that give just the faintest hint of room divisions. Materials and furnishings reflect the owners' love of the clean, streamlined forms in Japanese art and design.

BELOW: For a subtle sense of enclosure, sliding glass panels separate the entry from the dining room. The lower track is visible in the floor; the upper roller track can be seen in the photo at left. A ribbon of inlaid river rock leads from the walkway into the entry, blurring the distinction between indoors and out.

RIGHT: A roomy stainless-steel kitchen table with a granite inset slides from side to side for flexibility and access to storage underneath.

house tour ends 🏠

A compact guest cottage has a cheery, flea-market-chic vibe, thanks to brightly painted wood, rattan, and wicker furniture in complementary red-orange and blue-green, with jolts of other pure hues. Funky accents include the weathered mirror behind the sink and the galvanized-tub light fixture suspended over the breakfast bar.

BELOW: A pair of rattan chairs painted to match the armoire form a cozy corner seating area.

LEFT: Pale blue-green walls give the space a sense of cohesion, while the painted armoire commands attention. White upholstered chairs and cushions covered in black-and-white prints keep the look crisp and uncluttered.

house tour ends

153

BELOW: Situated between the living room and the kitchen, this storage and display unit subtly demarcates the two areas. The distinctive veneer is olive ash.

FACING PAGE, TOP: The owners of this late-20th-century home—one of them also the designer—longed for a warm, modern design with clean lines and natural hues. A cut-velvet sectional and oversize "dottoman" (so named by a young neighbor) deliver the posh, streamlined look. Cabinetry to the right of the mosaic fireplace stores electronic gear; out-of-sight wires run across the lighting cove to the TV and other components housed in the room divider (shown on the facing page, bottom).

BELOW: In the combined kitchen and dining room, the materials are a mix of shiny and matte: glass tile on the backsplash, slate on the island bar, and gray elm for cabinetry. A dropped soffit over the table gives the dining area its own sense of space.

house tour continues >

ABOVE: In the master bedroom of the home shown on the preceding pages, the designer bumped out the wall to create room for a bed under the windows and a dresser on the opposite wall. The result? A space that feels open yet cozy. Painting the niche mushroom brown emphasizes the architecture and balances the cool blue-green and gray hues of the walls and soft furnishings.

LEFT: A low-voltage system utilizing 10-watt bulbs lights the way upstairs to the master bedroom and bath. The transformer is hidden under the stairs.

FACING PAGE: A new-neutral palette for the master bath is carried out by limestone tile in the shower, glass tile on the backsplash and one shower wall, and slab limestone on the countertop. An inset at either end of the vanity adds just enough room to comfortably accommodate two sinks.

house tour ends 🏠

Color sets the stage for a collection of enchanting furnishings and accessories in this 1920s California cottage. Light bounces off sunny yellow walls, while green cabinetry in the kitchen cools things down. The cheery red cupboard looks antique but is really new, its convincing patina having been achieved with multiple coats of paint.

RIGHT: Bright as a California sunset, the pillow-strewn sofa dominates the sunroom. A rare four-hoop hickory chair has an open, airy look; behind the sofa, a handmade pond boat is the star of the space.

LEFT: Against light yellow walls, a red-and-green color scheme unfolds in the master bedroom. Camp blankets from the 1920s, '30s, and '40s help to establish a retreat-and-relax atmosphere; eclectic vintage pieces, from baskets to a horse marionette, add to the charm.

house tour ends

A Greek Revival home of elegant proportions called for an aesthetic as up-to-date as it is timeless. In the spacious family room, new upholstered furnishings mix easily with an antique tilt-top writing desk and metal-based "campaign" tables, named after military pieces that folded or collapsed.

LEFT: The view from the dining room into the sunroom is framed by arched paneled doors. Low on the wall, simple dentil moulding provides a visual foundation for the art.

RIGHT: To complement dark-stained trim on French doors and transom windows in the sunroom, the designer selected neutral-hued furnishings, many also dark in value. There's a casual quality, too, as an antique wicker chair joins a modern sofa with rounded cushions and an antique stool serves as an end table.

house tour ends 🏠

161

all about color

CHOOSING COLOR FOR A ROOM—OR FOR THE ENTIRE HOUSE—IS ON ALMOST everyone's decorating to-do list. And, more than any other part of the process, it can bring your project to a screeching halt. But you don't have to be afraid of color, because finding just-right hues for your home is easier than it sounds.

All you need is a grasp of a few simple concepts and a willingness to observe color all around you— in paint, flooring, furnishings, and accessories. This chapter lays out the basics to help you develop a color palette tailored to your personal style and situation. Included are custom color rings that illustrate the 12 pure hues in versions that are easy to use in today's decorating schemes. An "encyclopedia" of colors shows, at a glance, the infinite options. To make things even easier, we've assembled a collection of 16 ready-made Lowe's color palettes as inspiration, to use "as is" or to edit for your own decorating plan. For matches to these palettes, see the Lowe's color chip numbers on pages 420–423.

color basics

COLOR DOES MORE TO SET THE MOOD AND STYLE OF A ROOM THAN ANY OTHER design element. Wouldn't it be great to be able to choose colors with confidence, knowing you'll love the results?

This section explains color terminology, introduces an updated version of the color wheel, and shows you how to combine colors like a pro. The terms used here come from basic color theory, developed by artists, but they are just as applicable for decorating your home.

the language of color

To create a great color scheme, it helps to learn some common terminology. To begin with, the word "hue" is just another name for color. Turquoise and fuchsia are hues; so are softer colors like lilac and maize. All colors have three key characteristics— "value," "temperature," and "intensity." Understanding each of these is important when you are working with color.

value The lightness or darkness of a color is what's meant by its "value." Infinite variations exist for any color, from the lightest light to the darkest dark. Sky blue is a light value of blue, stone-washed denim a medium value, and navy a dark value. Light values appear to expand space, making a room seem larger, while dark values contract space, making a room feel cozier or more intimate.

temperature If you draw an imaginary line across the color ring (page 167) from yellow-green to red-violet, the colors to the left—yellows, oranges, and reds— are warm in visual temperature. These are considered "advancing" colors, because they seem closer to the viewer than they really are; that's why warm colors on walls make a room feel pleasantly snug. Cooler hues—those to the right of your imaginary line—are considered "receding"; they appear more distant than they are, making a room feel calm and spacious.

Light and medium values of cool blue make up the palette for this tranquil bedroom. Accents of warm yellow-green keep the scheme from seeming icy.

LEFT: Painting one wall an intense red provided the punch in this light-washed kitchen. Yellow walls and oak flooring contribute warmth, too.

intensity The third color characteristic describes the brightness of a color. The colors on the pure color ring are brilliant, or "saturated." Low-intensity colors, on the other hand, are more muted. Turn to pages 168–169 to see less intense versions of the 12 pure colors.

Try picturing two versions of a favorite color. As an example, chartreuse is an intense yellow-green; willow is a low-intensity (muted) version of yellow-green.

Designers consider intensity to be the "great unifier" of color. That is, you can combine any colors as long as they are similar in intensity; they just seem to go together. Take a look at the color palette cards at your Lowe's store and you'll see that various colors with the same intensity just "feel right" together. For example, bright red and soft sage may seem discordant, but a less intense brick red is compatible with sage.

If you have trouble distinguishing between value and intensity, think about the two characteristics separately. When looking at a color, first ask yourself, "Is it light, medium, or dark?" That's the value. Then ask, "Is it bright or dull?" That's the intensity.

BELOW: On a laundry room backsplash, low-intensity tiles in many colors harmonize, and walls painted pale yellow-green are similarly low-key.

using the color ring

If you're tempted to skip these pages—after all, who hasn't seen a color wheel?—stop for a moment and reconsider. Most of us never consult a color wheel when choosing colors for our homes, and for good reason. The colors shown on the typical color wheel—neon orange, bright red, pure violet—are not common in home decor, while the sophisticated, nuanced colors more typically found in today's home furnishings, such as celadon, aubergine, and cinnabar, don't even appear on the wheel. No wonder the color wheel seems useless.

But it's not! In fact, the color wheel is nothing short of magical. With a basic understanding, you can use this versatile tool to build a color scheme from scratch—or to fix one that isn't working.

It helps to simplify the standard color wheel, which generally contains 36 colors, to a color ring (as shown on the facing page) with only the 12 "pure" hues. Refer to this ring as you read about the different kinds of colors and how they are created.

primary colors Red, blue, and yellow are called "primary" because they cannot be created from other colors. Instead, in varying combinations and proportions, they make up all the rest of the colors on the ring. Intense primaries in large quantities can be overpowering; lower intensity versions—such as cranberry, indigo, and gold—are easier on the eye.

PRIMARY COLORS

SECONDARY COLORS

secondary colors Mixing two primaries results in a secondary color. Red mixed with yellow makes orange, blue mixed with yellow makes green, and blue mixed with red makes violet.

intermediate colors Sometimes called tertiary colors, these are made by mixing a primary with an adjacent secondary color. Red (a primary) and violet (a secondary) combine to make red-violet. Starting with yellow and moving clockwise around the color ring, the intermediate colors are yellow-green, blue-green, blue-violet, red-violet, red-orange, and yellow-orange. More complex than primary or secondary colors, intermediates are among the most versatile. Think, for example, of the color red-violet; made up of three-fourths red and one-fourth blue, it works with many other colors because it contains both red and blue.

INTERMEDIATE COLORS

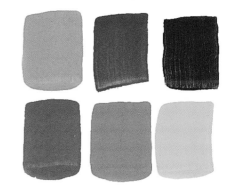

color relationships The position of one color on the ring in relation to another determines its affinities and contrasts. Adjacent colors (blue, blue-violet, and violet, for example) are called "analogous." Because these three share a common color—in this case blue—they are naturally in harmony with one another.

Opposing colors, like blue and orange, are "complements," meaning that they balance each other in visual temperature. Colors that are just approximately opposite each other are also well balanced;

they're known as "near complements." For instance, lavender blue (a version of blue-violet) is a near complement of yellow.

So what about those other colors, like celadon? Here's the secret to success with the color ring: recognize that the pure colors on the ring are the *source* of all the wonderful "real-life" colors used in decorating, most of which are created by adding some black, white, or gray. Pure orange, for example, is the source of spice, pumpkin, and peach. Being able to place real-life colors on the color ring—olive is just a dark yellow-green, iris really a light blue-violet—is the first step to using it effectively.

To make the leap from theory to practice, now turn the page and look at the four custom color rings. They show less intense versions of the 12 pure colors, in values ranging from light to dark. Just for fun, find a color you like on one of the custom rings (such as terra-cotta, found at the nine o'clock position on Color Ring 4); then turn back to the pure ring to identify its source (red-orange in this example). To find a cool contrast to terra-cotta, look across the custom ring to muted teal, a less intense version of pure blue-green. Once you realize that the colors you find in paint, flooring, and furnishings actually have places on the color ring, you'll be well on your way to building successful color schemes.

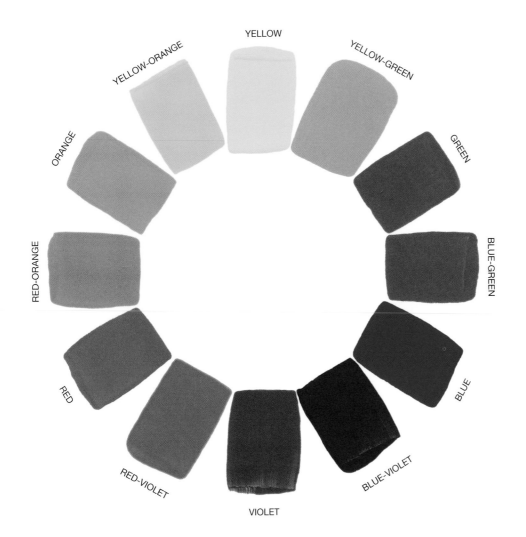

YELLOW
YELLOW-ORANGE
YELLOW-GREEN
ORANGE
GREEN
RED-ORANGE
BLUE-GREEN
RED
BLUE
RED-VIOLET
BLUE-VIOLET
VIOLET

custom color rings

The pure color ring is fine for introducing you to the 12 basic colors, but unless you're planning a palette of colors in their purest form, you'll need to see some other options. Color rings portraying the hues in values and intensities that you can easily apply to your home are more useful. The rings on these two pages display the 12 colors in four different values: very light, light, medium, and dark. All the colors on these rings are less intense than those on the pure color ring. In reality, you will probably combine colors that vary in value and intensity: that happens naturally when you gather different materials. But the rings can help you become aware of the kinds of colors you prefer.

color ring 1
Very Light-Value,
Low-Intensity Colors
These are the colors we normally associate with the word "tint." Very light, subdued colors, such as celery, chamois, and fawn, are often chosen for walls.

color ring 2
Light-Value,
Low-Intensity Colors
Still low in intensity, these colors are just a bit darker in value than those in Color Ring 1. Use them when you want quiet color that has a little more body.

color ring 3

Medium-Value,
Low-Intensity Colors

Versatile and easy to live with, these subdued colors of medium value—like mauve and lichen—are often used for upholstery and walls when you want a distinct color presence, but nothing too obtrusive.

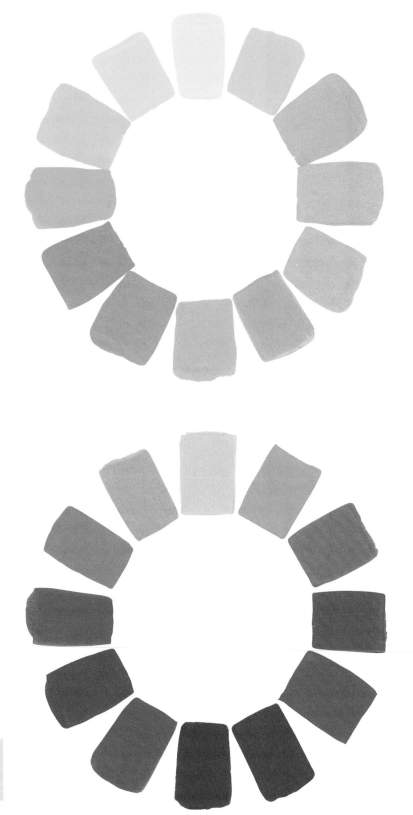

color ring 4

Dark-Value,
Low-Intensity Colors

Dark, subdued colors like eggplant and merlot add depth to a scheme. They combine naturally with rich woods, especially in rooms used at night—a dining room, perhaps, or a library.

 **QUICK TIP**

You may ask, "Why isn't brown on the color ring?" In fact, most browns are dark-value, low-intensity versions of red-orange, orange, or yellow-orange.

four strategies for combining colors

STUNNING EFFECTS OCCUR WHEN YOU COMBINE COLORS. Your least favorite color is suddenly perfect in the company of its complement, and unlikely combinations turn out to make beautiful blends. Take a look at the possibilities.

1 **monochromatic** One-color combinations are among the most elegant of schemes. In the airy bedroom at left, the values are light, but the blues vary just a bit from wall to easy chair to accessories; bleached wood floors stick to the pale theme. One-color rooms demand variety, or monotony can set in. Here, the bamboo bed frame and wrought-iron curtain rods supply dark accents, while picture frames painted a pale blue-violet are a bit of a surprise.

2 **analogous** Colors that lie side by side on the color ring, such as yellow-green and true green, are analogous. You can include up to four hues in an analogous scheme—for instance, yellow-green through blue—as long as only one primary (in this case blue) is present in the run of colors. A narrower analogous scheme of just two or three colors works best when there's a mix of patterns, textures, and finishes, as seen at right in the textured rug, lacquered tray, and patterned pillow. Neutrals play an important role in an analogous scheme, supplying contrast and a sense of visual calm.

3 complementary Schemes based on colors opposite one another on the color ring are complementary. The vibrant living room pictured at right features complementary yellow-green chairs and red-violet sofas. Adding intense accents of other colors softens the contrast of direct complements and keeps them from fighting. When using any complementary combination, feel free to wander a little around the color ring; sometimes near complements make more interesting color schemes than direct ones. It takes daring to use full-strength complements; if you do, add some neutrals to your palette and distribute the colors around the room.

4 complex Mixing colors that are spaced around the color ring results in a "complex" combination. It's not necessary to know the theory behind this kind of color scheme; just think of it as a sampling of both related and contrasting hues. In the contemporary living room at right, yellow-orange (the vase), yellow-green (the wall color), and blue-green (the chair) are accented by red-orange (the lamp), which lies opposite blue-green on the color ring. The blue-gray sofa and dark wood coffee table function as neutrals. The key to any complex color combination is balance; if some colors are neighbors on the ring (or near neighbors), introduce a bit of opposing color to round out the palette.

Lots of natural light allows you the luxury of selecting a subtle palette that might be lost in a darker room. In this low-key living room, plentiful daylight showcases a range of exquisite neutral hues.

how color works

Color doesn't exist in a vacuum; it's always interacting with the decorating "environment." Certain physical variables—particularly light—powerfully affect our perception of color. In turn, color can alter our awareness of physical space in striking ways.

color and light How the colors in your home look to you will depend on the time of day, the season, and the way a room is situated. As the day progresses from morning to afternoon, natural light becomes stronger, making colors appear more intense. Seasonal light varies, too: light is gentler in winter than in summer, when the sun is higher in the sky. North-facing rooms receive less direct sunlight year-round, and that light tends to be "cool"; south-facing rooms get more and "warmer" light. Conventional wisdom says you should balance the temperature in a room by using warm colors in north-facing rooms and cool colors in south-facing ones. But you can always ignore that advice and play up a room's natural characteristics instead by using colors of similar temperature.

Most light in your home is artificial, and the color of that light varies. (See "Shedding Light on Bulbs," page 299.) Warm light from standard incandescent bulbs amplifies yellows and reds but tends to dull the cooler colors. Halogen bulbs produce a whiter, brighter light. At one time, fluorescent light intensified blues and greens (it was therefore considered undesirably "cold") and muddied yellows and reds. Today's fluorescents come in a wide spectrum, however, offering cool and warm white light and everything in between.

Light fixtures themselves can contribute color to a room. Pendant lights that have brightly colored glass shades not only make effective accents but also color the light they give off. A warm-hued lampshade will cast its own glow, influencing the way other colors look and helping to establish a mood. (Be aware that the darker or more colorful the lampshade, the more it will tend to soak up light.)

It's a good idea to view your sample decorating materials under the kind of light you are planning for the room where they will be used.

color and space Using color to define or alter space is really about creating illusions. The rule of thumb is that light and cool colors visually expand space, whereas dark and warm colors make it seem smaller. Similarly, low-intensity colors make a room feel more spacious, intense ones to contract the space.

BELOW: When the ceilings are high, horizontal bands of color bring them down a bit to suggest a more intimate atmosphere. Choosing closely related colors in the same low intensity keeps the stripes from taking over.

continues >

LEFT: A combination of natural and artificial light offers the best of both worlds: daylight coming through windows or skylights, supplemented with task, accent, and decorative light as needed. In this contemporary kitchen, fluorescent downlights and hood lights bring out the colors of the honed marble (on the countertops and backsplash) and red birch cabinetry.

In an open floor plan, brilliant yellow and red divide the space into distinct, task-oriented areas. Cool green in between is a welcome visual break.

In practice, though, these optical effects are modified by many factors, such as the quantity and quality of light a room receives. Painting the walls a light color will brighten a naturally dark room but won't transform it into an open, airy space. A rich color won't necessarily bring intimacy to a large room. Sometimes it's best to evaluate what you have and go with it rather than work against it.

But do consider putting color to use when you want to subtly alter the apparent proportions of a room. Painting one end of a long, narrow room a warmer, darker color than the other walls can create the illusion of a better-proportioned space. In a square room, painting one wall a more intense color than the others can diminish the boxy look.

Color can affect the sense of space in adjoining rooms, as well. Carrying the same paint color and flooring from room to room makes for a smooth visual transition and opens up a small home. If you prefer distinctly separate spaces, on the other hand, you can use different colors for adjoining rooms (see "Layered Color," pages 216–217). Or combine these approaches with related but not identical colors for connecting spaces—perhaps a light, warm taupe for the entry and a darker, cooler taupe in the living room.

LOWE'S QUICK TIP

What color should you paint the ceiling? A time-honored approach is to use the same color on the ceiling as on the mouldings. Or ask Lowe's to mix a "half-formula" color consisting of half wall color and half white trim color.

a color encyclopedia

HERE'S A RULE YOU CAN RELY ON: ANY COLOR OR COMBINATION OF COLORS THAT makes you happy is the right one! If you have a keen color sense—a talent that a fortunate few possess naturally—you can combine colors freely and intuitively, knowing you'll enjoy the results. But many of us suffer paralyzing hesitation when it comes to developing a palette; after all, choosing colors on a hit-or-miss basis can cost both money and time. You may know your favorite color, or feel more comfortable with some colors than others, yet have no clue about what to do with that information. If you fall into this category, the color encyclopedia that follows can help you visualize the possibilities before you make your final choices.

Each of the 12 colors on the pure color ring (see page 167) is represented on two pages. Paint dabs on the lefthand pages illustrate different values and intensities of the color. The short text offers ideas for using the hue; photos show it in context. A color palette accompanies one of the photos in each color category, along with a description of the color relationships. Lowe's paint colors used in the palettes are listed on pages 420–423.

Browse this section, note the colors that especially appeal to you, and observe how they work in real-life settings. Then play designer—with increased confidence and a sense of fun—in your own home.

yellow

THERE'S NOTHING LIKE YELLOW TO LIFT THE spirits and lighten the mood. For an airy, monochromatic look, try yellow walls with vanilla trim; paint louvered shutters the same warm white. Or enjoy the dance of daffodil yellow and analogous apple green, with dashes of blue and red. Spice up medium-value yellows by adding complementary violet or near-complementary red-violet, or use soft rose to enhance a lower-intensity yellow. Saturated mustard yellow is powerful with Chinese red; pale yellow marries well with gentle versions of true green, blue, and pink. To create a springtime mix, combine yellow with mint green and analogous robin's-egg blue. If you like the energy of chrome yellow, jazz it up with black and white; if you dare, add stoplight red.

LEFT: Warm, sunny yellow is the primary hue in this Mediterranean-inspired kitchen. Olive green (a dark version of yellow-green) broadens the scheme of primary colors; granite and wood countertops introduce natural color.

yellow-green

YELLOW-GREEN IS A LARGE AND EXTENDED COLOR family, with many distant relatives. Familiar names like chartreuse and olive drab reflect the range of values and intensities you'll find within this category. Used full strength, yellow-green makes a powerful accent color—as piping on a cushion or beading on a lampshade. Create a high-energy analogous scheme by moving toward yellow and beyond on the color ring to include yellow-orange and orange. For a breezier look, go in the opposite direction and pair pale yellow-green with summery blue-green or blue. A low-intensity yellow-green like celadon harmonizes with warm beiges and creamy whites. To use yellow-green with its near complements (the colors on either side of red-violet), work with red for a warm combination or violet for a cooler one.

ABOVE: Cabinets painted two versions of low-intensity yellow-green separate from the neutral trim color and read as distinct pieces. Walls of rich violet—yellow-green's near complement—give the slender desk alcove visual impact.

green

GREEN HAS A FRESHNESS THAT PLACES IT ON almost everyone's list of favorite colors. Who doesn't enjoy a glimpse of green outside a window or feel that a room is incomplete without at least a touch of this living color? Because it is composed of yellow (a warm color) and blue (a cool color), green works well with every other hue. In the company of warm yellow, peach, and pink, green exerts a cooling influence. With blues and blue-violets, hues on the same side of the color ring, green becomes a cool cohort. It combines just as easily with yellow-green and blue-green, its color-ring neighbors. Sage, a very low-intensity green, wakes up in the company of muted plum and pink—near complements—or takes a leading role when paired with neutrals.

ABOVE: Sophisticated yet playful, this kitchen displays a palette that's unexpected for painted surfaces. Low-intensity green covering the cabinetry and banquette is beautifully in sync with primary-based accents of deep slate blue (on the island), bright marigold, and tomato.

blue-green

CLEAN AND REFRESHING, BLUE-GREEN REFLECTS the calming influence of blue, with a bit of warmth from its green parent. Blue-green harmonizes with hues on the same side of the color ring, in combinations that range from casually fresh (spa blue and apple green) to handsomely formal (verdigris and gold). As often as not, blue-green begs to be balanced with warmer hues; try it with cinnamon, terra-cotta, or even cherry red. Over large areas, a muted blue-green is easiest to live with; intense tropical versions work best as accents. Blue-greens have a prominent place in the history of design. The light-value blue-green associated with aged frescoes and weathered copper suggests old-world ambience. Williamsburg blue—really a blue-green hue—was a staple of Colonial palettes, and apothecary blue (a pale blue-green) flourished in the Federal period.

TOP: Muted blue-green cabinetry harmonizes with a yellow-green countertop because only one hue (green) separates them on the color ring. Celadon, lavender, cinnamon, and mustard are just a few of the colors in the glass-tile mosaic backsplash.

blue

THE BLUE FAMILY IS BROAD, RANGING FROM BABY blue through cornflower to ultramarine. This color has long connoted a spiritual quality, and a predominantly blue space is often calming and serene. Because it's the coolest of the cool hues, though, blue must be handled with respect—otherwise it can seem a little melancholy, even chilly and unwelcoming. Paired with white, blue comes across with invigorating freshness; visualize cumulus clouds over a cerulean lake, or a whitewashed Greek village silhouetted against the Aegean Sea. Blue and white have been a favorite combination in the decorative arts for centuries— think of Chinese ginger jars. To bring warmth to a blue room, pair chambray with buttercup, robin's-egg blue with pink, or azure blue with dark lime green.

RIGHT: Analogous blues and greens refresh an open living space. Though all are from the same side of the color ring, these cool hues vary in value and intensity.

blue-violet

BLUE-VIOLET IS THE COLOR OF GRAPE HYACINTH and, in its lightest form, the delicate haze on Concord grapes. In a monochromatic or an analogous scheme, blue-violet can expand the perception of space and make a small room's boundaries dissolve. Like its violet parent, blue-violet absorbs light and sometimes appears cold; energize and warm it by adding red-violet or its direct complement, yellow-orange. To create a balanced combination of colors equidistant on the color ring, team periwinkle with apple (a medium value of yellow-green) and salmon (a light value of red-orange). Consider a wall striped in pale blue-violet with creamy white or wispy apricot. Or take your color cues from nature and check the western sky at sunset, where you might see blue-violet streaked with coral, gold, and gray.

ABOVE: In this small but airy living room, periwinkle walls beautifully frame a built-in hutch; pale green highlights the inset. Related blues and sandy neutrals round out the light, cool scheme.

violet

AT ITS FULL INTENSITY, VIOLET—BETTER KNOWN as purple—tends to elicit strong reactions, both positive and negative. Some consider it a magical, mysterious color, while others find it dreary. But violet comes in many forms and moods. Dark versions such as eggplant convey formality and dignity when teamed with gray or taupe. Deep violet is luscious and dramatic paired with complementary gold, and cooled by sage green. Lighter, romantic hues like lilac combine easily with pinks of similar value and greens of similar intensity. To a monochromatic violet scheme that's light and low-key, add very pale gray or white; warm it with a bit of creamy apricot or yellow, the complement of violet. To see how nature mixes violet with other hues, take a look at primroses or violas, with their yellow centers and lush green leaves.

RIGHT: A modern palette consisting of true violet (the near wall), brilliant blue-green (the dining table and chairs), and intense yellow-orange (the pendants) is drawn from all around the color ring. A light-value version of yellow-orange repeats on the far wall, tying together the living and dining spaces.

red-violet

NESTLED BETWEEN RED AND VIOLET ON THE color ring, red-violet is warmer than violet but cooler than red. It has a jewel-like quality—envision the sheen of a Mission fig—that can endow a room with richness, especially in dark-value versions like merlot. Orchid is a lighter value, fuchsia a more saturated form. Intense red-violet is powerful when used on walls, but it also works beautifully as an accent for new neutrals (see pages 202–203) or in the form of silky sheer curtains. It also makes a dignified partner with brushed nickel, copper, brass, or any other metal finish. For a tropical palette, combine fuchsia (red-violet) with teal (blue-green) and mango (yellow-orange). If you need a fresh squeeze of color, add lemon yellow.

ABOVE: Intensity is the great unifier of disparate colors. Here, bright blue sofas and yellow-green window treatments are supported by rich red-violet walls. Blue-violet comes into play, too, in the geometric area rug.

red

PRIMARY RED IS HOT, EYE-STOPPING, AND A LITTLE risky. Because it's visually demanding and carries such emotional significance, intense red needs to be used with care. Lipstick red works with pink, even hot pink, in daring contemporary settings. Rich red combines with cadet blue in traditional schemes, or with complementary green and yellow-green in cottage-style florals or vintage tablecloths. True neutrals—black, gray, and white—balance the vibrancy of reds and make them "safer." New neutrals (pages 202–203) gain energy from deep reds like cranberry and Bordeaux or make calming partners for ripe tomato and chile reds. Full-bodied reds look wonderful glazed or polished, as on a Chinese red lacquered screen or red Venetian plaster walls. Keep in mind that warm colors—and none is warmer than red—appear to advance, making red rooms seem more intimate.

LEFT: A red room pulsates with visual energy, showing off the power of this hot hue. Red and orange silk pillows add sheen, while the yellow-green sofa provides both texture and visual relief.

red-orange

MORE COMPLEX THAN EITHER OF ITS PARENT colors, red-orange is warm and welcoming, the color of iron-rich earth and traditional clay flowerpots. Terra-cotta is a popular version that teams naturally with warm ocher (yellow-orange) and moss (yellow-green). But such a warm color also begs for cooler hues like awning green and nautical blue. A three-color combination of terra-cotta, sapphire (dark-value blue-violet), and olive satisfies the eye's desire for balance in visual temperature. Red-orange comes in lighter and brighter forms as well: shrimp, coral, salmon, and persimmon, to name a few. In its darker values it appears as russet and sienna. A natural for wherever people gather, red-orange works well on walls, enveloping a room with its glow and flattering guests. Used with its blue-green complement, red-orange supplies earthy warmth for a Southwestern palette.

BELOW: This contemporary living area crackles with saturated red-orange, calmed by low-intensity green and neutral gray. Celadon, moss, and salmon in the upholstery fabric expand the scheme, with just a hint of coolness coming from a pale blue-green.

orange

MIX YELLOW AND RED AND YOU GET ORANGE—
a juicy, beach-ball hue often considered too "hot"
for interiors. Few are bold enough to use it "as is"
on walls or major furnishings, but less concentrated
versions please almost everyone. The key to success
with orange is modulation in value and intensity.
Muted, light-value orange is flattering on walls; low-
intensity, dark-value orange becomes burnt umber or
brown, familiar colors for cabinetry and case goods.
At full strength, orange's true complement, blue, can
look harsh, but the colors that flank blue (blue-violet
and blue-green) make supportive partners. Three-
color schemes incorporating orange soften its impact:
imagine pale peach (orange), mint (green), and lilac
(violet), or maybe cinnamon, juniper, and eggplant.
Sometimes overpowering in large quantities, orange
is ideal for pillows, candles, or art.

ABOVE: What might appear at first glance to be a mono-chromatic combination actually contains bits of color from the opposing side of the color ring, producing a richer scheme. Yellow-green, blue-green, and violet calm the intense oranges; the neutral sofa provides the perfect foil for paisley pillows.

yellow-orange

RICHER THAN YELLOW BUT LESS ASSERTIVE THAN orange, yellow-orange has a luminous, vibrant quality that makes it a versatile color for the home. This cheerful hue abounds in nature, from mangoes to marigolds to butternut squash. Pine planking, natural wicker, even brass are examples of decorating materials with yellow-orange as their source color. Light, creamy versions are favored for walls where yellow might be too bright and orange too strong. Yellow-orange lends itself easily to elegant monochromatic schemes, but it also combines beautifully with blue-green and red-violet to form a complex combination (see pages 170–171). Think of saffron (yellow-orange), jade (blue-green), and plum (red-violet)—or, for a lighter look, papaya, aquamarine, and orchid. Yellow-orange is cooled by its complement, blue-violet; add yellow-green for a lively palette of periwinkle, honey, and lime.

ABOVE: Plaster walls
the color of a ripe papaya,
cabinets stained a rich
reddish-brown, and solid-
surface countertops are
decidedly warm in visual
temperature; gray-green
slate floor tile cools the
palette.

working with neutrals

THE TRUE NEUTRALS—BLACK, WHITE, AND GRAY—DON'T HAVE A PLACE ON THE color ring, but they nevertheless play an essential role in decorating. Sometimes referred to as "noncolors," true neutrals provide visual relief without adding color or altering existing color relationships. White walls, for example, let the focus fall on colorful art; black metal chairs set off, but do not compete with, a table painted intense red; gray slate counters balance brightly colored kitchen cabinets.

Texture always matters, but it's especially important with true neutrals, because their lack of color makes the interplay of light and shadow even more significant. The bounce of sunshine off glossy white paint, the variation of light perceived in a coarsely woven black damask, the shimmer of dove gray silk taffeta—texture plays with neutral colors in intriguing ways. Introduce different textures in a neutral scheme; the hand and the eye crave variety.

what about white? White is famous for creating that prized light-and-airy look. Walls painted white reflect both natural and artificial light; white ceilings reflect 10 percent more light than even the palest hue. White paint is a good choice for rooms with odd or irregular features, because minor flaws nearly disappear in the absence of color. Used on doors, mouldings, and fireplace mantels, white breaks up expanses of color and emphasizes architectural lines.

If you decide to paint your walls white, you'll quickly discover that not all whites are created equal, and almost none is pure. In fact, true-neutral white, devoid of all color, is rarely used on walls because it feels too cold and stark. Most white paints contain undertones of either warm or cool colors, typically creamy yellow, beige, or bluish gray.

When the styling is spare, true neutrals are enhanced by a dose of intense color and an expanse of warm-toned flooring.

LOWE'S QUICK TIP
Undertones are easiest to see in paint brochures, where samples are grouped for easy comparison. Or pick up paint strips that contain several whites and lay them side by side to compare.

basic black Black is everywhere in the decorating world, in both starring and supporting roles. Wrought-iron bed frames, metal floor lamps, and granite countertops are but a few examples of black in furnishings, accessories, and materials. Black is bold and sophisticated; as such, it's best used in small to moderate doses. (The classic black leather sofa and baby grand piano are notable exceptions.) Think of it as an accent, a sort of punctuation mark in a decorating scheme.

going gray Glamorous gray, often associated with Art Deco design, is sometimes called "the all-purpose neutral." A mixture of black and white, gray bridges the gap between other colors without taking over. In a contem- porary room with curry-toned walls and mahogany tables, for example, a charcoal gray suede sectional creates a "neutral zone" between the intensity of the walls and the warmth of the woods.

In decorating, gray often appears in the form of metal accessories and hardware— a silver tea service, satin-nickel drawer pulls, a polished-chrome floor lamp—or in natural materials such as slate, terrazzo, and concrete.

TOP: An offbeat mix of elements—hand-painted cabinet, shell-encrusted mirror frame, and stylish table lamps—looks both dressy and casual in crisp black and white.

LEFT: You can soften the edges of neutral metals with tactile materials. Close proximity to a cozy upholstered armchair keeps stainless-steel bar stools from looking cold.

New-neutral celadon (a grayish yellow-green) appears throughout this contemporary kitchen—on the bar stools, tile backsplash, and walls—and mixes beautifully with the cherry cabinetry.

a contemporary take on neutrals

Have you ever looked at a fabric or paint chip and wondered, "What color is that, anyway? Is it green? Or is it gray?" Chances are you were puzzling over one of the "new neutrals." These versatile yet difficult-to-describe hues are very low-intensity versions of the 12 colors on the color ring. To put it another way, new neutrals are colors that have been "neutralized," or neutrals that have been "colorized."

Although you're not likely to mix your own paint colors, it's helpful to understand where new neutrals come from. A new-neutral color is the result of adding a bit of one color to a larger amount of its complement, thereby lowering the intensity of the latter. (Usually white or black is added to lighten or darken the color.) For example, a small amount of red paint added to its complement, green, produces a less intense green: a new-neutral green. In the same way, a bit of green added to red creates a dull, new-neutral red.

Like any other colors, new neutrals can range in value from light to dark. Ecru, linen, and pearl are examples of light-value new neutrals; khaki, camel, and cocoa have medium values; and charcoal, coffee bean, and chestnut are dark. New neutrals vary in temperature, as well: a warm taupe and a cool bluish gray are both considered to be new neutrals.

These muted hues lend ambience and a hint of color to a room but never over-

whelm or stand out. New-neutral walls
envelop a room with nuanced color, making an excellent backdrop for art and the
perfect foil for treasured antiques. (Many
"historic" colors are in fact new neutrals.)
Their understated character also makes
these hues good candidates for decorative
paint finishes, which rely on subtle pattern
and texture for their appeal.

New-neutral colors are ideal for major
pieces of furniture like sofas, because they
won't lock you into one palette: you can
change smaller, less expensive, more colorful pieces while keeping the main (and
more expensive) one. The same is true
with flooring: you can change furnishings
without replacing the floor. A new-neutral
floor will also "anchor" the room in a way
a brighter, more distinctive color can't.

Once you determine the source color
of a new neutral, the color ring is invaluable
in working with these low-key hues. A
color described as "laurel leaf," for example,
is a dark-value, very low-intensity version
of yellow-green. For a complementary
contrast, you might choose merlot, a low-
intensity red-violet that lies opposite
yellow-green on the ring. To become
better acquainted with new neutrals, flip
through decorating magazines, picking
them out and trying to determine their
source colors. You'll be surprised at how
often these subtle hues appear in both
contemporary and traditional design.

TOP RIGHT: In this sumptuous neoclassical living
room, new neutrals pervade. Walls the color of latte,
oyster-white upholstery, and a multihued area rug
offer up layered color that feels as lavish as the room's
architecture. Re-covered in brushed aluminum, the
original fireplace mantel now adds its own flash of
true-neutral color.

BOTTOM RIGHT: A small, angular bathroom features
a mix of materials—plaster walls, slate tile, maple
cabinetry, and a solid-surface countertop—in new-
neutral hues.

sixteen ready-made
lowe's color palettes

THE PALETTES APPEARING ON THESE PAGES ARE MEANT TO INSPIRE, WHETHER you use a color grouping just as it is shown here or edit it to fit your own particular plan. See pages 420–423 for the Valspar paint numbers that correspond to the palette colors; for the truest color match, be sure to read the note on page 420.

palette 1

A delicate palette of new-neutral hues, with just a hint of color, evokes a feeling of calm. Pale peach and yellow convey a sense of spaciousness, while a wheat-toned beige and a brown that leans toward mauve add body and depth to the scheme.

palette 2

New neutrals with warm undertones blend beautifully in this quiet palette. Use either of the palest colors on walls for an airy effect. Chocolate brown "grounds" the sheer hues; a medium-value gray bridges the gap between light and dark values.

palette 3

Camel and warm taupe make pleasing companions for a weathered green. Pale papaya and earthen black supply light and dark values and bracket the new-neutral hues. Cover the walls with the lightest color or, for more body, the medium-value camel or taupe.

palette 4

For a room that is both tranquil and sophisticated, start with walls painted a warm white. The lighter gray is appropriate for silky curtain panels, fabric shades, or a finely proportioned chair; the darker gray and medium-value taupe are ideal for larger furnishings.

palette 5

A combination of palomino gold, dusty peach, slate blue, and soft plum draws from all around the color ring; light and medium beige function as neutrals. Use any of the darker hues on walls as a dramatic backdrop, or seek out lighter versions of these colors to achieve an ethereal effect.

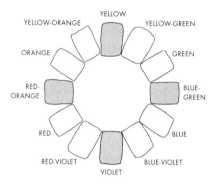

palette 6

A palette befitting a summer cottage includes pale blue, blue-violet, red-violet, yellow, and yellow-green. With such a variety of low-intensity hues, the options are many: imagine furniture painted forget-me-not blue with purplish pink accessories, all against a backdrop of delicate yellow or apple green.

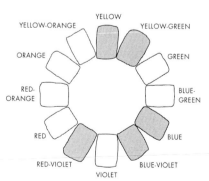

palette 7

Very low-intensity yellow-green and blue-green suggest a quiet kind of elegance. Though these hues are from the same side of the color ring, the blues are decidedly cooler than the greens, subtly balancing the visual temperature. Gradations in value give this palette variety; espresso brown acts as a dark-value accent.

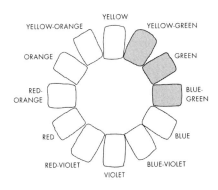

palette 8

A trio of balanced hues—red-orange, yellow, and blue—benefits from the addition of cool green. A similar intensity throughout modulates the colors and keeps the combination from looking harsh. In a bedroom, the lighter blue is ideal for walls, the medium blue appropriate for a comforter, an area rug, or painted furniture.

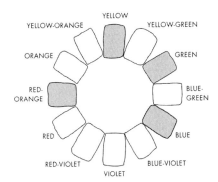

palette 9

A pairing of mineral blue and terra-cotta,
opposites on the color ring, is subdued
when the hues are low-intensity; the addition of fern green softens the contrast
between the complements. Light and dark
browns anchor the disparate hues and
broaden the spectrum of values.

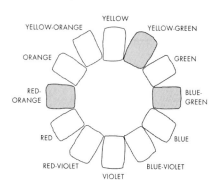

palette 10

You can never go wrong with nature's
color combinations. Warm greens and clay
colors predominate in this earth-inspired
palette; a range of values expands the
possibilities for walls, window treatments,
furniture, and flooring. Bark-colored brown
continues the natural theme.

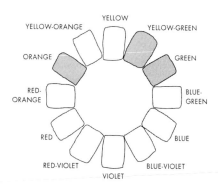

palette 11

A six-color palette, loosely based on a trio of green, orange, and violet, is diverse and complex. Aubergine and lichen green temper the warmth of sienna—a color inspired by iron-rich earth. Pale violet and two versions of gray lighten the scheme and provide visual rest points.

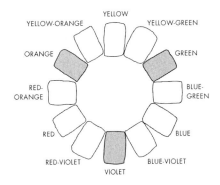

palette 12

Low-intensity red and blue are interpreted in a classic combination befitting a den or study; the addition of a green that borders on gold enriches and warms the cool blues. Use any of the colors on walls to create a rich atmosphere, or go with the warm beige for a more expansive effect.

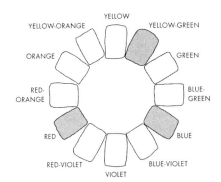

palette 13

Tropical colors—orange, yellow-orange, and blue-green—look fresh and energetic in combination. Use any one of them "as is" on walls for a lively look, or opt for lighter values to lessen the impact. Bright yellow-green and a muted red-orange add visual weight to the scheme.

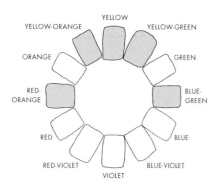

palette 14

Used together, complementary blue-violet and yellow-orange possess a clean, crisp quality typical of opposing colors. The addition of both light blue and medium red-violet—hues close to blue-violet on the color ring—increases the scope of the palette and keeps the combination from seeming formulaic.

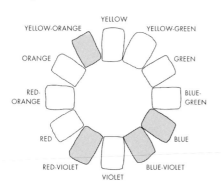

palette 15

Analogous hues on the color ring (see page 166) are naturally harmonious. Here, teal, spring green, and cadet blue make pleasing color cohorts; juicy red-orange from the opposite side of the ring warms up the cool trio. To expand the palette, vary the values, including both light and dark versions of one or more of the hues.

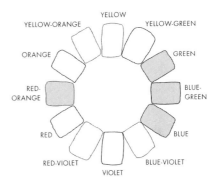

palette 16

Intense versions of complementary yellow-green and red-violet anchor this vibrant palette, while a pink that borders on coral and a refreshing blue-green add another warm-and-cool pairing. Light-value yellow-green calms the saturated hues.

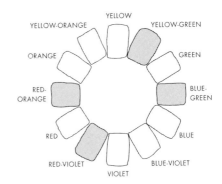

color, room to room

HARMONIOUS COLOR TRANSITIONS MAKE A HOME PLEASING, WHETHER A SINGLE COLOR REPEATS THROUGHOUT THE HOUSE OR COLORS CHANGE FROM ROOM TO ROOM.

when white is right
In a cozy vintage home with loads of charm, the homeowner/designer used analogous colors and generous quantities of white to refresh and connect adjoining rooms.

ABOVE AND RIGHT: A multipurpose island finished with high-gloss orange auto body paint and topped with stainless steel serves as a contemporary counterpoint to the original yellow tile on the countertops and backsplash. With this mix of warm and intense colors, clean white cabinetry and walls provide needed visual relief. A porthole in the door to the home office (shown at right) breaks up the expanse of white and leads the eye to the adjoining space.

LEFT: Extending the yellow of the kitchen countertop tile into the dining area, in seat cushions and the table base, establishes a sense of visual rhythm (see pages 244–245). Contemporary art picks up on the color theme.

RIGHT: In the compact living room, a sage accent wall and low-intensity colors for accessories and art set a serene mood.

feature continues >

color, room to room

nature's colors
A contemporary home in the woods takes its cues from the world just beyond its windows, connecting the indoor living environment with the outdoors.

LEFT: A tumbled slate backsplash set "on point," polished granite countertops, and full-overlay maple cabinets establish a palette of warm hues and organic materials.

ABOVE: In the modern master bedroom, dark-value, low-intensity mineral-blue walls accentuate note-worthy windows.

ABOVE: Though this fireplace and floating mantel are minimal by design, the subdued palette is anything but stark; a multicolored slate surround and new-neutral wall color contribute depth and sophistication.

LEFT: Deep, earth-toned green adds to the architectural presence of a stairway leading up to the second floor. Below the metal handrail, braided stainless-steel cables running horizontally contribute to an open, somewhat industrial look—and offer a sleek counterpoint to the natural theme.

feature continues >

color, room to room

layered color
Painting adjoining rooms in different hues presents the opportunity for a palette that reveals itself as you look from one space into another. The secret to success? Select colors of a similar intensity, even if they vary in value (see pages 164–165).

LEFT: Versions of blue in and beyond a minimalist bedroom display a subtle form of visual rhythm. The light, medium, and dark values of blue exemplify the design principle known as "theme and variation" (page 246).

BELOW: Low-intensity yellow and yellow-green facilitate the visual transition from dining room to living room. Orange appears as an accent color in both spaces, linking the two rooms.

FACING PAGE: Bathed in natural light, this low-intensity palette of camel (yellow-orange) and sea blue (blue-green) delineates a series of small spaces and accentuates striking architectural features. On the far wall is yet another color— "spice," a low-intensity version of red-orange.

practical design

PLANNING TO GIVE YOUR LIVING ROOM A NEW LOOK? OR ARE YOU THINKING about a whole-house makeover? Whatever the extent of your decorating project, it starts here, with design. Great design doesn't just "happen" in a home. It's a conscious, highly creative process—but not necessarily a mysterious one.

In fact, good design begins simply with knowing how you want your space to look and function, and bringing together the ideas and materials to make that happen. The step-by-step decorating plan in this chapter will help you with this process. You'll also get a crash course in design principles to help you put together your chosen colors and materials with style. Principles like "balance," "emphasis," and "harmony" may sound abstract, but they work like magic—even in a novice's hands. Practical strategies for arranging furniture, working with "problem" spaces, and incorporating accessories round out this idea-filled chapter.

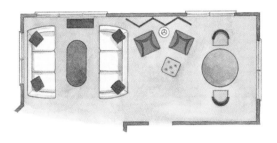

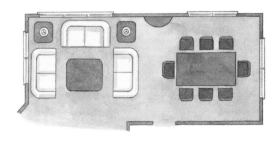

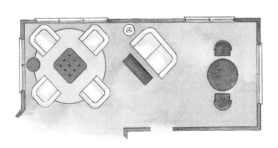

step-by-step to a decorating plan

DECORATING IS A LOT MORE FUN—AND A LOT LESS STRESSFUL—WHEN YOU HAVE a clear plan of action. In this section you'll learn how to develop a decorating plan, from setting goals to gathering materials to deciding what goes where in your home.

Careful assessment of your space is key to a successful decorating plan. In this home, the living room is open to the dining area, with a deep doorway on one side leading through a pantry to the kitchen and breakfast room—which opens to the dining room, completing a circular traffic pattern.

Once you've made the decision to decorate, it's only natural to want to jump in and get started. But before you pick up a paintbrush or begin shopping for furniture, take stock of your situation. The following five steps spell out a start-to-finish strategy. You need not follow these steps in this order, but take the time to read through them to get a feel for the process.

1 determining the scope of your project

It starts with a vision of what you hope to achieve. Then, to pin down the realities of your plan, you'll need a sketch of your room's floor plan—and lists, lists, lists.

make a wish list Do you plan to decorate a number of rooms or just add the finishing touches to a single room? A wish list can help you set priorities. If you're on a limited budget, start with the changes that will make the most difference, such as fresh wall color or a new sofa; then add to the scheme as your resources permit.

identify your givens "Givens"—those things you can't change, must keep, or

truly love—go hand in hand with a wish list. The most obvious given is the size and shape of your room; short of remodeling, you'll have to work with what you have. Architectural features—walls, ceiling, trim, floors—are also givens, along with furnishings that you want to keep or can't yet afford to replace. Although givens may seem like limitations, they actually provide a helpful place to begin.

assess your space Address your functional goals. Do you want to subdivide an open room to create separate activity areas? Do you need to arrange seating so it's more conducive to conversation? Can you move furnishings to create a more efficient traffic pattern?

A floor plan, drawn to scale on graph paper, can help you evaluate your space. Measure your room, noting doors, windows, and any fixed architectural features, and use these dimensions to draw up your plan. Using card stock, cut out miniature templates of furnishings, both what you already have and what you're considering. These need not be accurate; their purpose is simply to help you understand the relationship between your furnishings and the space they occupy.

Now consider a radical step: remove *everything* from your room and look at it empty. When you take away familiar objects, you'll see possibilities that aren't apparent when the room is full.

consider everyone Do you ever look at rooms in magazines and wonder who could actually live in them? Decorating your own home is about pleasing the people in your life, not about re-creating the latest look. Whom do you need to consider, besides yourself?

❖ Do you have or are you planning to have a baby? Comfortable crawling surfaces, safe materials, and washable finishes are a must.

❖ Do you have school-age children? If so, forgo the silk sofa until they're out of college; for now, a sturdy chenille in a blend of natural and synthetic fibers is a better choice.

❖ Is there an elderly or disabled person in your home? Think about ease of mobility and safety when you shop for flooring. Choose seating that is both comfortable and easy to get up from.

❖ Do you have pets? If your dog sneaks naps on the sofa now, he's not likely to mend his ways when you've reupholstered it. You may want to buy extra yardage to place on furniture when you're not on patrol.

ABOVE: Outstanding architectural features such as these soaring windows—a definite "given"—call for a minimalist approach to decorating.

BELOW: The wish list for this romantic bedroom retreat included faux-finished walls in a color called cognac, elegantly patterned bed linens, and an upholstered headboard that reaches to the ceiling.

2 defining your style

Focus on the feeling you want your room, or your home, to convey. Open and spacious, or private and cozy? Relaxed and casual, or ordered and formal? Brightly colored or quietly subdued? That's a lot to think about. Achieving the desired effect begins with discovering your personal preferences.

an idea file A folder full of inspiring examples can help you identify your preferences and then serve as a guide to gathering and auditioning decorating materials. Look through decorating books, magazines, and catalogs, tearing out or flagging every picture that appeals to you—whether it shows an entire room, a wallpaper pattern, or just a chair. Are richly colored walls inviting to you? Do you prefer patterned or solid-color fabrics?

Are you drawn to traditional upholstered furniture or to spare European-style pieces? Don't try to analyze why you like something; just collect images you love. Include family members in this process, because everyone's opinion counts.

a decorating questionnaire Now sit down with your idea file at hand and ask yourself the following questions:

❖ What's your environment? Think about your home's architecture and where you live. Have you chosen a traditional house or one with crisp, contemporary lines? Does your neighborhood incline toward formal, carefully maintained landscapes or relaxed, kid-friendly yards? These considerations will help you develop a decorating plan that's in sync with your lifestyle and surroundings.

❖ Can you identify a decorating style that especially appeals to you—East Coast

Formal doesn't need to mean stiff or unfriendly. Dressed in the pale colors and painted finishes of a Swedish farmhouse, this elegant living room is refreshingly unpretentious. The floor plan is formal, with matching chairs facing and flanking the sofa, but the classic seating pieces are upholstered in cheerful cotton fabrics that keep the look lighthearted; windows are likewise adorned. The effect is airy and welcoming.

traditional, California casual, minimalist modern, cozy cottage? Think about how you dress: sporty, elegant, classic, trendy? Knowing your personal style will help you to seek out compatible elements as you hunt and gather. Don't worry if you can't put a name to your look at this point; knowing what you like when you see it is enough for now.

❖ Do you enjoy basking in warm reds, yellows, and oranges? Or do you feel more relaxed in the presence of cool blues, greens, and violets? Identifying your preference for visual temperature is helpful when it's time to choose wall color and upholstery.

❖ Do you want a room that pulsates with visual energy, or do you long for a calm, soothing retreat? If you're after excitement, opt for vivid colors, and lots of them. For a quiet ambience, restrict your palette to neutrals, a single color in many variations, or closely related colors. See pages 170–171 for more about color combinations.

❖ Do you gravitate toward highly patterned and textured materials and finishes, or do you prefer minimal pattern and subtle texture? Your inclination will guide you in choosing everything from paint to fabric to flooring.

❖ What's your preference when it comes to furnishings? Do you like sleek seating and storage that's easy to move when the mood strikes, or more substantial upholstered pieces and built-in units for stowing books and displaying collectibles? Do you envision plantation shutters or lined curtain panels—or no window treatments at all? Turn to "Elements of a Room," pages 264–343, to see the range of possibilities.

A contemporary living space relies on simplicity and a one-color palette to convey a modern mood; a blend of materials and textures adds just the right note of interest to this spare style.

Time-honored furnishings in warm hues and comfortable materials typify the decorating style known as "new traditional." This family room—with its butterscotch walls, cast-form mantel, chenille-covered sofas, and varied woods—adapts equally well to everyday family life and to entertaining.

3 ready, set, gather!

Armed with your room sketch, your idea file, and a large tote bag, you're ready to "hunt and gather." Your goal at this stage is to collect things you love, without worrying about how you'll use them. That comes later.

Where do you gather? Start with a trip to your Lowe's store, where the paint, flooring, lighting, and window-treatment departments offer inspiration aplenty. If you live in or near a large city that has a design center with furniture, fabric, and lighting showrooms, visit there, too. Most design centers admit the public; to take home samples or order materials, though, you'll need to work through an interior designer.

Collect the largest samples possible. You can borrow wallpaper and window-treatment books from Lowe's for several days, along with flooring samples (wood, carpet, vinyl, and tile). Fabric stores will usually cut small swatches for you at no charge. Otherwise, buy the smallest piece you can, usually a quarter of a yard; later you may want to buy a full yard to see how the fabric looks draped over a chair or pinned next to a window. Some stores allow you to check out "memo samples," swatches from 9 to 18 inches square labeled with the fabric's name, code number, color, and fiber content.

If after a day or two of gathering you feel like a victim of sensory overload, just remember: you don't need to use everything you collect. Your goal is simply to assemble materials that inspire you. No commitments—not yet.

4 developing your palette

Whether you notice it or not, your personal palette naturally develops as you hunt and gather samples. One beautiful fabric leads to a harmonious paint hue; wall color and fabric together point you in the direction of tile or carpet. Bit by bit, sample by sample, your decorating scheme evolves.

When you feel you've collected enough, lay your samples on a large surface, such as your dining room table, and evaluate them. Plan to leave them there as long as it takes—days or even weeks. Alternatively, pin them to a large piece of foam-core board to create a movable observation gallery.

As you analyze your materials, consider the following points:

❖ As a group, do your gathered samples form a classic color scheme? Refer to the color rings on pages 166–169 and the color schemes described on pages 170–171. Unless you're working with all neutrals, your combination will probably be similar to one of these schemes.

❖ Do you need to gather more samples to expand or fortify your palette? If your colors are all warm and analogous, like yellow-orange, red-orange, and red, you may want to introduce a cooler color as an accent.

❖ Do you need one or more neutral colors among your samples to provide visual relief? If so, gather true-neutral or "new-neutral" materials (see pages 202–203) to include in the mix.

LOWE'S QUICK TIPS

Collect freely, without agonizing over your choices. At this point, you can't make a mistake.

❖

Be aware that the color you see on a paint chip or in a fabric sample will appear darker and more intense when it's applied to walls or furnishings.

Contemporary materials and an offbeat approach to decorating result in a new take on old-world glamour. The well-edited palette for this tiny bungalow is filled with surprises— a faux-ostrich-hide ottoman, vintage-style wallpaper, and a white shag rug. What ties it all together is the palette of neutrals enlivened with touches of deep red-orange.

5 finalizing your palette

At last, the time has come to make decisions. Designers some-times call this step "editing." With a sea of samples in front of you, your inclination may be to freeze. So many beautiful materials, so many choices! Let the ideas percolate, and stay open to the possibilities. If necessary, collect more samples; the hunting and gathering process often continues to the very end of a project.

Here are a few questions to think about as you begin to edit your samples:

❖ *Do I love what I see?* Keep only those things that please you, resisting the temptation to retain a material you think you need but don't really like.

❖ *Do I have too much of one thing?* If you've gathered four striped wallpapers, now is the time to select one of them and set the others aside.

❖ *Is there too much contrast?* Very light lights and very dark darks can be jarring in combination. Strive for a range that includes some medium values, unless you're going for a contemporary, high-contrast look.

❖ *Are my samples too subdued?* To play it safe, you may have unconsciously chosen all low-intensity colors. Try adding a few brighter notes.

Auditioning your samples comes next. You probably already have an idea of what you want to put where—it's just natural to visualize colors and materials in your room as you consider them. Now is the time to place your samples where you anticipate using them. Lay carpet samples on the floor; prop up wallpaper books across the room; drape fabric over a chair. In other words, have your room "try on" the materials.

These are some placement pointers developed by designers:

❖ The larger the area covered, the bolder a color will appear. A blue-green that appeals to you on a pillow will look stronger on your sofa and might seem overpowering on your walls.

❖ Plan low-intensity colors for walls, floors, and large furnishings. As a rule of thumb, the larger the area, the less intense the color should be. (You'll want to ignore this guideline, of course, if your goal is a saturated color scheme.)

❖ Bold patterns look even bolder over large areas. Focus on textures, solids, or subtle patterns for large furnishings and window treatments.

❖ If you're decorating several rooms, use most or all of your palette colors in one of the rooms, and one or two of them in the adjoining rooms. Use a color more than once in a room so it doesn't look like an "orphan."

Finally, when you think you're "there," ask yourself, "Do I still love these materials?" "Is the effect harmonious?" "Will I feel at home in this room?" If you've edited and auditioned thoughtfully, you'll answer yes to all three questions.

In the same house pictured on the facing page, red lamps bring color continuity to the compact entry area. Two ottomans upholstered in chinoiserie toile de Jouy (a one-color scenic pattern on a plain background) are scaled for the small space.

The juxtaposition of ornate wallpaper and minimalist accessories keeps the look light-hearted.

LOWE'S QUICK TIP

It's essential to view your collected samples as a group, because that's how they will be perceived in your room.

key starting points for room design

YOU MAY ALREADY OWN A STRIKING WORK OF ART OR AN HEIRLOOM RUG, OR maybe you want to feature a particular fabric or a favorite color in your home. Perhaps you're beginning with an architectural "given," such as a fireplace. Here are some examples of decorating with these popular starting points.

1 an architectural feature As a significant presence—and often the focal point—in a room, an architectural feature like a fireplace or built-in cabinetry is a natural starting point for a decorating scheme. Other features can steer you in a design direction, too: a cathedral ceiling with exposed beams suggests a different approach than a 10-foot ceiling with elaborate crown moulding.

If you have a fireplace or other prominent architectural element, let its proportions dictate the scale of major furnishings such as the sofa and chairs. The fireplace material should also factor into your choice of other elements; to complement a rock fireplace, you might introduce another element

with pronounced texture (perhaps an area rug), as well as smooth materials (wood and leather, for example) to counterbalance the rough stone. Consider the undertones of the surround—whether it's stained wood, ceramic tile, or plaster— as part of your palette and apply those hues elsewhere in the room.

In the great room shown below, the homeowners designed the precast concrete fireplace with function and aesthetics in mind. A raised hearth for extra seating was a must, with a mantel deep enough to serve as display space but shallow enough to keep guests from hitting their heads upon standing. Space to stow firewood under the hearth is a nod to practicality, and the

visual weight of the wood helps ground the entire unit.

In a room with a fireplace, furniture placement is usually the biggest issue. Should the sofa face the fireplace or not? Here, the homeowners opted to place the chenille sofa opposite the fireplace, an arrangement that takes advantage of the view through noteworthy windows—another "given." A media center, shown on page 288, faces the window wall.

A neutral finish on the fireplace allowed almost total freedom in color choices for this room, and though the homeowners went with a nuanced palette of browns, hues range from cinnamon to mocha to dark chocolate. Varied stains on the wood—beams, ceiling, casings, and screen—keep the look elegant yet relaxed.

2 **a paint color** What better place to begin your decorating plan than with a paint color that appeals to you? Start by visiting the Lowe's paint department, where you can collect paint chips from the Valspar and Olympic lines of paints, including special collections by Eddie

Bauer, Laura Ashley, Waverly, and Martha Stewart. You'll find ready-made palettes that group congenial colors (unlike paint strips showing light-to-dark values of a single color); if you choose a paint color from a palette card, you can confidently use the other colors elsewhere in the same room—in accessories, for instance.

Who can mistake the chosen color in the playful living room above? Walls of vibrant spring green (a version of yellow-green) and a deeper green patterned rug envelop the room in high-energy color. When you work with such a strong hue, repeat it in slightly varied form in other areas of the room and in accessories to establish a pleasing repetition. On the color ring (see page 167), look in the "neighbor-hood" of your color for a few companionable hues. These nearby colors, referred to as "analogous," are almost always harmonious because they share common colors. In this example, blue (just a few colors away from yellow-green) exerts a cooling influence on the warm, intense greens. A side table painted bright teal fits right in with the upbeat scheme.

feature continues >

key starting points for room design

3 a key fabric Many people are more powerfully attracted to fabric than to any other decorating element and will fasten onto one with have-to-have-it commitment.

On the practical side, beginning with a fabric is a good idea if you're planning to paint. It's easy to find paint colors that work with fabrics you've gathered, more challenging to find fabrics that work with a paint color you've already chosen.

A multicolored fabric provides you with a ready-made palette of harmonious hues; in effect, the fabric designer has done the creative work for you. You might use one of the colors in your chosen fabric on the walls, a second color for the flooring, and one or two of the remaining colors for upholstered furnishings and window treatments. In general, the larger the surface to be covered (walls, ceiling, and floor), the more neutral the color should be; save intense colors for accent pieces.

In contrast to a multicolored fabric, a predominantly one-color fabric offers you the opportunity to build a unique color scheme. In the warm, welcoming study shown below, the homeowner chose a cheerful palette of blue, yellow, and white to brighten what was once a dark space. The swirl-patterned fabric on the ottoman served as the catalyst; it introduces a major color and, with its light-to-dark values of blue, adds visual weight (see page 239) to the seating area. White cotton duck slipcovers and window treatments act as neutral players, while a dark wood side table and curtain rod echo the room's conspicuous "given," wood shelving that extends across one wall.

4 **artwork or rug** If you're fortunate enough to possess a painting or other work of art that you love, it's immensely satisfying to use it as the catalyst for your decorating plan.

The painting atop the mantel in the 100-year-old home pictured above has a casual, abstract feel, yet it's a successful springboard for the color scheme in a traditional room. Yellow-green paint accentuates the lines of cabinetry that appears to be original to the home but is actually new; an indigo overmantel provides a contrasting backdrop for the art. Creamy yellow walls and white trim define and

lighten the space, while bits of color from the painting reappear in chairs, pillows, and other accessories.

A rug is another place to begin a decorating plan because it presents you with a well-thought-out color palette. One tried-and-true strategy is to use a light- or medium-value color from the rug (often the background) on the walls of the room, a medium-value color for the flooring, and darker-value colors for major furnishings. Keep in mind the concept of using neutral colors for large areas like walls and upholstered pieces, saving intense colors for accents and accessories.

two subtleties of good design

THE COMBINATION OF PATTERNS AND TEXTURES CAN EITHER ADD TO OR DETRACT from the success of a room's decor. What makes the difference? In this section we look at the design subtleties of pattern and texture.

Common colors unite naturalistic, stylized, and geometric patterns in a formal living room; variation in pattern scale—from small to medium to large— keeps the look serene.

Did you know that you should evaluate patterns from a distance to see their over-all effect? And that strong patterns can coexist harmoniously in a room if they are separated? Read on for tips that will enable you to work successfully with pattern and texture in a room.

pattern

Faced with an array of florals, checks, stripes, and plaids, you may well experience a moment of "pattern panic." Relax. A little pattern know-how can alleviate your anxiety and help you choose and combine patterns—in fabric, wallpaper, and flooring—with confidence.

pattern scale The size of the motifs or design elements in a pattern is known as "scale." Keep in mind that from a distance, small-scale patterns tend to read as just texture or even as a solid color. Medium-scale patterns are the most versatile, because they retain their design impact yet rarely overpower other patterns. Choose large-scale patterns with care; they can appear even bolder when covering a sofa but may look fragmented on a small chair.

pattern style Patterns generally fit into these style categories: naturalistic (typically flowers and leaves), stylized (simplified motifs), abstract (nonrealistic images), and geometric (stripes, dots, plaids). Browse the samples in stores or look through decorating books and magazines to view the possibilities. Advertisements are an excellent resource, because they frequently show patterns up close.

pattern combinations The following principles are meant to guide you as you gather, edit, and audition materials, but they are not rules. Rooms pictured in magazines often defy these guidelines with great success.

❖ Start with one pattern as your design inspiration; make it one that you absolutely love.

- ❖ Err on the side of caution and use just three or four patterned fabrics in a room.
- ❖ Vary the style of your patterns, combining a curvy leaf pattern with a plaid, for example. Nature-inspired patterns like florals marry well with stripes.
- ❖ Combine patterns that differ in scale. To a large-scale floral, you might add a medium plaid and a smaller-scale stripe.
- ❖ Look for three places where you can distribute patterns in a room. Clustering patterns in one area can make a room look lopsided; spreading them throughout the room creates a sense of visual equilibrium.
- ❖ Unite different patterns with a common color, such as a similar violet running through a floral, a stripe, and a plaid.

LOWE'S QUICK TIP

Wallpaper books—you can check them out at Lowe's—are a wonderful source of pattern ideas. Analyze the photos in the books and you'll begin to see how the pros put it all together.

NATURALISTIC

NATURALISTIC

STYLIZED

ABSTRACT

GEOMETRIC

GEOMETRIC

color in powerful ways. Rough-textured materials like tapestry have tiny valleys that absorb rather than reflect light, decreasing the intensity of the color. Smooth, shiny surfaces such as satin, on the other hand, reflect light and increase the color's intensity.

Texture also affects the "value" of colors (see page 164), or how light or dark they seem; colors on shiny surfaces will look lighter than the same colors on textured surfaces. Canary yellow, for instance, will seem perceptibly lighter in chintz than in wide-wale corduroy.

When it comes to paint, texture can accentuate the positive—or hide a multitude of minor sins. High-gloss paint spotlights architectural details, such as handsome mouldings or window casings, but it also draws attention to defects like cracks or bumps. The matte finish of a flat paint absorbs light, and its slight texture can melt imperfections into insignificance.

texture tips Combining textures, like combining patterns, is a balancing act. Too little texture gives a room a flat, dull appearance; too much is visually confusing. Here are some basic guidelines:

❖ Use a mix of textures, just as you would patterns. Toss a pebbly knit throw on a leather sofa, or juxtapose smooth silk and plush chenille.

❖ In a room with minimal or low-key color, such as a new-neutral (see pages 202–203) or monochromatic scheme (see page 170), texture is the greatest source of visual interest. Play it up.

❖ Solid-color textured materials are timeless. Use them among patterns to create places for the eye to rest.

Texture can be quiet, as illustrated by a quilted coverlet and upholstered headboard. Dark case-good pieces (see pages 328–329) are the perfect foil for the subtle colors and textures of the bedding; the pillow injects a bit of pattern.

texture

We experience texture in two ways: with touch and with vision. Our bare feet tell us when a wood floor has been sanded so that the grain is perceptible; our fingers tell us that chenille is soft and cushy. Designers call this "tactile" texture.

Some patterns in fabric and wallpaper only *appear* to be textured—they imply light and shadow, creating the illusion of dimension. Paint appears textured when its flatness is altered by faux finishes. Designers refer to this effect as "visual" texture.

Tactile texture—how rough or smooth a surface is—animates a room and modulates

❖ Different textures work best together if they are in the same color range. Soft mohair and rough blanket wool in a similar cocoa color will naturally harmonize.

❖ When your palette contains several distinctly different colors, unite them with similar texture—a gleaming wood table and shimmery silk curtains in a dining room, for example.

❖ The effects of texture make it nearly impossible to match colors exactly in different materials such as carpet, fabric, and paint. Strive to combine colors that are congenial, not perfectly matching; it's more interesting if they vary just a little.

ABOVE: A contemporary Tibetan rug, a leather accent ottoman, and an easy chair covered in chenille display a variety of textures; related colors unite the disparate materials.

LEFT: Textured fabrics and gleaming finishes—most of them the color of copper—bounce light in a contemporary great room. When the scheme is monochromatic (see page 170), like this one, texture takes on added significance.

making a sample board or scrapbook

INTERIOR DESIGNERS PREPARE "PRESENTATION BOARDS" TO SHOW THEIR CLIENTS the ideas and materials they envision for a project. You can easily adapt this concept to create a portable sample board or scrapbook for your own decorating plan. The greatest advantage of this handy tool is that it will open your eyes to any holes in your plan. And when you take it with you to shop, it will be useful to salespersons as they help you choose compatible materials.

creating your sample board Start with a piece of foam core, illustration, or mat board, approximately 15 by 20 inches (or larger, if you're comfortable carrying a bigger board). Look for your board at an art supply, framing, craft, or office supply store. You'll also need paper and fabric scissors and all-purpose glue (not a glue stick) strong enough to adhere your samples firmly to the board.

Arrange your gathered samples—including paint chips, color palette cards, wallpaper swatches, and window treatment materials—on your board. For a neat appearance, affix fabric samples to lightweight cardboard first, folding raw edges to the back and gluing in place. Add photos from decorating magazines or catalogs that convey the look you're after. Once you're satisfied with the arrangement of your samples and photos, attach them to the board with glue.

Fabric, paint, and flooring samples glued to a piece of mat board can help you organize the elements you need to carry out your decorating scheme. When in doubt, keep your sample board simple.

LOWE'S QUICK TIP
Carry your sample board in a canvas tote or other bag to protect it.

a decorating scrapbook

An alternative to a sample board is a scrapbook. You'll need a binder, album, or scrapbook with removable pages sturdy enough to support your materials without buckling. (Pages that come out allow you to view your gathered materials as a group.) Include a few pocket pages for odds and ends.

Draw a simple floor plan of your room, roughly to scale, including major furniture pieces. Make photocopies of your sketch, enlarging it a little if necessary to better show the furnishings. Glue the sketch to one of the binder pages or put it in a clear plastic sleeve. If you've collected photos that inspired your decorating plan or capture the mood you want to create, add them. Include pictures of furnishings, wall coverings, flooring, window treatments, and accessories clipped from magazines or catalogs.

Organize your samples—paint chips, color palette cards, fabric swatches, wallpaper samples, and so on—and glue or staple them to the pages. Leave space near each sample to note where it will go in your room. Use pocket pages for materials that can't be glued. Attach fringe or other embellishments to the lower edges of the appropriate materials.

You now have a sample board or scrapbook to show family and friends. More important, you can consider new materials in the context of what you already have. Bit by bit, your efforts will add up to a winning plan.

Here's how the pros put together a sample board. A few samples and photos are glued directly to the foundation board, while others are raised on small pieces of foam core board. The layering of elements creates slight shadows, adding drama to the presentation.

a primer of design principles

HAVE YOU EVER THOUGHT ABOUT WHY SOME ROOMS "WORK" AND OTHERS DON'T?
Color is always a factor, but well-thought-out design is just as important. Fortunately,
the principles of good design are not professional secrets.

Here we present a quick course in design principles, followed by tips for arranging
furniture, altering the perception of space, and adding accessories.

balance

Balance is a good place to begin, because
it is relatively easy to understand and put
into practice. Three kinds of balance apply
in decorating: symmetry, asymmetry, and
radial symmetry.

symmetry Imagine an entry with a console table, a mirror hanging above it, and
a matching sconce on either side. If you
drew a line down the center of this picture,
each half would be a mirror image of the
other. That's symmetry: if it's on one side,

it's on the other as well, creating a serene
and satisfying effect.

Symmetrical balance pleases us because
it's orderly and predictable, demanding
little effort on our part to figure it out. The
effect is restful and dignified.

To achieve symmetry, start by placing
matching furnishings on either side of a
central point. The furnishings need not be
identical; the secret is to imply balance
by using pieces that have the same visual
weight (see "What Is Visual Weight?" on
the facing page).

RIGHT: Symmetrical bal-
ance is ideally suited to
a dual-sink bathroom
decorated in traditional
style. Stripes echo the
repetition established
by identical mirrors,
lamps, and accessories.

FACING PAGE, TOP:
Asymmetry is at work
in this casual setting, in
which lightweight (both
visually and literally)
accessories at one end
of the mantel balance
the large, "heavier" art
near the center.

FACING PAGE, BOTTOM:
Each element in this ele-
gant setting is rounded,
from the floral arrange-
ment and the chandelier
to the modified barrel-
back chairs. Radial
symmetry works well in
dining situations, where
it fosters an atmosphere
of conviviality.

asymmetry With asymmetry, furnishings or pieces differ in visual weight yet still appear balanced. Less predictable than its symmetrical counterpart, asymmetry is typical of contemporary design.

Think of a seesaw from your childhood. Remember how a small child at one end of a seesaw could balance a larger child sitting closer to the center on the other side? That's how asymmetrical balance works in decorating: visually lighter objects, or groupings of accessories, placed farther from a central point visually offset heavier objects placed closer to the center.

If you're not sure how to achieve asymmetry, begin by arranging your furnishings symmetrically; then add or shift pieces to break up the formality.

radial symmetry In radial balance, visual weight radiates in circular fashion out from a central point. In most decorating situations you don't have to work at creating radial symmetry; it occurs naturally if you have a strong center point. Still, it's helpful to recognize this kind of balance, especially if you want to accentuate it. A pendant light centered above a round dining table establishes radial symmetry; a sofa and armchairs arranged around the imaginary center of a room feel balanced.

WHAT IS VISUAL WEIGHT?

Visual weight cannot be measured; it's all about perception. Here are a few examples:

❖ Large objects are visually heavier than small ones. An oversize club chair, for instance, visually outweighs a diminutive slipper chair.

❖ Materials that are actually weighty—limestone, for example—are visually heavier than light-weight materials, such as a painted floorcloth.

❖ Dark, warm, intense colors like black, russet, and red seem heavy. Light, cool, low-intensity colors such as straw, azure, and willow appear less weighty.

❖ Complex patterns are "heavier" than plain ones.

❖ Opaque materials are heavier than transparent ones. A stone pitcher appears heftier than a clear glass one.

Intricate detailing on a Victorian mantel contrasts with the graphic painting above it, adding emphasis to this focal-point fireplace. An eye-catching fabric and an octagonal coffee table support the room's clean-lined, contemporary look; new-neutral walls (see pages 202–203) form a restful backdrop.

LOWE'S QUICK TIP
Think about how to develop your focal point first; then think about how to support it with rest points.

emphasis

Emphasis is really a two-part concept comprising a "focal point" and "rest points." Both are necessary to the principle; you can't have one without the other. The term "focal point" refers to the object or area that attracts attention; rest points are those elements that provide visual relief. Without a focal point, a room can be as monotonous as a dripping faucet; without rest points, it can feel as chaotic as rush-hour traffic. Rooms that have both—areas of emphasis and visual relief—are the most satisfying.

find the focal point How do you know what constitutes a focal point in your room? Whatever catches your eye first is usually the natural focal point—a fireplace with a carved mantel, for example, or a bay window with a garden view. Once you've identified the focal point, give it its due. Accessorize a handsome mantel with beautiful objects; install window treatments that enhance a fine window casing or frame the view.

Because of its size, a sofa or an armoire is a natural object of emphasis. Similarly, media centers often become focal points—intentionally or not—in open-plan great rooms. If an oversize entertainment center attracts unwanted attention, counterbalance it with an equally large-scale piece of furniture in a color that gives it greater visual weight.

create rest points Focal points get most of the attention, but rest points are crucial to a successful decorating plan. These are more difficult to define, but when a room lacks places for your eye to pause, you know it—immediately. Think of rest points as supporting characters in a play; they are not the stars, but they are essential to the story. Floors and walls play supporting roles; when you have a strong focal point, keep these surfaces low-key and noncompetitive. Neutral furnishings also provide a place for the eye to rest in a room featuring a prominent area of emphasis.

Between the focal point and the rest points, a decorating scheme must have other elements of interest as well. In a room with a focal-point painting and understated walls, you might choose sconces that command a little *more* interest than the quiet wall, and a neutral sofa that attracts a bit *less* interest than the focal-point painting.

ABOVE: A focal point can be just as effective in a foyer as in a living room. Here, a wall of stone literally brings the outdoors in, creating a natural visual pause. The contemporary art, supported by richly colored pillows and a traditional rug, is the star.

LEFT: Wide, alternating bands of curtain fabric emphasize a graceful bay window; minimalist linens and a gleaming hardwood floor provide the rest points.

Small-scale furnishings are appropriate in the bedroom alcove below. The delicately scaled table doubles as a writing desk; the armchair wears a sheer slipcover, and a slender black frame repeats the slim lines of the desk and chair. The same design elements—chair, table, art, and accessories—are equally harmonious on a larger scale (right).

scale and proportion

Successful design always includes appropriately scaled furnishings that are in pleasing proportion to one another. Scale and proportion go hand in hand, and it's well worth the time it takes to learn what each term means and to distinguish between the two.

Simply put, *scale* is the size of an object or element. A tiny floral print is small-scale, a 5-inch plaid large-scale. Designers usually refer to scale as being small, medium, or large, but of course there are infinite possibilities, from very small to very large. Scale is also relative: large-scale objects look even larger when grouped with small ones, while small-scale objects look smaller still in the presence of large ones.

Whereas scale logically refers to the size of objects, *proportion* is a subtler concept. It's about the *relationships* between objects or furnishings. Even the novice instinctively knows when something is "in proportion" or "out of proportion." A hefty ottoman is perfect with a generous sectional, for example, but a Queen Anne table looks out of place next to an immense recliner—they are proportionally (not just stylistically) alien to each other.

Scale and proportion apply to pattern, too. A miniprint gets lost in a high-ceilinged dining room but looks just right in a small attic bedroom. Conversely, a large-scale floral might dominate a cozy bedroom yet look at home in that same dining room.

As you shop for and arrange furnishings, ask yourself if the pieces are in pleasing proportion to each other. Is the coffee table in proportion to the sofa? Is the area rug in proportion to the seating arrangement? Is the lamp in proportion to the chair it accompanies? Proportion is just as important when choosing accessories. Arrange chunky earthenware on a large wood table; group delicate porcelains on a glass-topped, slender-legged table.

In the end, achieving correct scale and proportion is all about comfort, for you and your family. Much traditional furniture is scaled for comfort, which explains its enduring popularity. Contemporary designers often use overscaled furnishings to provide a sense of fun and drama; if you like this look, use fewer pieces so they don't consume the space. In children's rooms, you may want to scale down the furniture to kid-friendly size.

The furnishings and accessories in this restful living room are in pleasing proportion, from the crisp, simple fireplace surround to a traditionally scaled sofa and wing chair. The effect is elegant yet restrained.

rhythm

Of all the design principles, rhythm may be the most fun to work with. When a room has visual rhythm, a sense of vitality carries you along, as if to a destination. Rhythm is surprisingly easy to achieve once you're aware of how it occurs in a room. The following techniques set the principle in motion.

repeat it Think of this kind of rhythm as a musical beat, with repeating patterns, textures, shapes, and lines instead of notes. In a formal living room, for example, you might put round silk bolsters on a tuxedo sofa with slightly rounded arms and a round presentation urn atop a demilune (half-circle) console table. This simple repetition of round forms makes the room pulse with a quiet rhythm; varying the sizes and materials makes the effect engaging rather than monotonous.

Vertical lines—in the narrow Craftsman door, the balustrade, even the shorebird sculpture at the turn of the stairs— establish visual rhythm in a traditional foyer.

go from small to large There's something satisfying about similar elements that increase in size. A bathroom with a countertop of small square tiles, a stack of bath towels folded into squares, and large squares painted on the walls illustrates the kind of rhythm that's known to designers as "progression." The basic shape—a square in this example—repeats, but in increasing size.

This concept is especially relevant when it comes to accessories. Imagine a collection of rectangular picture frames atop a piano, arranged from short to tall, front to back.

LEFT: A contemporary dining room exemplifies the design principle of progression. Similar shapes repeat—in stemware, candle shades, and chandelier—but vary in size. The corner sculpture, though boxier, plays a part in the small-to-large repetition of forms.

Curvilinear furnishings and a monochromatic palette give a modern living room a sense of movement and ease. The absence of pattern strengthens the sense of transitional—flowing—rhythm.

Bamboo nesting tables—these serve as nightstands in a guest room—display progression in its simplest form.

make it flow "It just flows" is a phrase often used to describe what designers call "transitional" rhythm, that sense of subtle visual motion within a room. For instance, curved lines—an arched doorway, a camelback sofa, a circular area rug—lead your eye smoothly around a room, from one design element to the next.

Furniture placement is essential to creating rhythmical flow in a room—see "Furniture Arrangement" on pages 248–253.

include contrast A mere repetition of shapes, lines, patterns, or colors is boring if it's not interrupted by a contrasting element. In decades past, rooms sometimes exhibited a dull sameness— all small-scale patterns on walls and upholstery, for example, with "suites" of matching wood furnishings. Today you're freer to mix styles and scales and throw in a surprise or two. Hang an ornate carved mirror over a contemporary glass-topped table, contrasting the period detail of the mirror with the sleek, hard lines of the table. Introduce contrasts in texture—bumpy tapestry, plush mohair, smooth leather—to set up a lively, almost syncopated sense of rhythm.

A one-color scheme
possesses a natural
harmony, yet it requires
striking variations to
keep the look lively.
Yellow unifies this dining
room; patterns that differ
widely in style and scale
supply the element of
surprise.

harmony

Pick up any design magazine, and you won't read long before encountering the words "harmony" and "harmonious." They will probably be describing an atmosphere of well-being. What is the design principle of harmony, and how can you realize it in your home?

Even without taking a course in interior design, most of us can recognize the presence of harmony. It's a feeling that results when two opposing qualities, unity and variety, coexist. Think of it as a kind of design equation: unity + variety = harmony. In other words, when parts of a room are *similar* enough to make the room feel unified yet *different* enough to make it interesting, the space is harmonious. Interior designers put it another way: they speak of "theme and variation." A room should have a con-

sistent, unified theme yet include enough variety to keep the look fresh.

To apply the concept of harmony, first consider its components.

unity   The easiest way to achieve visual unity is through repetition and similarity. Use colors from your palette to unify rooms that adjoin, for example, or repeat geometric shapes to create unity within a room. Repetition and continuity automatically unify a room.

Too much unity, though, can lead to monotony. Imagine a room with the same floral pattern on all the upholstered pieces and the window treatments. Even without seeing the room you can feel its excess. In the same way, an all-beige room composed entirely of solid-color materials with smooth textures is likely to be boring. That's where variety comes into play.

variety In a harmonious room, everything seems to "belong," but one or two elements of surprise make the visual experience a little richer and less predictable. The variation can be as subtle as slight differences in one color, or as pronounced as a chic, two-tone leather sofa atop an antique Persian rug. Unlikely combinations can add up to pleasing variations.

As with unity, however, too much variety can tip the scales toward disharmony. Authentic Victorian design, with its profusion of color, pattern, and texture, is considered oppressively overwhelming by today's sensibilities. You could, however, reinterpret elements of that style in a way that avoids visual confusion—perhaps choosing a wallpaper pattern of simplified Victorian motifs on a more open background.

ABOVE: Harmony results when a decorating plan includes both theme and variation. Crackle-glaze walls, gauzy curtains, warm-toned woods, and a new-neutral chair are similar enough to be unified (theme) yet different enough to be interesting (variation).

BELOW: Even in this small space, the harmony equation is at work. A slatted chair, an upholstered headboard, and leafy wallpaper could not be more different, but they coexist peacefully, thanks to the unifying effect of a neutral palette.

LOWE'S QUICK TIP
When striving for variety, push beyond what feels safe; then pull back, if necessary. It's all part of the process.

The arrangement of furnishings in this spacious great room welcomes visitors with seating that faces an entrance and directs attention to the focal-point fireplace.

furniture arrangement

"Just for fun, let's rearrange the furniture." Sound familiar? But before you begin, read the furniture-arranging guidelines that follow and decide which ones are relevant to your situation. These pointers aren't in any particular order, because arranging furniture requires thinking about a number of factors simultaneously. That's the challenge.

clear out! There's nothing like a clean slate to open your eyes to the possibilities. As labor-intensive as it is, invest the time to remove everything from the room and see the space without the distraction of furnishings. You'll be glad you did, once you see the new arrangement that results.

revisit your givens Review your givens (see pages 220–221), because an immovable element such as a built-in media center or a bank of windows will be an automatic starting point for furniture placement. Stand in each entrance (an entrance is also a given) to analyze the room's strengths and weaknesses as they appear from that viewpoint.

consider your focal point Plan to arrange seating so that your family and visitors can enjoy your focal point (see pages 240–241), whether it's a baby grand piano, the view, or a painting. If you have more than one focal point, create seating for each: a pair of love seats positioned perpendicular to a fireplace, for example, and a floor lamp and chairs adjacent to bookcases. A single strong focal point, like a given, will limit your furniture-placement options; if your room has more than one, you'll have more choices.

start with the sofa Because of its bulk, the sofa is often the cornerstone of a living room furniture plan. Taking into consideration the goals of facilitating conversation and directing foot traffic (see pages 250–251), first situate the sofa and then build out from it, adding chairs, tables, and lamps. (Don't feel that you must place the sofa against a wall; see "Float Furnishings," page 250.)

make an entrance Seating that faces you as you enter a room is welcoming, whereas the back of a sofa says "Stay out!" Sometimes there's no way around placing a chair or sofa with its back toward the entrance, as when you group pieces around a fireplace opposite the room's main entrance. But even in that situation, you can try to arrange the pieces so that one or two seats face the doorway.

LOWE'S | QUICK TIP

A floor plan drawn to scale can help you visualize how your furniture will look in different arrangements —see page 221.

ABOVE: Charming—and challenging—architectural givens in this bonus room dictated a plan that revolves around the sectional sofa; secondary seating follows naturally.

BELOW: In this small sitting area opposite the dining room table, the sofa must go under the window. The arrangement of the side chair, Eames lounge chair, and glass-topped coffee table makes the space feel open yet cozy.

float furnishings Lining the walls with furnishings is a typical approach, but in a living room this arrangement tends to put an uncomfortable distance between people when they're seated. In other rooms, such furnishings may feel like isolated elements, subverting the sense of a unified space. "Floating" furnishings can make for a more convivial atmosphere—and pulling sofas and other furnishings away from the walls buys valuable space for wall units and foot traffic.

The typical floating arrangement consists of a sofa and chairs arranged to create a cozy, unified seating area. Furnishings that float need not always be parallel to the walls: a bed placed on the diagonal opens up a room. An area rug that's also on the diagonal strengthens and anchors such an arrangement. Even when an area rug is parallel to the walls, you can float furnishings on it diagonally.

encourage conversation The number-one activity in rooms where people gather is conversation, so it's important to cluster seating in a way that makes chatting easy. A circular or elliptical arrangement with a central space approximately 8 to 10 feet across allows guests to hear and see each other clearly; any greater distance destroys the sense of intimacy.

Sofas placed at right angles—one against the window wall, the other floating in the room—define the conversation area in this great room. A chair and matching stools increase the seating capacity without closing off the inner room; the low table unifies the grouping and provides a generous surface.

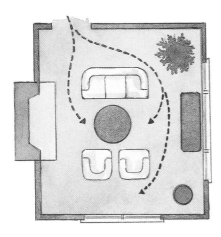 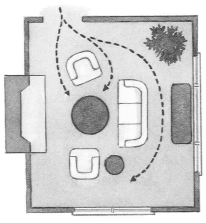 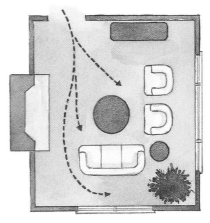

control traffic Work out a plan that guides foot traffic around, rather than through, conversation areas. One traditional arrangement consists of love seats flanking a view window, creating an "inner room" (see page 252) that you can enter but not walk through.

Allow 30 to 36 inches between major furnishings for easy passage. Between a coffee table and sofa, or between chairs, allow 18 inches. In a bedroom, your first consideration will be the placement of the bed; dressers, tables, and lamps should be added with ease of movement in mind.

think up and down We tend to consider first how furnishings are arranged on the floor, but it's just as important to look upward to see how they relate to one another vertically. Interior designers use the term "eye-mapping" to describe the up-and-down path our eyes follow as we look around a room. If the furnishings are all about the same height and accessories are at the same level, a room is likely to seem static. But when your eye travels across the back of a sofa, goes up a lamp, and then skips along the top of a window treatment and down to a painting, the effect is lively and satisfying.

ABOVE: Consider potential traffic patterns when you arrange your furnishings. In the first example (above left), the sofa blocks the view of the room for entering guests, and they must walk around it to be seated. In the middle scheme, the back of the angled chair is less obtrusive, and guests have better access to the seating. The arrangement in the third example welcomes guests and permits the freest circulation within the room.

BELOW: The arrangement of furnishings in this bedroom sitting area is a fine example of eye-mapping. The up-and-down movement begins at the patterned curtain and travels down to the lamp and chair, up to the art, and then across the front of the armoire.

The arrangement of chairs and tables in this loft establishes an inner room and allows easy movement to both the dining area and the view; each chair has access to either the coffee table or a side table.

subdivide for success Open floor plans and spacious great rooms are typically considered a design plus, but sometimes these spaces can feel too big. To avoid the "ballroom" effect, you can divide a large room into sub-areas based on activity. Designers sometimes call these inner rooms.

Start by creating a main conversation area; the backs of the seating can form the boundaries of this space. (As previously mentioned, try to place at least one piece facing the main entrance to the room.) A secondary area might consist of two club chairs, a table, and a reading lamp near a window. The dining space is another natural sub-area with a dedicated activity.

Arrange furniture compactly to hold each activity area together; use area rugs to delineate and anchor inner rooms. Simply changing the direction of a rug can redefine the imaginary perimeter of an inner room.

plan for convenience The easier it is to move chairs and tables to accommodate guests, the more comfortable and versatile a living room or family room will be. Occasional chairs and ottomans are ideal for drop-in visitors; including a few of these movable pieces will make your room more livable.

leave room for light Allow enough space between furnishings to accommodate lighting. When light spills behind, in front of, and between pieces, it enhances the sense of space. Table and floor lamps supplement general lighting and create height between elements, enhancing eye-mapping.

stand back and critique With your furnishings in their new positions, stand back, evaluate what you've done, and ask yourself these questions:

❖ *Is the room lopsided?* If so, rearrange the furnishings, symmetrically or asymmetrically, to achieve a better balance. Pay particular attention to the visual weight of each piece as you work to improve your arrangement; for example, a solid wood cube used as an end table will seem to take up more space than a slim-legged rattan table. (See "What Is Visual Weight?" on page 239.)

❖ *Are there too many pieces in the room?* Take out one or two to see if you like the look of less furniture and the resulting increase in floor space. Consider substituting dual-function pieces—an ottoman/coffee table or a coffee table/storage unit—if you decide you have too much furniture.

❖ *Are the furnishings all rectangular or square?* Curved pieces—a round coffee table, a round ottoman, or an overstuffed club chair—can soften a room containing mostly rectangular pieces.

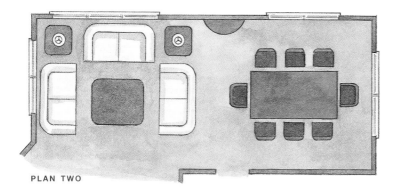

ONE SPACE, FOUR OPTIONS

A combined living and dining room demands a flexible furniture plan for everyday living and occasional entertaining. Whatever the arrangement, ease of movement is a must. All four of these plans fit the bill.

PLAN ONE: Three inner rooms make maximum use of the space. Facing sofas facilitate conversation and take advantage of the view windows. Two comfortable chairs with a shared ottoman are positioned in front of a folding screen, creating a cozy place to read the newspaper or chat.

PLAN TWO

PLAN TWO: A trio of love seats accommodates the most guests in a single seating area; each piece has access to both an accent table and the coffee table. A demilune console table against the wall visually separates the two inner rooms.

PLAN THREE

PLAN THREE: In this circular seating plan, four chairs positioned on a round area rug share an ottoman. A separate love seat provides additional seating for larger gatherings. The bistro table is ideal when it's just dinner for two.

PLAN FOUR

PLAN FOUR: A quarter-round sofa and a chair-and-a-half welcome guests into the conversation area; the circular coffee table creates a sense of rhythm by repeating the sofa's curves. Placing the dining table lengthwise emphasizes the shape of the room.

spatial illusions

When it comes to space, you may think your rooms are either too small or too large. Whether they strike you as confining or overly vast, there are ways to alter the sense of space and transform problem spaces into rooms that feel "just right."

"grow" a small room When small rooms feel uncomfortably close, you can make them appear roomier. Here's how:

❖ Use light color values to make a room feel larger. The standard approach is to paint the walls white, but colors like chamois, spa blue, and celadon can be just as space enhancing.

❖ Choose sofas and chairs with open arms and exposed legs that allow light to spill around and under them for an airier effect. Glass-topped tables don't interrupt the view, making rooms look and feel larger.

❖ Use modest-size furnishings that don't leave a large "footprint"—just don't use so many small-scale pieces that your room looks like a dollhouse. You can also ignore conventional wisdom and include a larger piece or two to visually anchor the room. It all depends on the look you're after.

❖ Maximize precious floor space with open vertical storage: a tall hutch, for example, or floor-to-ceiling bookcases.

❖ Hang a mirror to visually expand space and to bounce light and color around the room. A mirror that is positioned to reflect the view of the outdoors from windows on an adjacent wall will imply another window.

A chaise placed on the diagonal echoes the ceiling line in an attic hideaway. Arranging furniture on an angle makes a small room more dynamic, though you do lose floor space.

A neutral gray sectional and a metal-and-marble coffee table increase the sense of space in a small living area; exposed furniture legs and the absence of an area rug add to the illusion of a larger room.

The concept of a "keeping room," an old-fashioned mixed-use space adjoining the kitchen, inspired the designer of this great room. Soft yellow walls and green cabinets set a warm tone, while a mix of furnishings and accessories seems to soak up the space. Exposed rafters and plank flooring add an earthy touch.

cozy up a spacious room

Large rooms are a blessing—who doesn't love extra space?—yet they present their own design challenges. Here are some strategies for making large rooms more intimate and livable:

❖ Cover walls with warm, deep, or intense colors such as persimmon, indigo, or apple green; they will visually fill a room and contract space.

❖ Rather than treating the room as a gigantic conversation pit—no one wants to shout across a vast expanse of carpet—create several inner rooms (see page 252).

❖ Purchase furnishings that present an unbroken surface all the way to the floor—a sofa with bun feet, a skirted chair, or a solid desk—to absorb space.

❖ Choose a complex color combination rather than a monochromatic one (see page 170). A large space that combines tangerine, violet, and lime green—three contrasting colors—will seem cozier than an all-blue room.

❖ Employ lighting to help separate a large room into smaller areas. (For more information about lighting, turn to pages 296–299.)

A sand-and-sun palette and an assortment of patterns and textures make a master suite feel like a beach retreat. Natural-fiber rugs, wicker, and dark wood break up the space just enough to give it an intimate atmosphere.

applying the finishing touches

NO DECORATING SCHEME IS COMPLETE UNTIL YOU ADD THE FINISHING TOUCHES, and arranging these essential elements so they look their best is one of the final—and most enjoyable—steps in the whole process.

Finishing touches include traditional accessories like vases and mirrors as well as table-top arrangements, flowers, art, and collectibles. The possibilities are infinite and the strategies for their arrangement diverse, as you'll see on these and the following pages.

gathering and arranging accessories

Accessories are like jewelry for your home. Without them, the best-designed room can still look "under-dressed"; with them, a room looks polished.

Anything that captures your imagination and expresses your style can be an accessory. Some items may be practical as well as decorative, such as a clock in an entryway or a folding screen dividing a room; others are strictly ornamental, like blown glass or topiary. Whether they're hardworking or just for show, your accessories should be objects that you love.

A glossy chocolate brown accent wall acts as a backdrop for framed photos casually propped on top of and underneath a white side table. Lucite and crystal candleholders sparkle in the light from a contemporary lamp.

shopping strategies The most common mistake novices make is to underaccessorize a room. Unless you have a huge stash from which to choose—and few homeowners do—you'll need to acquire some new decorative pieces.

Searching for accessories is a hunting-and-gathering process, just like choosing fabric, flooring, or paint. Designers urge you to take your time when looking; the worst approach, guaranteed to disappoint, is to pick out everything in one frenzied shopping expedition. As you did when you were gathering other decorating materials, cast a wide net and consider all of your options.

perfect placement Where should you put accessories? The most logical places are where you naturally look: opposite the front door as you come in, where your eye falls when you look from one room into another, behind a sofa or on top of an armoire, at the end of a hall. You can also position eye-catching objects to indicate where you want your guests to look—for example, a sculpture in the line of vision to a view window.

ABOVE: A vintage jelly cupboard has been accessorized with salvage pieces in keeping with garden-style decor, including a pair of green-painted brackets, a bit of decorative lattice, and faux-stone birds.

LEFT: An antique pine hutch shows off a fine collection of majolica, glazed earthenware inspired by shapes and motifs from nature.

LOWE'S QUICK TIP
Home furnishings stores and design showrooms that display fully accessorized room settings are excellent sources of inspiration.

Warm hues repeat in each of three small accessories. Even on such a modest scale, transitional rhythm (that sense of visual flow) comes into play, as attention moves smoothly from one object to another and back again.

❖ Use both symmetrical and asymmetrical balance to organize objects. For instance, matching lamps placed at either end of a console table will visually "ground" a collection of vases arranged asymmetrically in the center.

❖ Try this designer formula: "shiny, matte, tall, and fat." When combining accessories, include things from each category, like tall, shiny candlesticks grouped with a rotund vase and a matte-finish plate.

BELOW: A bedside grouping illustrates the design formula of "shiny, matte, tall, and fat."

beginner basics Formal rules of accessorizing have given way to a respect for individual style and fresh perspectives. Conventional dictates aside, a few guidelines are still helpful.

❖ The "odd-number rule" suggests that you group an uneven number of objects together; three or five is typical. An even number can work if the pieces vary significantly in size and visual weight (see page 239).

❖ Novices tend to use accessories that are either too small or all the same size. Include larger pieces among smaller ones to add drama to an arrangement.

❖ A small entry hall is the ideal spot for accessories that are seen to best advantage at close range, such as a delicately painted chest. A big living room where small accessories might be lost can accommodate pieces that will be noticed from afar.

- Repeat a color in at least three different objects and three areas of the room to make a strong visual connection. In a black, cream, and taupe living room, for example, black tapestry pillows, a black wrought-iron lamp, and a black lacquered bench can tie the scheme together.
- To achieve cohesion in a grouping of accessories, unite pieces of different sizes and shapes with a common color (such as burnt orange) or material (perhaps brushed metal).
- Accessories offer the perfect opportunity to introduce a daring accent color that's outside your palette. If you simply repeat your palette colors in your accessories, the effect is likely to be boring—or, as designers shudder, "matchy-matchy."

- Leave unequal spacing between the objects in a grouping; this allows each one to be seen clearly and also provides needed visual rest points.
- To start afresh, "clear the landscape"—that is, remove all accessories—and study your room. Audition your favorite piece in different locations; then add others one by one. You'll quickly appreciate that they can be used effectively in a number of spots.
- Finally, get organized and dedicate specific storage space for your unused accessories. Putting them all in one place will encourage you to keep a mental inventory and remind you to rotate them more often.

A tiny powder room is ideally suited to small-scale accessories. Wallpaper in a larger scale gives your eye a place to rest and keeps the room from feeling confining.

These are a few approaches that designers take with tabletop arrangements:

❖ Think in threes or fives. Five candles are more appealing than four, three vases more graceful than two.

❖ On any large table, build your arrangement in three dimensions—height, width, and depth—by starting with the tall elements in the center and then working outward.

❖ In a fresh centerpiece, include materials that spill over the sides of the vase onto the table, as if they are growing. Long, low containers are ideally suited to trailing arrangements.

❖ To keep a dining table display from appearing isolated, arrange smaller elements so they extend out toward the place settings.

❖ Make a dining table arrangement low enough for guests to converse without having to peek around flowers or candles. Candle flames should be well above or below eye level.

❖ Simplicity is sometimes the best choice for formal occasions. Put white candles in glass candlesticks of varying heights to cast an elegant glow. White flowers—tulips, roses, lilies—allow gilded china to take center stage.

ABOVE: A grand tabletop arrangement befits an elegant console table and a large-scale mirror. The frilly display of flowers adds height to the scheme and balances a grouping of smaller, more formal accessories.

RIGHT: Colorful tableware and neutral linens are as much a part of this design as the lush centerpiece of foliage and hydrangeas. The long, low arrangement decorates the table in whimsical style yet allows guests to converse freely without obstructing their lines of sight.

tabletop arrangements

If there's an interior designer lurking within you, you'll enjoy the opportunity tabletop arrangements give you to play with color and design on a small scale, usually for only a modest investment.

The principle of balance (see pages 238–239) definitely comes into play when you accessorize a tabletop. Symmetrical centerpieces work on any dining table, no matter what its size or shape. Radial symmetry is ideal on any round table. Asymmetrical centerpieces—in which each half of the arrangement is different yet the overall composition seems balanced—are graceful on a console table, an accent table, or a sideboard.

gems. Such an arrangement typically consists of just one kind of flower, cut to short stems and packed tightly in a rounded vase.

❖ At the florist's, ask for a "hand-tie"— a bunch of flowers individually chosen, arranged, and tied by the florist; you provide the vase.

❖ To create a cottage-garden bouquet, loosely arrange flowers of different sizes, shapes, and heights in your hand. Fasten the stems with a rubber band. Place your bouquet in the container to check the effect; remove and trim the stems to the desired length. Put the flowers back in the container and cut the rubber band, letting the arrangement fall gracefully into place.

LEFT: A garden urn's luscious arrangement of hydrangeas, roses, sedum, and purple sage recalls the "presentation urns" of the late 1800s.

BELOW: A French country bouquet begins with all-of-a-kind bundles of flowers and greenery, each secured with a rubber band or florist's wire. The bundles then go into the container, bunch by bunch, for a dense, lush effect.

fresh flowers

Fresh flowers are nature's accessories, delighting the senses and brightening any decorating scheme. Try these tips for creating pleasing displays:

❖ Think scale when you choose flowers for tabletop arrangements; the blooms and their containers should be in proportion to the table and the room.

❖ If you're unsure of your skills, stick to a monochromatic scheme—like all pinks, or all ivory with green accents. A one-color arrangement is guaranteed to impress, and your bouquet will seem larger than it really is.

❖ For a vertical arrangement, cut your tallest stems so they're one and a half to two times the height of your vase. Fill in with medium and short stems on the sides.

❖ Try a pavé arrangement, named for the French jewelry fashion for small, close-set

displaying artwork

Arranging art is itself an art, and many a homeowner freezes at the prospect of hanging even a single picture. A few guidelines can make the process less intimidating.

❖ Over a fireplace, hang a single work of art or a grouping that takes up roughly the same amount of space as the fireplace opening below.

❖ The standard guideline for grouping artworks is to leave 1½ to 2½ inches between the frames. Very diverse subject matter calls for a little more space; related works, such as botanical prints, look best hung close together.

❖ Position art at eye level. In a dining room, that means hanging it lower than usual, since viewers will be sitting. In an entry or hallway, hang art higher.

❖ To get an impression of how multiple pieces of art will look as a unit, arrange them first on the floor. Or tape pieces of paper, cut to the sizes of your art, on the wall to try out potential arrangements.

❖ A single painting hung above a sofa should extend approximately two-thirds of the sofa's width. If you have a narrower piece, add smaller ones to compose a larger unit.

Feel free to mix approaches when displaying art. Two framed pieces rest atop the rail in a mudroom, along with other accessories; three portraits below are hung along a horizontal axis.

LAYOUT PRINCIPLES

Each of the three common display strategies illustrated here begins with an imaginary point of reference.

❖ *a horizontal axis* This plan works well when you have three pieces of art. Hang the center piece first. Now imagine a horizontal axis running through its midpoint. Hang the flanking pieces so their midpoints align with that horizontal axis.

❖ *a vertical axis* For four pieces of art, this approach is ideal. Hang two pieces on one side of the vertical axis and two on the other. Offset the horizontal spacing to avoid creating a "cross" of negative space that would destroy the sense of a cohesive unit.

❖ *a perimeter* Establish an imaginary perimeter for the space you want the grouping to occupy and hang the pieces so their outer edges "touch" that perimeter. Again, avoid creating a cross of negative space in the center.

VERTICAL AXIS

PERIMETER

HORIZONTAL AXIS

showcasing collections

Because collections have such personal significance, it's important to arrange them in ways that enhance their beauty and meaning. The most successful arrangements look as though they were effortlessly composed. Here's how to achieve that effect:

❖ Color can be the tie that binds a collection of otherwise diverse objects, such as a grouping of white porcelain, mother-of-pearl, and ivory pieces.

❖ Take the time to audition your collection in various locations until you find just the right spot for it. Effective display always involves experimentation.

❖ For maximum impact, cluster items. If they vary in size, place shorter, smaller objects in front and taller, larger ones in back for a sense of depth. You can also create subgroups within a collection, arranging some pieces in a circle, for example, offset by others in a straight line.

❖ If your prized objects are similar in size, a gridlike arrangement—or even a single row—gives equal emphasis to each one and visually organizes the grouping.

❖ Show off small objects on a wall, shelf, tabletop, or windowsill. Large objects like urns and garden finials can be placed on the floor—flanking a fireplace, grouped in a corner, or marching up a flight of steps.

❖ Use display devices such as pedestals, plate stands, books, cubes, and miniature easels to raise your treasures. Keep these devices inconspicuous, though, so they don't detract from the collectibles themselves.

❖ The very nature of a collection serves to unify it. Adding pieces that differ in size or material introduces a little variety.

❖ Plates or other objects that you plan to hang on the wall can be arranged on the floor first to arrive at a pleasing configuration.

❖ To show off bowls that are decorated on the inside, display them low—on a coffee table, for example.

A wall of built-in shelving in the entry treats guests to individual displays drawn from the home-owner's collection of shells and baskets.

elements of a room

WHETHER YOU ARE SETTING OUT TO BUY A NEW SOFA OR TO REPLACE THE FLOORING all through your house, choosing decorating elements takes you on a path much like the one you followed to develop your overall plan. You need to determine your needs, consider your options from a practical as well as an aesthetic standpoint, learn where you can find what you're looking for, and draw up a shortlist of choices.

This chapter travels that path for each decision you're likely to face, from choosing between paint and wallpaper to finding the perfect countertop material or planning a lighting scheme. Use these pages as a resource as you narrow your selections.

A good place to begin is the Project & Video Center at Lowes.com, where you'll find Buying Guides for many of the materials discussed in this chapter—flooring, paint, cabinetry, countertops, and more. Also check out the hands-on features in the Interactive Design Center, where you can "audition" materials such as paint and moulding in rooms of various styles.

As you consider the different elements of your decorating scheme, you may be inspired to undertake some projects by yourself. Go to it! Even a novice can create stunning effects with decorative paint techniques; the more skilled may choose to install new flooring or crown moulding. You'll find step-by-step instructions for more than 25 achievable projects starting on page 345.

walls and ceilings

Decorative paint in the adjoining kitchen (left) and wallpaper in a powder room are in pleasing contrast to plain-painted walls and a faux-finished ceiling in the entry area. To see more of the paint treatments and wall coverings in this home, turn to pages 276–277.

WALLS AND CEILINGS MAKE UP THE LARGEST SURFACE IN ANY ROOM, PRESENTING a powerful—sometimes overwhelming—design opportunity. How do you decide which of all those paint and wallpaper options are appropriate for your decorating plan?

Paint, plain or decorative, has the power to make a big change in a home for a relatively small investment. Plain paint never goes out of style, and a wealth of choices in colors and finishes—from glossy to flat—guarantees that you'll get the look you want. Decorative paint techniques such as antique glazing or wispy clouds can add depth and texture. And some paints actually contain texture—"sandstone," "granite," or "brushed suede"—to give a subtle granular or fiberlike finish to walls.

Wallpaper is enjoying a resurgence. Grass cloth and other natural-look textures suit many contemporary homes, while traditional styles continue to be valued as a way to add pattern and texture to a room. You'll find textured wallpaper specifically designed to cover cracked walls or even paneling. Paintable wallpapers that mimic tin ceilings, stucco, and other embossed or textured surfaces let you choose whatever color suits your scheme. You can even paste torn wallpaper to walls for a faux-stone effect.

LOWE'S QUICK TIPS

No matter what type of wall treatment you choose, adequate prep work is crucial to success. For guidance, refer to "Preparing a Room" in the Lowe's book *Complete Home Improvement and Repair.* To learn how to mask adjacent surfaces and apply a base coat of paint, turn to pages 346–347. At the very least, wash your walls with trisodium phosphate (TSP) or a premixed, no-rinse TSP substitute before painting or wallpapering.

❖

If your ceiling isn't flat, or if you're just trying to cover a bad joint between the ceiling and the wall, consider painting both surfaces the same color to minimize the imperfections.

where to begin Review "Step-by-Step to a Decorating Plan" on pages 220–231 to determine the scope of your project. It's important to identify your givens and assess your space before selecting paint or wallpaper, because what you have to work with will in great part determine your decisions. Then answer the following questions:

❖ Are your walls textured, or relatively smooth? Heavily textured walls aren't appropriate for some techniques, but smooth walls make almost any paint technique or type of wallpaper possible.

❖ Are your walls in good condition? Wallpaper and some decorative paint finishes can mask minor defects, while a glossy or uniform paint treatment will highlight them.

❖ How will the room be used? Some paints and wallpapers are much easier to clean than others, so they are suited to high-use areas like kitchens, bathrooms, and kids' rooms.

❖ Will you do the work yourself? Many treatments are easy enough to master with a little practice, but it does take time to learn the techniques, gather materials, complete the job, and cope with surprises along the way.

❖ What's your budget? Investing in a few cans of paint is an inexpensive way to make a dramatic change, but the cost of some wallpapers and professionally applied decorative finishes can add up quickly. Be sure to factor wall treatments into your overall budget.

getting help If you don't have an interior designer assisting you, ask for help from the pros at Lowe's. Bring photos of furnishings you plan to keep and samples of fabrics or other materials you are considering (see "Making a Sample Board or Scrapbook," pages 236–237). At Lowes.com you'll find guides to choosing and buying paint and wallpaper.

A trompe l'oeil fireplace complete with candlesticks and a portrait turns this cozy attic space into an imaginative retreat for children.

Toile de Jouy wallpaper depicting French country scenes envelops a cottage bathroom in old-fashioned charm.

plain paint

Two important considerations come into play when you are selecting paint for your home: color and sheen.

color Choosing just the right color can be the most time-consuming part of the painting process—mainly because judging a color on the basis of a paint chip is impossible for all but the most experienced eye. Turn to "All About Color" on pages 162–217 for help. The paint department at Lowe's offers mistake-proof color palettes, groupings of harmonious colors; a sales associate can also computer-match a color sample for you.

sheen A paint's sheen, or finish, affects both its appearance and its performance. The shinier the paint, the lighter and brighter the color will look—and the more durable and easily wipeable the surface will be.

❖ "Flat" or "matte" paint is nonreflective, making it the most forgiving finish for imperfect surfaces. This finish is best suited for ceilings and rooms in low-traffic areas because its rougher texture is more difficult to clean than other finishes.

❖ "Eggshell," "satin," and "low-luster" paints are a bit more lustrous, with eggshell having the lowest sheen of the three. These paints are easier to wipe down than a flat finish, so they are appropriate for kitchens, bathrooms, and kids' rooms.

❖ "Semigloss" paint, which has a medium luster, is very stain resistant and easy

LATEX VERSUS ALKYD

Water-based latex paint is what you will find at Lowe's. It's nearly odorless, dries in hours rather than days, and cleans up with just soap and water. Latex paint has excellent sheen and color retention and is resistant to chipping.

Alkyd (oil-based) paint, a petroleum solvent, is restricted in many municipalities and states because of the volatile organic compounds (VOCs) it gives off. While alkyd at one time was favored over latex for woodwork because of its durability and cleanability, water-based paints now perform just as well and are kinder to the environment—and to the health of homeowners and painters.

In a living room corner, deep-toned walls provide a suitably glamorous backdrop for patterned window treatments and an intricate Venetian-glass mirror.

LOWE'S QUICK TIP
Start by choosing the decorating elements that offer a finite number of possibilities—furniture, window treatments, flooring. Then turn your attention to paint, where the options are truly endless.

to clean. It is popular for wood doors and trim and for areas prone to moisture, grease, or heavy wear, such as bathrooms and kitchens.

❖ "Gloss" paint reflects the most light and is sometimes referred to as enamel because of its shiny, lacquerlike finish. While it gives the most durable surface, gloss paint also highlights imperfections, so it's important to smooth out rough spots and to fill and sand any holes before you apply it.

ABOVE: Tongue-and-groove paneling was painted several shades of aqua for a soothing yet contemporary look in this bedroom. A fanciful painted headboard and wicker nightstand continue the solid-color approach.

LEFT: Pale camel-colored walls play a supporting role to the warm tones of wood flooring, built-in seating, and window casings.

HEALTHIER PAINT

Poor indoor air quality is a known health risk, and according to the Environmental Protection Agency (EPA), one of the main causes of unhealthy air in homes is the presence of volatile organic compounds (VOCs). These occur at high levels in alkyd (oil-based) paint (no longer sold in many areas); they are present to a far lesser degree in latex paints.

The EPA has set a standard for paint to be called "low-VOC," but in fact a paint labeled as such may be significantly better than that. (The EPA standard is 250 grams per liter for low-VOC flat latex paint; the independent Green Seal organization requires 50 grams or less for its certification.) You will also see paint labeled "zero-VOC." While this is a bit of a misnomer (color pigments add VOCs), so-called zero-VOC paints do have extremely low levels, usually under 10 grams per liter. At Lowe's, look for Olympic Premium paint, a zero-VOC product.

No matter what paint you choose, always ventilate the room you're painting by opening windows and operating fans.

ABOVE: A multicolor mottling technique is well suited to textured walls. Here, four glazes— caramel, bark, camel, and dark chocolate— intermingle over a creamy golden base coat.

RIGHT: A two-step porcelain crackle finish involves a layer of porcelain crackle medium over the base coat of paint, followed (24 hours later) by an application of colored antiquing glaze.

decorative paint

If you're yearning for a look that goes beyond solid-color walls but have little painting experience, you're in luck. Even a first-timer can transform plain walls into a beautiful blend of color, pattern, texture, and light by using one or more decorative paint techniques. (See pages 348–357 for a variety of decorative paint projects.)

The possibilities in decorative paint have mushroomed in recent years, thanks to the wide availability of specialty paints, glazes, and tools. In the paint department at Lowe's you'll find materials and how-to brochures for creating such special effects as linen weave, Venetian plaster, and lime washing.

Knowing which technique is right for you and your walls involves answering a few questions:

❖ Do you want your walls to have a pronounced texture (such as "Papier Collé," page 354) or a more delicate, ethereal appearance (like "Cloudy Skies," page 348)? Match the technique to the degree of visual and tactile texture you desire (see pages 234–235).

❖ Do you need a treatment that will camouflage an imperfect wall? Some paint techniques, such as faux plaster and various stone effects, are well suited to walls that have minor surface irregularities.

❖ Will you be doing the work on your own or hiring a professional? If you're a do-it-yourselfer, practice first on 2-by 2-foot pieces of primed hardboard. (Hardboard is available at Lowe's in 4-by 8-foot sheets; have it cut into smaller pieces.) If you are hiring a professional painter, ask for a finished sample before you agree to the job.

❖ What's your skill level, and how much patience do you have? Forgiving finishes like stenciling and mottling are easiest for beginners; save the more challenging techniques such as dragging or strié until you've gained a little experience.

❖ Will the treatment be covering a large expanse of wall, or will it be broken up by windows, doors, and cabinets? The more features you have to work around, the more complicated it is to execute a technique.

wallpaper

Wallpaper remains unsurpassed for adding history and character to a room. It is also a good way to hide small imperfections in walls. The most popular wallpapers are made of a continuous, flexible vinyl film applied to a paper backing. These usually come prepasted; you use water or a liquid referred to as "prepasted wallpaper paste" to attach the strips.

Hanging wallpaper requires a few inexpensive tools, adequate time, and a little patience, but it is definitely something first-timers can do; turn to pages 359–363 for instructions.

Aside from pattern and color, wallpapers are differentiated by some practical characteristics. Here's a review of wallpaper terminology:

Scrubbable Cleans with a brush and detergent; good for kitchens.

Washable Cleans with occasional soap-and-water sponging.

Stain resistant Releases stains such as grease or coffee when cleaned, leaving no residue.

Abrasion resistant Withstands scraping and rubbing as well as scrubbing; excellent for hallways.

Colorfast Won't fade in sunlight.

Prepasted Uses water or prepasted wallpaper paste to adhere the paper to the wall.

Peelable Can be dry-peeled, leaving the backing on the wall; fine if you plan always to redecorate with wallpaper.

Strippable Can be completely dry-peeled, leaving little paste or adhesive residue on the wall.

ESTIMATING WALLPAPER QUANTITIES

Start by measuring the overall height and width of each wall, using a steel tape measure; round up to the nearest foot. Multiply the height of each wall by its width; add all the wall figures to get the room's rough square footage. Use the same technique to find the square footage of door and window openings, this time rounding down when you measure. Subtract these areas from the rough square footage.

Plan on 25 usable square feet for each single roll of wallpaper if the pattern repeat (printed on the back of the roll) is less than 6 inches. With a repeat of 7 to 12 inches, you will probably get only 22 usable square feet; if the repeat is 13 or more inches, count on only 20 usable square feet.

To figure how many rolls you need, divide the room's total square footage by the usable square feet of wallpaper in a roll. Round up to an even number, if necessary—rolls are sold in doubles.

LEFT: Wavy stripes in nautical blue carry out the seaside theme in a child's bathroom. Vinyl wallpaper is a good choice for high-moisture areas.

LOWE'S QUICK TIP
Be sure to order all the wallpaper you need, and some extra. Rolls ordered later may come from a different print run and may not match those purchased earlier.

decorative paint effects

PAINT BY ITSELF IS GREAT FOR REFRESHING A ROOM, BUT SOMETHING SPECIAL happens when it's mixed with glazing liquid and applied using decorative tools and techniques. What was ordinary opaque paint becomes a sheer curtain of color that can be spread thin for a translucent effect or layered and manipulated for a denser, more sophisticated look. Some treatments are simple enough for the novice, while others take a practiced hand, and perhaps a helper. Murals are best left to a professional—or an adventuresome, artistic amateur. You'll find instructions for achieving a wide variety of techniques in decorative painting books sold at Lowe's.

TROMPE L'OEIL

a mural painted directly onto the wall can add whimsy or drama to a room, depending on its style and subject. Some muralists incorporate words into their images, or even let a text border serve as the sole ornamentation. *Trompe l'oeil*, a French term that translates as "fool the eye," is meant to trick the viewer into perceiving the painting as a real scene or object. This can be a cost-effective means of giving a space what it lacks naturally—a charming view, for instance, or a distinctive architectural feature. At left, real folk-art accessories mix with painted-on objects to brighten a kitchen corner. Murals and trompe l'oeil are best suited to smooth walls. Ask the artist about maintenance, as touchups can be difficult. To avoid overpowering a room, limit this effect to one or two walls.

STENCILING

stenciling is a time-honored technique that lets you add color and pattern to walls even if you don't have the skill of a muralist. Readymade stenciling patterns are available in many designs, or it's easy to create your own (see "Stenciled Lampshade," page 406). Typical places to apply stencils are just below the ceiling or at chair-rail height, depending on the style of the room. A more involved option, shown at left, is to use a large-scale stencil motif and a number of glazes to create an allover, floor-to-ceiling pattern. Stencils can also be used to highlight an interesting architectural detail, like an arch or a beam, or to decorate wood furniture and floors (see page 281).

DRAGGING

dragging involves pulling a dry paintbrush or other tool through a wet glaze to reveal thin, irregular stripes of the base-coat paint color. *Strié* is executed in vertical lines, producing a subtle texture and pattern that makes an ideal backdrop for art and antiques. An overlay of horizontal brush lines creates the look of linen. At left, dragging in gently undulating lines introduces movement and under-stated pattern to a casual, eclectic decor. *Combing,* a less formal dragging technique, is worked in both directions with a comblike tool to produce a checked, basketweave, or plaid design effect.

geometrics are a good starting place for beginners, requiring just painter's tape, a carpenter's level, and a little planning to produce crisp, tailored patterns (see "A Tape Trick," page 358). Vertical stripes draw the eye upward, heightening a room; horizontal stripes appear to widen a wall. Diamonds add dramatic pattern and movement to a room—and require especially careful measuring, marking, and taping. At right, the look of a mortared limestone wall has been created with the use of painter's tape and tinted glazes. A cautionary note: stripes, both vertical and horizontal, have a way of emphasizing out-of-plumb walls.

texturing paint techniques can enhance a room by giving walls both visual and tactile texture (see page 234). Stone effects that mimic granite and marble lend an organic look to earthy decors. *Venetian plaster,* illustrated at right, has a lustrous, silky smooth surface with subtle, tone-on-tone coloration, ranking it among the most elegant of wall finishes. Related techniques include *faux fresco, textured imprints,* and *bas relief*—all created with plain wallboard joint compound and basic tools. Such quiet textured techniques also work beautifully as a base for other applications, like stenciling.

mottling finishes go by different names, like *colorwashing* and *parchment,* but they're all variations of the same basic technique: translucent glazes are swirled and pounced (see page 349) over a base-coat color to create a seamless finish that varies ever so slightly as it moves across the wall. A one- or two-color glaze applied with a cheesecloth pom-pom yields a sheer, ethereal finish, like the antique glazing pictured at right. It takes two glazes—sometimes more—to achieve the mottled look of aged bronze, copper patina, or leather. Mottling techniques that call for more than one glaze can actually be easiest for beginners, because layers of different-colored glazes can disguise a less-than-perfect application.

GEOMETRICS

VENETIAN PLASTER

ANTIQUE GLAZING

architectural features

FROM THE MOST ELABORATE CROWN MOULDING TO THE SIMPLEST BASEBOARD, trim can add architectural interest to almost any home—even one that is otherwise lacking in character. When selecting trim (often referred to as millwork) for the interior, look to your home's exterior style and proportions for design inspiration and guidance.

Traditionally, interior moulding has been made from softwoods such as pine, poplar, and basswood, or from hardwoods such as oak. Clear (stain-grade) wood moulding is formed from single lengths of knot-free lumber and is meant to be finished clear or stained. Paint-grade wood moulding may have cosmetic flaws and joints that can't necessarily be disguised by paint.

In recent years, wood composites such as medium-density fiberboard (MDF) and other types of fiberboard have gained popularity. Less expensive than wood, composite is also less prone to warping, takes paint better, and is more impact resistant. Because wood-composite moulding almost always comes preprimed, it can usually be finished with a single coat of paint. On the down side, the mouldings are heavy, require a brad nailer for installation, and will accentuate undulations in an uneven wall.

You'll also find mouldings made of extruded polymer that has a paintable white surface or an applied film resembling wood grain.

Besides moulding, you may want to consider architectural accents such as columns, mantels, decorative appliqués, and ceiling medallions; many of these are stocked in the moulding section at Lowe's. Some are made of wood, but you'll find a wide variety of decorative elements made of polymer. These are less expensive, easier to work with, and stronger than traditional plaster.

CROWN MOULDING

PLATE RAIL

crown and baseboard mouldings are designed to conceal seams where walls meet the ceiling and floor. Not only do they mask any unevenness in the joint, but when stained or painted they define a room and give it style. *Crown moulding* draws the eye upward and visually heightens a room; smooth or carved, it comes in various sizes. Narrow *decorative moulding* is typically carved in rope, dentil, or basketweave pattern. *Baseboard moulding* is the simplest of the trims; corner blocks eliminate the need to miter joints, and plinth blocks ease the transition from baseboard to door casings. Baseboard and crown moulding are good projects for the confident DIYer; see pages 364 and 374 for step-by-step instructions.

rails are strips of trim attached horizontally to a wall. *Chair rails* typically measure $2\frac{3}{8}$ to 3 inches wide and are installed at or slightly above chair height (typically 3 to 4 feet from the floor). The area below the rail, called the dado, is usually given a heavier treatment such as paneling, the upper part a lighter and more decorative treatment like wallpaper. *Plate rails*, ideal for displaying a china (or other) collection, are narrow shelves running high around the wall (1 to 2 feet below the ceiling), with a lip or groove in which plates rest. (A *peg rail* is a variation on a plate rail; see page 366.) *Picture rails* make it easy to hang and rearrange art without hammering nails into walls; pictures hang on invisible wire or decorative cording from S-shaped hooks that grip the moulding.

BEADBOARD PANELING

paneling brings architectural significance and style to otherwise unremarkable rooms. It may cover the whole wall or only the lower half (often referred to as wainscoting), in which case it is finished at its upper edge with panel moulding. Such mouldings are routed in back to fit over the upper edge of the paneling. (To install *beadboard* paneling, as shown top right, see page 368.) *Frame-and-panel* walls, featuring wood, wood composite, or polymer panels framed by moulding, stained or painted, are usually accompanied by distinctive baseboard and crown mouldings.

a fireplace mantel is a natural focal point in any room, and dressing it up can have a big impact. Lowe's stocks mantel kits in prefinished oak, mahogany, and maple as well as white-painted wood, with Federal, Colonial, and dentil detailing. Although wood and stone surrounds are traditional, tiles made of porcelain, marble, or slate offer durability and a multitude of design possibilities. Stained or etched concrete and resin are two contemporary options. Check local codes to determine the distance required between the mantel and the upper edge of the firebox—and be aware that removing a mantel may uncover existing problems with the firebox structure that could necessitate costly repairs.

MANTEL

banisters, comprising the staircase handrail and supports, are worthy of special treatment if they're in a prominent spot like the main entry. The staircase pictured here features white-painted balusters topped with a scrolled, stained handrail, a style well suited to this traditional home. In contemporary homes, materials such as iron and steel can make banisters focal-point features; a decorative paint treatment is another option.

BANISTER

columns and pilasters can create a sense of height and add period atmosphere. Columns are rounded and sometimes provide structural support; pilasters (shown here) are rectangular and almost always ornamental, usually protruding from the wall on either side of a noteworthy entryway. Both can be made of wood, plaster, cast concrete, stone, or newer materials such as extruded polymer and molded foam.

PILASTER

well-dressed walls

HOW DO YOU DECORATE A TRADITIONAL HOME IN A STYLE THAT'S formal yet fresh—and suitable for an active young family? Interior designer Tres McKinney and decorative painter Peggy Del Rosario used an array of paint techniques and wall coverings to infuse the rooms in this 100-year-old house with a lively spirit and a sense of ease. To this decorative mix they added sophisticated, often unexpected furnishings. The result is a lush and elegant home, with walls that showcase an exquisite selection of materials and finishes. Turn to page 266 to see a photo of the home's vestibule, where wallpaper and paint finishes hint at the visual delights within.

BELOW: Walls painted a soft mustard hue are the perfect foil for vibrant artwork and handsome case goods in the dining room. Patterned portieres frame the view into the formal entry at right.

ABOVE: Charming wallpaper in the children's bath complements the bombé (rounded-front) vanity and tile backsplash, setting off the frame-and-panel wainscot and other crisp white trimwork.

Grass cloth in a rich pomegranate color provides the design canvas on which elegant cabinetry and wall accessories are layered in this guest bath. The subtle horizontal pattern of the wall covering supplies a sense of visual equilibrium to the small space.

Over a deep mustard base coat, painter del Rosario applied a sheer, watered-down glaze the color of limestone, then broke it up with a cheesecloth pom-pom to create a Swedish Gustavian effect. The patterned window treatments and a generous banquette add yet more character to this eat-in kitchen.

flooring

Tumbled travertine tile reveals the natural "bubbles" in this ancient form of limestone. Sealing is a must for limestone and travertine.

LOWE'S QUICK TIP
You'll see the term "grade" when you shop for flooring. "Above grade" means on a raised foundation, "on grade" on a concrete slab, and "below grade" in a basement. Some flooring can only be installed above grade; laminate, on the other hand, can go above, on, or below grade.

ALTHOUGH FLOOR COVERINGS MAY SEEM LIKE SUPPORTING PLAYERS in a room, they usually cover a large area, giving them an important role. And of all the furnishings you buy for your home, flooring will see the most wear. In choosing it, you'll want to consider durability, maintenance, functionality, and comfort.

Flooring is a working component, not just an aesthetic choice, and it represents the second-largest surface in a home, after walls. That means flooring will account for a significant portion of your total decorating budget.

The major categories of floor coverings are wood, in all manner of finishes and construction; soft flooring, in the form of carpet, rugs, and matting; resilient flooring such as vinyl and laminate; and hard flooring, including concrete as well as ceramic, porcelain, and stone tile. As you ponder your many options, try to answer the following questions:

❖ How much can you spend? In comparison to your wall coverings, window treatments, and furniture, installed floors are a long-term investment, and prices reflect that. But even high-end looks can be achieved within reasonable means. Porcelain and vinyl tile can simulate stone, for example, and "hand-scraped" laminate flooring can look like real wood. Whatever material you decide to go with, factor installation costs into your budget; a sales associate in the flooring department at Lowe's can provide information on professional installation services.

❖ What's the look you're after? Do you want the natural feel of slate, the rustic appearance of distressed wood, the high-tech appeal of concrete, or perhaps the sleek, formal look of marble?

❖ How do you want the room to relate to the rest of the house? Similar floor coverings throughout provide visual continuity; conversely, a mix of flooring helps delineate areas and lets you tailor the flooring to the room's function. If you plan to use different floor coverings under one roof, make them harmonious in color, value (see page 164), and scale (see page 242), and think about how you'll make the transition from one material to another.

❖ Do you want the floors to be a prominent feature, or to act as a low-key backdrop? A patterned area rug commands more attention than neutral cut-pile carpeting; multicolored slate tile will be noticed more than will porcelain tile that's all the same color.

❖ How does the room function? Kitchens, bathrooms, and other heavy-use areas call for durable, water-resistant coverings like tile, whereas a formal dining room can sustain a more delicate flooring such as mahogany with a decorative inlay border.

❖ What kind of support do you need underfoot? Saxony carpet is an enduring favorite for bedrooms because it is cushy. Vinyl is popular in the kitchen because it cleans up readily and is easy to stand on. Slipping is an issue in bathrooms, so a slightly textured porcelain tile is safer than polished marble.

❖ Is noise control an issue? For hallways and stairs, consider a plush, cut-pile carpet to insulate against sound.

❖ Are you going to do the work yourself? Know what's involved before you commit to installing your own floor. In general, tile floors are the easiest because you're working with manageable units; engineered flooring and laminate take time and patience but are also achievable. Leave installation of carpet, linoleum, and concrete to the pros.

CORK

LINOLEUM

FRIEZE CARPET

SHEET VINYL

PORCELAIN TILE

BIRCH LAMINATE

wood flooring

WOOD IS A CLASSIC, NATURALLY APPEALING FLOOR MATERIAL THAT FITS IN beautifully with almost any home's decor. It ages gracefully, feels good underfoot, and is relatively easy to care for. Oak, maple, birch, and cherry are perennial favorites, but options abound (including exotic woods such as eucalyptus), and every species has its own unique color and graining.

Wood flooring falls into two broad categories—solid and engineered. Each has its aesthetic and practical advantages, as outlined below. Also included here is laminate flooring, which mimics wood and is stocked near the real thing. To become better acquainted with all the choices in wood flooring, browse the hundreds of samples at your Lowe's store; many can be checked out for several days.

SOLID OAK

ENGINEERED PECAN

solid wood is any wood flooring that is all one piece from top to bottom. Available in strips (2¼ or 3¼ inches wide) and planks (up to 8 inches wide), it has tongue-and-groove edges that fit together. Oak, pictured here, and maple are among the most popular choices in solid wood. You can buy solid wood flooring either with a factory-applied chemical finish or unfinished. The latter must be sanded and finished on-site after installation; because of environmental regulations, the finishes are less durable than the factory-applied ones, though the look is more traditional.

engineered wood is made by laminating a hardwood veneer to a layer of plywood; a micro bevel on each edge smooths the transition from strip to strip. (Once seen as a negative, these tiny bevels are actually useful for capturing debris that would otherwise scratch the surface.) Engineered wood is easier to install and maintain than solid wood and has greater dimensional stability—that is, it doesn't shrink or expand when exposed to moisture, heat, or pressure. In general, the thicker the veneer layer (typically ⅜ to ¾ inch), the more durable the flooring; check the warranty to determine a product's life expectancy. Engineered flooring comes in many species—oak, maple, walnut, hickory, cherry, ash, pecan (shown here), and exotics—with a durable factory-applied finish. Strips are generally 2¼, 3, or 5 inches wide and are often "ganged" to form wider planks that are easier and faster to install. Most engineered wood is attached to the subfloor by means of a floor stapler. Sometimes it can be glued or "floated" over foam underlayment; refer to the manufacturer's instructions before you proceed.

parquet flooring is made up of small strips of hardwood arranged in patterns—herringbone, checkerboard, and stripes are classic designs. Parquet is usually purchased in readymade, prefinished 12- by 12-inch sheets (sometimes referred to as "tiles") attached to a mesh backing. These are stapled or glued to the subfloor—easy for do-it-yourselfers, making this a great way to get a wood floor. Because of the many seams, parquet floors are not suitable for areas where moisture is present, notably bathrooms and kitchens.

PARQUET TRIM

stenciled floors are another way to introduce pattern under-foot or to turn an unremarkable surface into something special. Stencils work especially well as borders or to define spaces within a room. Though they are typically applied with paint, in the example pictured at right stains were used instead to add lilting prose to a distressed wood floor. Sealing with two coats of polyurethane protects the design.

STENCILING

laminate floors have come a long way as a convincing alternative to real wood. A photograph of wood is sandwiched between a top layer of melamine resin and a base of high-compression fiber core. When shopping, pay attention to the thickness of the melamine "wear layer"; generally, the thicker the wear layer, the better the warranty. (Laminate flooring can't be refinished.) Choices include oak, hickory, mahogany, bamboo, walnut, beech, maple, cherry, and pine look-alikes, as well as slate and other stone. Some wood patterns have a rustic, hand-scraped look; others are embossed to match the grain of the wood image. Laminate can be installed over existing wood, concrete, vinyl, and tile flooring. The required foam pad also functions as a moisture barrier and helps muffle sound.

LAMINATE

bamboo, though technically a grass and not a wood, has become popular as a sustainable, renewable flooring choice. Ask about the hardness of any product before you buy; bamboo harvested before maturity may dent and scratch easily. You'll find bamboo in two grain patterns—horizontal (wider strips that reveal the "knuckles") and vertical (thin strips turned on their sides, forming a subtle stripe). The stain is either natural (blonde) or carbonized (golden brown). Like engineered wood flooring, bamboo comes in prefinished tongue-and-groove strips; these can be installed with a floor stapler or glued.

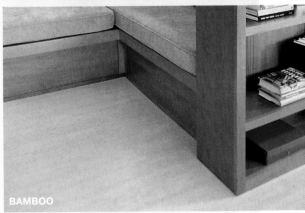

BAMBOO

soft floor coverings

CARPETS, AREA RUGS, AND MATTING CAN DISGUISE DAMAGED FLOORING, PROVIDE warmth and softness underfoot, reduce noise, conserve energy, and serve as focal points in a decorating scheme.

Wall-to-wall carpet typically plays a subordinate role in a room's decor, contributing color and texture and, less frequently, pattern. It may be made of natural fibers (wool, cotton), synthetic fibers (nylon, Olefin, polyester, acrylic), or a blend. Cost varies considerably depending on weave density, design complexity, and fiber. Wool is the most expensive and durable natural fiber, nylon the most durable and easy-care synthetic.

To determine the quality of a weave, bend the carpeting to see how much backing shows through: less is better. Also ask how many fiber tufts per square inch it has: the more, the better. Some people prefer commercial grades of carpeting, because of their durability and their understated appearance. You'll find a large and diverse selection of carpets at Lowe's, and you can arrange for installation as well.

PLUSH CARPET

SISAL-WEAVE CARPET

cut-pile carpet features fiber tufts that are cut straight across; their length and density determine the look and feel of the carpet. *Plush,* shown here, is the shortest cut-pile carpet; it's good in bedrooms because of its softness, but it shows footprints and vacuum tracks more than any other type of carpet. *Frieze,* a "hard-twist" carpet (made of tightly twisted, heat-set tufts of yarns) sometimes described as "curly," is a good choice for high-traffic areas because its random texture doesn't reveal footprints; some shag carpet is actually frieze. *Saxony* carpet, another type of cut pile, is not as tightly twisted as frieze and shows footprints more. *Textured* cut-pile carpet has a multicolored look that effectively disguises footprints. In general, the shaggier any cut-pile carpet, the more it will hide foot-traffic patterns and insulate against sound.

loop-pile carpet has a tailored look; because it has no cut or frayed ends, this flooring is more durable and easier to clean than cut-pile carpet and doesn't show footprints. *Berber* has slightly varied loop lengths and is typically available in neutral colors. *Sisal-weave* carpet, shown here, is woven in tiny, tight loops that offer the look of sisal matting but the feel of carpet; it's much easier to keep clean than real sisal. Loop-pile carpet does not offer quite the sound insulating quality of cut-pile carpeting.

cut-and-loop-pile carpet achieves subtle pattern and texture effects by having some yarns looped and others cut. These variations make cut-and-loop-pile one of the best styles for hiding traffic patterns and withstanding general wear and tear. Geometric patterns like the one pictured here stand up well to heavy use, disguising the wear pattern.

carpet panels provide a versatile, easy-to-install alternative to wall-to-wall carpeting or area rugs. Typically sold in 24- by 24-inch squares, 10 per carton, they have an antimicrobial treatment and soil and stain protection (like carpeting) that makes them durable. Each panel has an attached pad that serves as a moisture barrier and provides extra comfort. You can create your own custom design by mixing colors and patterns, as seen here.

area rugs can define an inner room (see page 252), protect high-use areas, and provide design focal points. They may be handmade or machine made of synthetic or natural fibers, knotted or woven. Cost can vary dramatically, so determine the size you need and set a budget. Also think about shape: for instance, you might choose a round area rug to give an otherwise angular room soft curves. To extend the life of your rug and protect the floor, be sure to use a nonslip pad.

matting is a natural material that is both neutral and sophisticated. Although economical to purchase, matting is considerably less durable than tile or wood flooring and not as soft to stand on as carpeting; sisal and sea-grass mats can stain easily. Here, Japanese *tatami* mats add warmth and texture to a wood floor. Made of grass reeds stitched together in a double layer, tatami mats are traditionally filled with rice straw; polyester fiberfill is a synthetic alternative filling. The edges are bound with black fabric tape in 6- by 3-foot sections (these were sewn together to cover a larger area). The fibers are soft and smooth to the touch, and the mats can be cleaned with a vacuum.

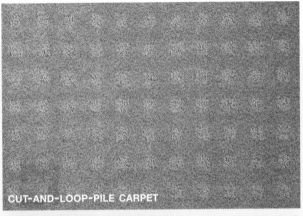

CUT-AND-LOOP-PILE CARPET

CARPET PANELS

AREA RUG

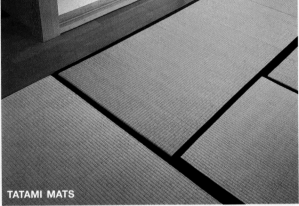

TATAMI MATS

resilient flooring

SMOOTH-SURFACE FLOORING WITH A BIT OF GIVE IS REFERRED TO AS "RESILIENT." From vinyl to cork to linoleum, resilient floors are softer and quieter underfoot than many other flooring surfaces, relatively easy to install and maintain, and resistant to both moisture and stains. That makes them perfect candidates for kitchens, entries, bathrooms, and laundry rooms. As a category, resilient flooring is less expensive than most other flooring, though price varies widely depending on the material. Its very resilience makes this flooring prone to dents and tears from sharp objects or heavy appliances, but often such damage can be repaired. Proper installation is essential; moisture can collect in poorly jointed seams and cause problems.

LINOLEUM

CORK

linoleum is an environmentally friendly flooring composed of renewable organic materials: linseed oil, ground wood or cork, resins, and mineral pigments on a jute backing. Tough and long wearing, it comes in a variety of bright or muted hues that extend through its entire thickness, almost always with a mottled appearance. Linoleum is sold as a sheet product but is often laid in wide bands of alternating colors. Some linoleum has a protective coating bonded to the surface; otherwise it must be polished to resist spills and stains. It should be installed by experienced professionals.

cork is enjoying a renaissance as homeowners rediscover all its desirable qualities: it is easy on legs and feet, has insulating properties, looks luxurious, and is an environmentally sustainable product. Once limited to shades of brown, cork is now stained in a whole array of colors. It can be purchased in sheets, tiles, and planks, some of which feature click-together installation. Different-size granules create various surface textures, but cork is almost always filled and finished to a completely smooth surface. Once it's installed, you can wax it or apply a urethane or acrylic finish to protect the surface. Note that cork can be dented by furniture and may fade with prolonged exposure to sunlight.

sheet vinyl consists of several layers: a protective top coat makes the surface easy to clean and scuff resistant, a clear vinyl "wear layer" protects against rips and gouges, and a printed vinyl layer creates the design. Sheet vinyl comes in 6- and 12-foot widths in numerous colors and patterns, some of which convincingly imitate stone, tile, and even wood. Because it is a continuous piece, sheet vinyl is excellent at repelling water. The top coat will last for years, but eventually you will need to apply an acrylic finish made for no-wax floors. A smooth subfloor is a necessity—any imperfections will telegraph through the vinyl and be visible forever. You may need to install new underlayment (see page 381 for instructions).

vinyl tile comes in two versions, commercial and self-sticking. *Commercial-grade* vinyl composition tile (VCT) is 12 or 18 inches square and comes in boxes of 45 same-color pieces; flecks of color running through the thickness of the tile help hide dirt and disguise damage and wear. *Self-sticking* vinyl tile (also called "peel and stick") is essentially the same material as sheet vinyl in the form of 12-inch tiles. Some are embossed, or feature a beveled edge that mimics stone; 4- by 36-inch "planks" imitate wood flooring. Better-quality self-sticking tiles are stiff, have a thick top layer, and are protected by a solid no-wax coating that will last for years. VCT doesn't have this coating, so you'll eventually need to apply an acrylic finish made specifically for VCT. (For instructions on installing VCT, see page 377.)

laminate comes in planks that imitate tile—complete with simulated grout joints—and also in 16-inch squares. See page 281 to read about the characteristics and requirements of this type of flooring. The "click" forms of laminate are not rated for wet areas, but glue-down products are, if installed according to the manufacturer's specifications.

leather is migrating from furniture to flooring, primarily in the form of tiles ranging from 4 to 24 inches square. This high-end product offers a luxurious yet natural look as well as softness and insulating properties. Like leather for furniture, leather tiles come in various colors and textures. The surface will get scuffed and scratched, but many consider these natural markings a plus.

SHEET VINYL

VCT

LAMINATE

LEATHER

hard flooring

DURABLE, BEAUTIFUL, AND NATURAL—IT'S HARD TO BEAT STONE, PORCELAIN, AND other ceramic floor tiles when it comes to these qualities. Similarly durable is concrete, possessing its own beauty. With today's sealers, all these materials become virtually impervious to food spills, water, and mud, making them practical for kitchens, bathrooms, and entries. (Seek out tile labeled for use on floors—it's thicker and more durable than tile for countertops and walls.) Any natural stone, such as marble and slate, is porous and requires sealing. Be aware that the sealant will enhance the color of the stone and can also change the color of the grout; you can get a sense of the effect by wetting a sample of each.

The luxurious look of hard flooring can come at a steep price: natural stone is one of the most expensive flooring categories. Porcelain tile varies widely in price but is usually less expensive than stone. And all hard flooring shares certain drawbacks. Anything that falls on it (from glassware to small children) will take a beating. It can be tiring to stand on for long periods. And unless radiant (underfloor) heating is installed, it almost always feels cold. Finally, most hard flooring is heavy, so the subfloor must be strong enough to support it. If you feel "give" when you walk across your floor (known as "deflection" in the flooring trade), you run the risk of tiles cracking or grout failing unless you replace or strengthen the subfloor.

PORCELAIN TILE

TERRA-COTTA TILE

ceramic is a sometimes confusing category that encompasses four types of tile: glazed, porcelain, quarry, and terra-cotta. A glasslike material baked onto *glazed ceramic* tile forms a hard surface that's impervious to water; to render the tile skid resistant, the surface may be textured, or the glaze itself made bumpy. (White-bodied glazed ceramic tile—colored only on the surface—is not recommended for floors but is appropriate for use as a backsplash.) *Porcelain* tile, shown top left, is a type of ceramic made by firing fine, white clay at a very high temperature. Typically manufactured to resemble tumbled marble, limestone, or travertine, this tile is extremely durable. *Quarry* pavers are made from natural red clay, fired but unglazed; these aren't slippery when wet, but they must be sealed to prevent staining. The rugged surface of quarry tile develops an attractive patina with wear. *Terra-cotta* tile, shown bottom left, is similar to quarry tile but is more porous and less durable; it's also unglazed and needs sealing.

marble is an elegant metamorphic limestone distinguished by its eye-catching mineral veining, like the Carrara marble pictured here. Marble occurs naturally in many colors, from white and gray to brown, ocher, and black. Although less porous than limestone, marble is softer and more porous than granite; food and dirt will leave permanent stains, so plan to seal and maintain the tile surface. Tumbled marble is softer-looking and a bit more textured than polished marble, which can be slippery when wet.

MARBLE

slate is an extremely dense metamorphic rock that tends to split along natural grains and fissures, giving this stone its characteristic irregular surface and color variations. Like marble, it is found in a wide range of natural colors, most commonly gray, green, blue, and black, less often buff and rust. The slate shown here is gauged, meaning each piece was milled to a uniform thickness, while retaining its "cleft" surface. Slate can also be honed to a smooth finish, or even polished for a silkier look. Some slates are very porous; for them, sealing is a must.

GAUGED SLATE

limestone and travertine are sedimentary types of stone that have been layered and compressed over millions of years. Travertine results when hot water percolates through limestone, leaving small pockets in the stone. Both limestone and travertine are typically neutral in color, making them ideal for almost any decorating style. Both also share an undeserved reputation for being too soft for flooring—some are, in fact, as tough as granite. They come in tumbled (seen here), honed, and polished finishes, all of which must be sealed.

TUMBLED TRAVERTINE

concrete floors can be stained just about any color, or they may have "integral color," meaning the hue is added when the concrete is mixed. At right, gray concrete was acid-stained after installation to give it a rich, warm color. Concrete is porous and needs to be sealed and properly cared for, or it will stain; over time it acquires a rich patina. The most obvious drawback? It is hard—on legs and joints, on dishes that are dropped, and on anyone who falls. It is also subject to cracking. Besides poured-in-place concrete, you will find concrete tiles in various textures, some mimicking marble, limestone, or other natural materials.

ACID-STAINED CONCRETE

cabinetry

CABINETS TYPICALLY COST MORE—SOMETIMES MUCH MORE—THAN MOST OTHER components in a room, so it's important to evaluate your options for style, performance, and price. Three features define cabinets: box construction, door and drawer fit, and door and drawer style. Storage capability, of course, is important. Major manufacturers offer all sorts of organizational features that maximize capacity and convenience, from vertical spice drawers to swing-out pantries. Making cabinets easier to use are soft-closing mechanisms that slow down doors and drawers and keep them from slamming shut.

box construction Cabinets vary in the way the cabinet "box" is put together. Think of this box as having five sides, with an open front.

FACE-FRAME CABINETS, the traditional style, have a wood frame attached to the front edges of the box. Doors and drawers fit into the frame opening. Because the frame reduces the size of the opening, drawers are narrower than the full width of the cabinet, slightly decreasing their storage capacity. Door hinges may or may not show.

FRAMELESS CABINETS, also called "Euro-style," have no frame attached to the face of the box. Open the door and you see the box edges; close the door and they are covered. Hinges are attached to the inside of the door, so they don't show. Drawers can be sized to practically the full dimension of the box, maximizing the storage capacity. Frameless cabinets can look contemporary or traditional, depending on the style of the door.

door and drawer fit Doors and drawers fit into the cabinet box in one of the following three ways.

A media center constructed of cherry is a striking example of face-frame cabinetry with partial-overlay, frame-and-panel doors. Open shelves with matching interior supply display space and lighten the unit's visual weight; crown moulding finishes the piece in style.

FLUSH-INSET doors and drawers close flush with the frame on face-frame cabinets, like those on fine furniture. This traditional style is the most expensive, because such a precise fit requires a high degree of craftsmanship and takes a lot of time to produce.

PARTIAL-OVERLAY doors and drawers have a lip that overlaps the box frame on a face-frame cabinet while still revealing some of it. Usually traditional in style, these are less expensive than flush-inset doors and drawers because there is some "play" in the fit.

FULL-OVERLAY doors and drawers cover the box completely on both face-frame and frameless cabinets, with as little as ⅛ inch of space needed for clearance between doors and drawers. (On well-made cabinetry with full-overlay doors, you can't tell whether the cabinets are face-frame or frameless until you open the doors.) They can look either contemporary or (with the addition of moulding) traditional.

door and drawer style Doors and drawers come in two basic styles: frame-and-panel and slab. You'll often see these styles mixed in a kitchen—typically frame-and-panel doors with slab drawers.

FRAME-AND-PANEL doors are the most widely used. A recessed, raised, or flush panel fits within a frame made up of two horizontal "rails" and two vertical "stiles." Cathedral-style frame-and-panel doors with arched tops are sometimes used on upper cabinets; lower doors have square or rectangular panels. Shaker-style doors have rails and stiles that butt together to form right-angle corners; doors with mitered corners are less common.

SLAB doors and drawers can be solid wood, but they are more often made up of several layers of wood. They're used most frequently in contemporary settings, but slab drawers can coexist nicely with frame-and-panel doors in a more traditional scheme, too.

ABOVE: A vanity and adjoining three-bin clothes hamper offer vintage style along with modern practicality. The frameless cabinets feature full-overlay, frame-and-panel doors and drawers, finished with classic bin pulls and simple knobs.

RIGHT: Shallow glide-out drawers accommodate baking accessories in a base cabinet.

LOWE'S QUICK TIP

The supporting pedestal for a base cabinet is recessed slightly to make room for your feet when you stand close to the cabinet—hence the term "toe kick." On furniture-style cabinetry like the media center shown on the facing page, the frame extends straight down to the floor, a style referred to as a "flush toe."

cabinets

VISIT THE KITCHEN AND BATH DEPARTMENTS AT LOWE'S AND YOU'LL FIND EVERY-thing you expect in cabinetry—and then some. Base and wall cabinets are the mainstays of kitchens and bathrooms, but you'll also see islands with legs, cabinetry that conceals range hoods, appliance panels that cover everything from refrigerators to trash com-pactors, and bathroom vanities dressed up with carved moulding. Details like corbels (decorative brackets), glass door inserts, and special hardware (which you may need to order separately) can give cabinetry a custom look.

When it comes to wood, cherry and maple are among the most popular kinds, with alder and birch rapidly replacing oak and hickory as runners-up. White thermal foil (created by binding a durable vinyl film to engineered wood) is a crisp, clean alternative that looks right at home in both traditional and contemporary settings. Variations on the basic frame-and-panel door let you customize cabinetry with beadboard or Mission-style panels.

Kitchens and baths aren't the only rooms where cabinetry has a place—you can order window seats, entertainment centers, wine cabinets, desks, and office shelving. Add crown moulding and hand-applied glazes to give these pieces the look of fine furniture.

FRAMELESS

COMBINATION

PARTIAL OVERLAY

combination cabinets in a classic white kitchen (far left) showcase a variety of box, door, and drawer options. Upper cabinets are face-frame construction with flush-inset doors; hinges are visible but unobtrusive. The base cabinets are frameless, with full-overlay doors and drawers that completely cover the box. Slab drawers combine nicely with frame-and-panel doors for an unclut-tered look.

frameless cabinetry in a bathroom (top near left) features full-overlay doors and drawers that appear traditional, thanks to frame-and-panel fronts with narrow bead trim. Legs minimize the look of the toe kick and make the cabinet seem more like a piece of furniture than a built-in unit.

partial overlay doors and drawers over-lap the box frames on the face-frame oak cabinets shown near left—the most popular combination of box construction and door and drawer fit. The corners are mitered on these frame-and-panel doors; the drawers are slab style.

full-overlay doors and drawers made of maple cover the frameless cabinets completely in the bright, contemporary kitchen at right; minimalist hardware is in sync with the sleek slab doors and drawers. Above the sink, a niche in the cabinetry provides display space and houses task lighting for the cook.

a hutch in a dining area (near right) incorporates beadboard panels, glass inserts, crown moulding, and undercabinet lighting, making this built-in unit look more like a freestanding piece. A granite countertop complements the hutch's warm-toned birch.

an appliance door for a flush-with-the-counter refrigerator gives a seamless look to a wall of fir cabinetry (far right). The adjacent base and upper cabinets are traditional face-frame construction, with flush-inset, frame-and-panel doors and drawers. Glass inserts in the upper cabinet doors break up the expanse of wood.

decorative glass inserts give upper cabinets an open, airy look. The Shaker-style, full-overlay pantry doors shown at near right feature quilted glass; clean, simple maple cabinetry pairs well with the boldly patterned glass. In the kitchen pictured far right, panes of wavy water glass have enough pattern to slightly obscure the cabinet's contents. The flush-inset doors feature unobtrusive hinges; handsome crown moulding adds a fine finishing touch.

FULL-OVERLAY DOORS

HUTCH

APPLIANCE DOOR

QUILTED GLASS INSERTS

WATER GLASS INSERTS

counters

AN APPROPRIATE COUNTERTOP MATERIAL ADDS STYLE AND CHARACTER TO A ROOM, but even more important is the work surface it provides for countless tasks. Whether you're buying a countertop for a kitchen, bathroom, home office, or utility room, take into account its durability, cost, appearance, and maintenance requirements.

Think about how you will use your countertop. In general, a continuous surface without grout lines is easiest to keep up. Marble and granite are durable, but if you do damage the surface, you'll need a professional to polish out the defect, and you may be left with a slight dip. Solid-surface materials are mendable using a fine abrasive pad and a cleanser; if you burn the surface, however, you'll need a pro to repair it. And be aware that prolonged or pooled moisture on laminate countertops can cause the seams to fail, making the substrate swell and the top layer de-laminate.

A backsplash—that vertical extension of the countertop just behind the work surface—is both a practical feature and a potential focal point. Its utilitarian purpose is to protect the wall and keep liquids and debris from slipping down behind the counter. A backsplash may be the same material as the countertop or different— a tile backsplash paired with a granite countertop, for example. (Where the two materials meet, the joint needs to be sealed with a bead of flexible grout.) For plastic laminate, solid surface, and engineered stone, a 4-inch backsplash is usually calculated into the price of the countertop.

As you go through your selection process, consider which counter characteristics are most important in each different area of your home.

Mosaic glass tile on the backsplash and tumbled travertine on the countertop offer contrast in texture, color, and scale. Eased (slightly rounded) trim pieces soften the edges.

kitchens These are the most challenging rooms to outfit with countertops because so many activities take place here, from preparing and serving food to cleaning up. Traditionally the same countertop surface is used throughout, but you can easily mix materials to satisfy your needs—a butcher-block top on an island prep area, perhaps, with cool marble as a baking counter and heat-resistant stone next to the stove. If you opt for a single material, increase its versatility and prolong its life and looks by using cutting boards, heatproof trivets, and dish racks.

bathrooms A countertop material for a bathroom needs to be impervious to water, stain resistant, and easy to clean. While ceramic tile was once the countertop of choice, a counter without grout lines is easier to clean and maintain—and gives you a smooth surface on which to set grooming products. Many of today's popular countertop materials—solid surface, engineered stone, and natural stone—fit the bill nicely.

other rooms Countertops should suit a room's particular purpose. For an office, a smooth, hard surface that's not cold to the touch, like Richlite (see page 295), is appropriate. Some solid-surface and laminate products have an antistatic feature that prevents interference with computers and other electronic equipment. In sewing rooms and playrooms, counters should be impervious to damage from scissors and markers. For a utility room, choose a material that can withstand the chemicals in cleaning products.

COUNTERTOP EDGINGS

The visible edges on countertops need to be finished in some fashion. A self-edge—one made of the same material as the countertop—suits natural and engineered stone, solid surface, plastic laminate, and tile. A self-edge may be integral to the countertop (like a no-drip edge on plastic laminate) or applied (like surface bullnose or V-cap trim pieces on a ceramic tile countertop). The edgings shown here are appropriate to use for any slab material, whether it's natural stone, solid surface, or engineered stone.

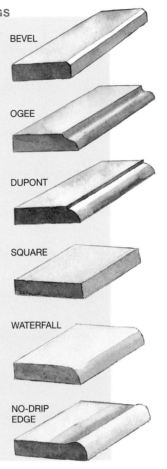

BEVEL

OGEE

DUPONT

SQUARE

WATERFALL

NO-DRIP EDGE

An ogee edge on a dark marble countertop adds a tailored touch to a bathroom vanity; lighter marble forms the low-profile backsplash. Polished nickel fixtures harmonize with both surfaces.

countertops

YOU PROBABLY RECOGNIZE MANY OF THE COUNTERTOP MATERIALS AVAILABLE today, and you may already have a preference based on appearance alone. But take the time to learn the characteristics of various surfaces—including maintenance requirements—before you make a commitment. Costs vary widely, depending on the material, but prefab counters in standard depths and standard edge treatments (see page 293) are almost always the least expensive options.

Look for more information and inspiration in the kitchen and bathroom showrooms at Lowe's, where specialists can answer your questions and show you the many choices in countertop materials.

PLASTIC LAMINATE

plastic laminate comes in a dizzying assortment of patterns and textures that mimic granite, concrete, even wood, in addition to contemporary color choices. Laminate is one of the easiest countertop materials to install yourself. On the minus side, it can be damaged by heat, sharp objects, and abrasive cleansers; burns, stains, and deep scratches can't be repaired. Corner seams may be visible. Some solid-color (not patterned) laminates are "color-through," meaning the color isn't just on the surface. That makes scratches less noticeable and seams less apparent.

PORCELAIN TILE

ceramic and porcelain tile is durable, water resistant, and heat resistant. Glazed ceramic tile is a popular countertop choice. Porcelain, shown here, is a type of ceramic fired at a higher temperature; it's more expensive but also more durable, and it can be made to look like natural stone. While the need for regular grout maintenance has been a deterrent for some, narrower grout lines, a wider range of grout colors, and better sealers have reduced this drawback. Twelve-inch porcelain tiles are ideal for standard countertops (which have a depth of 24 inches), providing a fairly large, uninterrupted surface with fewer grout lines. Tile varies in price, but it is usually less expensive than solid or slab surfaces. Installing tile is well within the capabilities of the do-it-yourselfer—see pages 389, 392, and 394.

SOLID SURFACE

solid-surface countertops made of acrylic or polyester are nonporous, making them hygienic, stain resistant, and easy to maintain. Solid-surface countertops can be fabricated to include an integral sink (the countertop and sink are one seamless piece). Another option is an undermount sink, which fits below the countertop material. Solid-surface countertops may be one color, as shown here, or patterned to resemble stone. Either way, they are significantly more expensive than laminate or tile. Extremely hot items can damage this material.

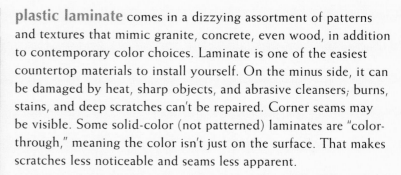

natural stone choices run the gamut from granite (pictured here) to marble, limestone, travertine, soapstone, and slate. A stone slab is a striking feature in a kitchen, but stone tile is easier to install and much less expensive. Stone characteristics vary considerably: granite is heat resistant and waterproof and will last forever if properly maintained, while marble is softer and more susceptible to staining and damage from food acids. All stone should be sealed to inhibit staining; tumbled stone (worn down at the edges and slightly distressed) or honed stone (buffed to a dull sheen) will need sealing more often than polished stone. However, honed stone won't show surface scratches as much as polished stone, and polished stone is more prone to acid damage. Polished surfaces may also create glare under direct light.

GRANITE

engineered stone, often referred to as quartz composite, consists of natural quartz particles mixed with an acrylic or epoxy binder. Because it is nonporous, quartz composite is one of the safest surfaces for food preparation; it also resists stains, heat, and scratches. Because of its color consistency, some people find engineered stone static in appearance compared to natural stone. It is generally more expensive than solid-surface materials.

ENGINEERED STONE

Richlite is an environmentally friendly product made of resin-treated paper derived from sustainable forests. It has a natural look and soft feel akin to wood; unlike wood, Richlite is heat resistant to 350 degrees. It also resists moisture and stains; keeping the surface sealed makes it even more stain resistant. Richlite will scratch, but minor damage is not noticeable because the color runs all the way through. And because it is so strong, this surface can span longer lengths than other materials without supports—for a cantilevered eating counter, for example. Richlite is more expensive than solid-surface countertops.

RICHLITE

other surfaces include concrete, stainless steel, and butcher block. *Concrete,* shown here, is chosen for its somewhat industrial look and rich, earthy colors; the color may be added when the concrete is mixed or applied as a stain after installation. A good sealer is a must, because concrete is porous. Be advised that concrete countertops may develop hairline cracks, and that it is sometimes difficult to find experienced fabricators. *Stainless steel* is a nonabsorbent countertop option, hygienic and easy to keep clean. Choose brushed over polished surfaces to minimize scratches; these can be buffed out by a professional fabricator. *Butcher block* offers the warm look of wood but is porous and requires significant maintenance, especially when installed near a sink. The most durable blocks have an end-grain work surface composed of thick pieces running vertically.

CONCRETE

lighting

GOOD LIGHTING IS THE RESULT OF A WELL-THOUGHT-OUT PLAN THAT LAYERS different types of illumination, using a variety of fixtures. Success can be measured by how much you use and enjoy a room; an appropriately lit space supports the room's activities—and just feels good.

Designers separate home lighting into four distinct categories: ambient, task, accent, and decorative. All of these contribute to the functionality and overall comfort of a room.

ambient lighting This general overall illumination fills in the shadows with a soft level of light—enough, say, for dining or conversing with friends, playing with the kids, or just passing through the room. Ambient light gives a room a subtle glow and makes people look their best. The most effective ambient lighting comes from indirect fixtures, gently illuminating the perimeter of the room and reflecting off the ceiling and walls.

task lighting Strong, focused illumination is needed for any area where a particular activity takes place, such as cooking or reading. Adjustability is essential, as is shielding (hiding the bulb from sight). When possible, light sources crossing each other are better than one overhead fixture; this arrangement all but eliminates shadows.

In an open kitchen, a combination of fixtures provides ambient and task lighting: recessed downlights in the coffered ceiling, a fixture suspended over the island, and undercabinet lighting above the cooktop.

accent lighting Similar to task lighting in that it consists of directional light, accent lighting has the primary purpose of accentuating a feature such as a work of art or an architectural element. Low-voltage halogen bulbs often are used because their clean, white light is ideal for highlighting china, crystal, or artwork. Although it may not be obvious, accent lighting also adds to the ambient light in a room.

decorative lighting Some fixtures draw attention to themselves as objects and can be regarded as accessories. The traditional chandelier is the classic decorative fixture; sleeker options include low-voltage pendant fixtures. Decorative strip and rope lights can add sparkle and warmth to a room while also highlighting architectural features. Whatever the fixture, it should also contribute ambient or task lighting.

room-by-room lighting

Each space in a home calls for a lighting plan that's appropriate to the room's intended use. Here's an overview.

entries Warm lighting creates a welcoming atmosphere. Avoid high contrast in light levels between the outdoors and the foyer, however, and between the foyer and the adjoining room. A ceiling-mounted fixture is often sufficient; to minimize shadows, choose one that throws light up onto the ceiling rather than straight down. Add soft fill light with wall sconces or a table lamp that has an opaque shade.

living spaces Flexible, layered lighting is called for here. Soft, adjustable levels of ambient light set a congenial mood for entertaining or relaxing. Include task lighting for reading or handwork and accent lighting for artwork or collections. Built-in architectural devices such as soffits and valances effectively house ambient fixtures; sconces and torchères are good ambient sources, too. In a living area with a televi-

sion, be sure there's enough ambient light to prevent a sharp contrast between the screen and the room; light spilling from an adjacent room can help. Position floor lamps to the side of the room to avoid annoying reflections and to reduce glare.

dining rooms Typically, a fixture such as a chandelier drops down over the center of the table. Ideally it will be at least 12 inches narrower than the dining table and hang at least 30 inches above the surface of the table; if the ceiling is higher than 8 feet, raise the chandelier an additional 3 inches per foot. A dimmer switch allows for full light while serving, lower light while dining. Don't expect a central fixture to carry the load of lighting the entire space; recessed lights soften shadows, sconces minimize glare, and a table lamp illuminates a buffet. (Avoid placing a recessed light where it will shine directly over a seated person's head.) A track lighting system with adjustable pendants gives you more flexibility than a single suspended fixture.

A fanciful metal chandelier supplies ambient light to an eat-in kitchen; antique mica shades over low-wattage incandescent bulbs produce a warm glow. Downlights brighten the corner even more.

kitchens

Recessed ceiling fixtures housing compact fluorescent lights (see facing page) are ideal for kitchens. To layer this kind of lighting, alternate fixtures on two switches; that way you can have some lights on and others off when you want a lower light level. Sufficient task lighting above the sink, island, cooktop, and countertops is essential; fluorescents shine in these locations because they provide even, energy-efficient light. The best task lighting is located between the cook's eye level and the work surface, which is why undercabinet fixtures (mounted as far forward as possible) are a mainstay in kitchen lighting plans. Hoods with built-in lights brighten cooktops; pendants effectively illuminate sink and island areas. Kitchen dining areas often feature a decorative pendant or chandelier—but keep in mind that kitchen fixtures need to be cleaned more often than those in other rooms.

RIGHT: Pendant fixtures flanking the mirror function like sconces and maintain the uncluttered look of this minimalist bathroom.

BELOW: To provide flexible lighting for reading, this wall-mounted, swing-arm lamp operates on a dimmer. The lamp's satin-nickel finish works with both traditional and contemporary decorating schemes.

bedrooms

A range of lighting effects is required in a bedroom, soft enough for relaxation and bright enough for late-night reading. Torchères, wall sconces, and soffit lighting all provide flattering ambient light. Downlights (see page 300) can bathe a bedroom in gentle illumination or direct light to the headboard area. Bedside reading lights should be adjustable, in both position and brightness. Wall-mounted swing-arm lamps do the job without taking up precious nightstand space; plug-in models eliminate the need for hard-wiring.

bathrooms

Lighting here needs to be bright enough for grooming, without harsh shadows. Mirror lights are best positioned along the sides rather than centered above; make sure light is directed toward one's face, not onto the mirror. A bathroom larger than 100 square feet should have general overhead lighting as well, close to the tub and shower; this may be part of a ceiling-mounted fan. Any light fixtures in the shower must be sealed and approved for wet rooms. Finally, consider a plug-in night-light for safe passage.

LOWE'S QUICK TIP

Occupancy sensor switches turn incandescent lights on manually, then shut them off automatically when no motion is detected in the room after a set period of time. In many locales, these are mandated for new construction and remodels. Some areas also require dimmer switches on incandescent fixtures to conserve energy.

SHEDDING LIGHT ON BULBS

Throughout the country, the trend in lighting is moving decisively in the direction of high-efficiency bulbs and fixtures. If you're planning to build a new home or to overhaul the lighting in your existing home—especially in the kitchen or bathroom—start by checking local building codes. If you can, work with a professional lighting designer who is knowledgeable about regulations in your area.

A short course in the main types of light (and requisite bulbs) is a good place to begin exploring your options.

INCANDESCENT light, warm and flattering, is produced by a tungsten filament burning slowly in a glass bulb filled with inert gas. The pear-shaped A bulb is the most familiar example—but be aware that in many areas it is slated to be discontinued and replaced by high-efficiency fluorescent lights.

FLUORESCENT lighting meets stringent standards for energy efficiency better than any other light source. A fluorescent tube uses a quarter to a third of the energy that its incandescent counterpart takes to produce the same level of illumination; this means that a 26-watt compact fluorescent light (CFL) can replace a 100-watt incandescent bulb. And though they cost more initially, fluorescent lights can last 10 times longer and cut operating costs by three-quarters. Californa's energy code now requires that at least 50 percent of the wattage in both new and newly remodeled homes be high-efficiency—which means, for the most part, using fluorescent lights in any permanent fixtures. CFLs with screw bases can replace incandescent bulbs in most traditional fixtures, letting homeowners conserve energy and reduce utility bills without remodeling.

Older fluorescent tubes were criticized for noise, flicker, and poor color rendition. Electron ballasts and better shielding have remedied the first two problems, and new technology has produced many more options in the color of light emitted by fluorescents; you can match the warmth of incandescent bulbs or the full spectrum of sunlight.

In areas that have a code like California's, any hard-wired kitchen fixture must accept a high-efficiency CFL with a pin base. These pin-style fixtures are rated for specific tube sizes and types; when choosing your fixtures, be sure you know which tubes they accept.

HALOGEN light bulbs containing halogen gas produce a whiter, purer light than incandescent bulbs and last longer. Because they are smaller and brighter than incandescents, halogen bulbs are great candidates for task and accent lighting and for use in tiny, sleek fixtures. However, these lights give off significant heat (never place them near fabric), cost more, and must be used in fixtures specifically designed for them. Many halogen bulbs are low-voltage, requiring a transformer to convert 120 volts into 12, either as part of the fixture itself or in a remote location like an attic or a closet.

LOWE'S QUICK TIP
Don't be confused when you see the term "lamp" in reference to a light bulb. That's the industry term for a bulb or tube used in a fixture, not for the fixture itself.

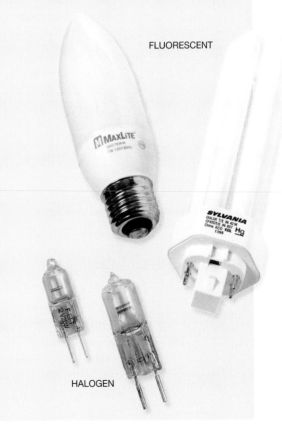

FLUORESCENT

HALOGEN

light fixtures

FINDING THE RIGHT COMBINATION OF LIGHT FIXTURES CAN BE DAUNTING—THE variety is impressive, and growing all the time. How do you decide? A visit to the lighting department at Lowe's is a good first step. You'll find an array of fixtures illuminated with bulbs of the correct wattage, allowing you to see how each one looks when lighted. As you consider a fixture, notice how it directs light: narrow and focused (for task or accent lighting), in a broad spread (for general or decorative lighting), or somewhere in between? An effective approach is to determine what type of light you need, then look for the beam patterns that will supply it.

INDIRECT FIXTURE

DOWNLIGHTS

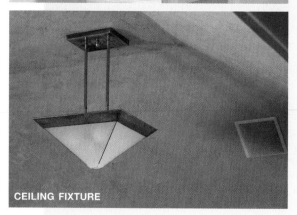

CEILING FIXTURE

indirect fixtures attached to the wall, ceiling, or underside of a cabinet bounce soft illumination off adjacent surfaces. The light source is shielded from view by architectural devices such as coves, valances, and soffits, so there's no glare. Usually indirect fixtures are used to provide general lighting, but they can also light an area where a task is performed, such as a desktop in a home office. At left, xenon bulbs (cooler-burning spin-offs of halogen bulbs) are mounted on a track hidden under the upper cabinets.

downlights—recessed ceiling units—provide general light from above without the visual intrusion of a ceiling-mounted fixture. Trim pieces—rings, baffles, reflector cones, lenses, and diffusers— are modular accessories that create different effects. The trim ring (the flange that fits flush with the ceiling) and baffle (the cone-shaped unit that fits into the ceiling hole and surrounds the bulb) typically come as one piece. For a seamless look, choose a unit that blends with your ceiling. *Puck lights* are partially recessed mini-downlights that accept tiny halogen bulbs. Use them to light display cabinets or niches, mount them under cabinets to brighten work areas, or install them above cabinets to wash upper walls with gentle light.

ceiling fixtures covered by a shade or a bowl are unbeatable for ambient lighting and the chance to inject style into your lighting scheme. They're also a safety feature, making it easy to light up a room before you walk into it. Just remember that you'll need other kinds of lighting in the room, too; alone, a ceiling fixture can make a room look dreary at night. Another ceiling option, *track lighting*, offers versatility and ease of installation—it's a popular alternative to recessed fixtures if you can't or don't want to poke holes into the ceiling. Tracks accept individual fixtures that swivel and move, directing light where you need it; they can also accept pendants. For high-tech style, check out low-hanging cable lights, flexible track lights, and monorail systems.

undercabinet task lights, often called "light bars," are slender lights that are mounted under upper cabinets to shine down on countertops, illuminating the work surface and eliminating shadows. You'll find undercabinet fixtures designed for fluorescent, halogen, or xenon lights, less frequently for incandescents. Lengths vary from 12 inches to more than 48; some fixtures are "linkable," meaning that you can connect them to make a longer run. Both plug-in and wire-in fixtures are available.

suspended fixtures provide stylish illumination in the form of chandeliers and pendants. A *chandelier,* that most traditional of suspended fixtures, typically drops down from the ceiling on a chain, has several arms, and uses small, low-wattage decorative bulbs. A halogen chandelier is ideal for a dining area—halogen light makes crystal and china sparkle. *Pendant* fixtures (shown here), which hang from cords or stems, are available in both fluorescent and low-voltage halogen versions; the shade is what sets the style—retro or modern, elongated or rounded, opaque or clear. A suspended fixture mounted over a table should hang safely away from diners' heads, and the bulb should be above eye level.

sconces are wall-mounted fixtures, pointing either up or down. They can be used in pairs, often flanking a fireplace or a mirror, or singly down a hall. For general lighting, choose sconces that direct the light upward; if sconces are being used to illuminate stairs or a buffet, a downward cast is appropriate. Either way, make sure the bulb itself is hidden; mount the sconce so the bulb is situated *above* eye level if the light shines upward, *below* eye level if the light shines down.

portable light fixtures such as desk, table, and floor lamps are by far the simplest and most flexible lighting option. As you shop, pay close attention to the lampshade, as it will determine the light's effectiveness: the wider the shade at the bottom, the greater the spread of light. The hardworking desk lamp pictured here features a lever arm that adjusts easily to the task at hand. Floor lamps serve a variety of functions: a swing-arm version is useful for reading, a torchère or a floor lamp provides general lighting, and a decorative lamp brightens a room while contributing style. Think about where a lamp will be plugged in—you don't want the cord lying on the floor in a high-traffic area. The trend is for shorter cords, for both safety and aesthetics.

UNDERCABINET TASK LIGHTS

PENDANTS

SCONCE

DESK LIGHT

FLOOR LAMP

low-voltage lights the way

A LIGHTING PLAN was part of a whole-house remodel for this contemporary home with sloped ceilings. The homeowners wanted stylish, energy-efficient fixtures that could deliver a range of lighting effects, varying from room to room. Low-voltage systems with halogen bulbs met all their requirements.

"Simplicity and versatility were key to the design," says lighting designer Angie Ferone. "The house, with its beautiful views, called for a plan that would give the homeowners a lot of options."

Low-voltage systems utilize transformers that convert standard residential power from 120 volts to 12. Individual fixtures on track, rod, and cable systems appear to float in space but—on a more practical level—accommodate a mix of bulbs for a variety of different lighting effects from the same track. Halogen bulbs, chosen for their low-voltage efficiency and true color rendition, supply ambient, task, and decorative light throughout.

In the stairwell of this tri-level home, a low-voltage cable system runs at an angle from the skylight down to the ground floor. Glass tubes, slit on each side, fit onto the wires to shade 20-watt halogen bulbs. On the wall, sconces with frosted-glass shades can be rotated for different lighting effects.

A rigid right-angle track rod hanging from thin cables surrounds the custom-made hood above the kitchen island; a single thick cord powers the fixtures. At either end, a small light twisting down from the track supplies a whimsical touch.

ABOVE: The lighting designer worked out the shape of the flexible track beforehand, based on the planned furniture arrangement, and then attached the individual halogen fixtures. Because the ceiling slopes, the supporting cables had to be different lengths to level the track at the desired height (9 feet in this room). Wall washers add ambient light and play up the rich red wall color.

BELOW: In place of a conventional dining room chandelier, the owners chose a contemporary fixture that attaches to the sloped ceiling by means of cables, like the track system in the living room. A curvy cord supplies the power to halogen bulbs.

Just inside the front door, six low-voltage halogen pendants connect to the existing junction box and fan out on individual cables. Some cables attach to beams, others to the planks between the beams.

window treatments

WELL-CHOSEN WINDOW TREATMENTS DO MORE THAN ADD THE FINISHING TOUCH to a decorating scheme. They are often essential, hard-working components of a room, filtering the morning sun and softening harsh afternoon glare, providing privacy and offering an extra measure of security. They conserve energy, helping you warm or cool a room with a flick of the wrist. They may even help control noise. And every window covering contributes to—or detracts from—the overall style of your home.

As you explore the possibilities on the following pages, think about what jobs you want your window treatments to perform in different rooms. Privacy, for instance, is more important in bedrooms than in kitchens, and more important at night than by day. Blinds, shades, and shutters adjust easily as needed to modulate light and shield the interior from view.

Window treatments can alter the aesthetics of a room. You can "heighten" a window by mounting curtains or valances high above the casing. Sheers can disguise an undesirable view, just as draperies that blend with the wall will put the focus on what's outside. Shutters add architectural presence to a plain room, while an arched, upholstered cornice softens a room and draws the eye upward.

Given all the options, and all the magic they can perform, you'll want to place your window treatments artfully. Here are some guidelines for treatments mounted outside the window opening:

❖ Curtains and draperies typically begin about 5 inches above the window opening, but you can hang them anywhere between the ceiling and the opening.
❖ Valances usually hang from about 8 inches above the window opening, but it depends on the valance length and how much of the window you want to cover. The more glass a valance covers, the more light you'll lose.
❖ Floor-length treatments traditionally end ¼ to ½ inch short of the floor, but they may also "puddle" on the floor. (If so, be careful not to vacuum them up!)

Sumptuous silk makes a formal yet loosely structured top treatment for a window tucked into a dormer. An embroidered-sheer London shade completes the look.

When there is little space between windows, inside-mount treatments are the best choice. Plantation shutters control the light in this small study and give a bank of windows architectural significance.

❖ "Apron-length" curtains or draperies generally end approximately 5 inches below the window opening. In Victorian homes with tall, elegant baseboards, they may extend to the upper edge of the moulding.

shopping for window treatments You'll find a wide selection of curtain panels and valances in the window treatment department at Lowe's, along with accompanying hardware in many finishes and styles (see page 314). Also stocked are mini, wood, and vertical blinds, plus roller and bamboo shades. You can special-order pleated, cellular, and Roman shades from major manufacturers; sample books usually can be checked out for several days. There are sun-filtering shades that keep damaging rays from coming in but let you see out (these are not intended as privacy shades). In-store samples of shutters are on display for special order. For the widest selection of standard blinds and shades, shop online at Lowes.com, then pick up your treatments at your nearest store.

Home-decorating fabric stores often have workrooms where you can have window treatments made, start to finish. For a fee, they will send someone to your home to measure your windows, plan the placement of hardware or mounting boards, install the finished treatment, and steam and "dress" fabric treatments so they break correctly when opened and closed.

INSIDE VERSUS OUTSIDE MOUNTS

One of the biggest decisions you must make when planning your window treatments is where they will be mounted.

Inside mounts fit entirely within the window frame or opening, close to the glass, and end at the sill or lower edge of the opening. A clearance of ¼ inch on each side of a shade or blind allows it to function smoothly. Curtains mounted inside the window frame usually are hung on tension rods.

An outside-mount treatment covers the entire window and is installed on the window frame or above the frame or opening. Curtains or draperies can be positioned either to clear the glass when opened or to leave part of it covered; outside-mount shades generally extend 1 inch beyond the casing on each side of the window, or 2 inches beyond the window opening if there is no casing.

Each mount has its advantages: inside-mount treatments show off beautiful window casings; treatments mounted outside offer better insulation, prevent light seepage at the sides, and make windows appear larger.

Soft Roman shades draw up from the bottom for daytime privacy; simple matching valances give the windows a more finished appearance.

curtains and draperies

CURTAINS AND DRAPERIES ARE THE SOFTEST OF THE WINDOW-TREATMENT OPTIONS, with fabric that soaks up noise and "cozies up" hard expanses of glass and wall.

Most curtains are hung from rods by means of rings (with or without clips), making the hardware just as important as the fabric. (For hardware options, see page 314.) To prevent hand-traversing curtains from becoming soiled, attach a curtain wand to the leading edge of each panel. Standard curtain panels range from 63 to 84 inches in length, 40 to 59 inches in width, with some sheers as wide as 90 inches. For nonstandard sizes, you may need to make your own panels (see page 400) or have them custom-made. Headings (the upper edges on the panels) vary from flat to rod pockets to a number of different pleated styles.

If you're going for an airy, casual look, unlined curtains are fine. But for a more substantial appearance, choose lined panels. A lining gives a panel body and improves the way it hangs, protects the decorative fabric from sun and dust that drifts through the window, and presents a finished look from the outside.

Standard draperies, hung from traverse rods and operated with cords or wands, are less common today, but they are a good choice when you want a simple, efficient means of opening and closing the panels.

DRAPERIES

PLEATED CURTAINS

draperies are pleated panels hung from hooks that attach to slides on a traverse rod; a cord or wand moves the slides along the track to open and close the panels. Sheer draperies are left unlined; draperies made of medium-weight or heavy fabrics are almost always lined. Pleat options are numerous; at far left, sheer draperies with widely spaced reverse pleats hang from ceiling height, softening the windows in a chic bedroom.

pleated curtains, attached to rods with rings or clips, have the finished look of draperies but open and close by hand and hang from decorative rather than traverse rods. Preferences in pleat styles change as often as any other decorating trend. At near left, "Paris-pleat" curtains are a focal point in a formal library. Decorative wood hardware gives the impression of draperies, but these curtain panels don't move.

ROD-POCKET CURTAINS

rod-pocket curtains have a stitched channel (pocket) that allows them to be gathered onto a rod. They are by nature stationary, because it's difficult to pull them back and forth over the rod. Rod-pocket curtains can be lifted to the side with holdbacks or with tiebacks made of fabric or cording, or they can be allowed to hang straight and puddle on the floor. In casual settings, rod pocket curtains often have a heading above the pocket, forming an instant ruffle when the rod is threaded through.

TAB-TOP CURTAINS

tab-top curtains are simply panels that hang from narrow fabric strips (tabs). They adapt easily to a variety of windows, hardware, and fabrics. Few tab-top treatments move across a rod as easily as do curtains on rings, so think of them primarily as stationary panels. The tabs may be made from the same fabric as the curtains, but often they contrast. At right, a patterned curtain edged with a solid-color fabric dresses up bamboo shades.

SHEERS

sheers diffuse light, provide partial privacy, and soften the glare and hard surface of glass. They are especially effective for masking an unattractive view and ensuring daytime privacy without blocking light. Sheers with woven or printed patterns or decorative embroidery can easily stand on their own; plain sheers are traditionally layered under more substantial curtains or draperies. The patterned sheers pictured at right are held to the sides with fanciful metal holdbacks.

CAFÉ CURTAINS

café curtains, which cover only the lower half of a window, are a minimalist choice in every way. They're typically shortened versions of stationary rod-pocket or tab-top curtains, but you can use rings or grommets (shown here) to make it easy to open and close the panels. These cotton duck café curtains are mounted directly onto the window frame. The versatility of café curtains—their ability to provide privacy while admitting light from above—makes them a classic.

shades

SHADES ARE AS PRACTICAL AS THEY ARE GOOD LOOKING—THEY CONTROL LIGHT, provide insulation, and ensure privacy. Use them alone or team them with curtains, valances, or cornices for a more decorative effect. Compared to curtains or draperies, shades require less fabric, making them more economical than voluminous fabric treatments. And their trim profile makes them well suited to situations where space on one or both sides is limited, such as corner windows.

Think ahead about how you want to install shades in your room; see "Inside Versus Outside Mounts" on page 305 for guidance. Fabric shades must be lined to hang well; the lining also protects the face fabric from dirt and sun damage, insulates the window, and provides a uniform look from the exterior.

WOVEN SHADES

ROMAN SHADE   LONDON SHADE

woven shades made from split wood, bamboo, reeds, or other fibers offer distinctly natural color and texture. You'll also find synthetic shades that look like the real thing. If left unlined, woven shades allow natural light to enter—but also reveal some of the interior from outside when the room is illuminated. Some manufacturers offer light-filtering and room-darkening liners. Woven shades can roll up or fold up, like the ones shown at left; they're often teamed with curtain panels for added insulation and privacy. If you choose a woven shade as your primary window treatment, look for styles with matching valances and concealed hardware. Woven shades with fabric edgings work well in tailored decorating schemes.

roman shades, flat panels that draw up into neat horizontal folds, supply a crisp, clean look using minimal fabric. Soft-fold or "hobbled" Roman shades form loops of fabric rather than flat folds. Whether tailored or more loosely structured, the accordion effect is achieved by pull cords that run through rows of rings attached to the back of the shade. Cordless shades are raised and lowered by means of a handle. Top-down or bottom-up versions let you lower the shade from the top, raise it from the bottom, or both.

london shades have a more relaxed look than Roman shades, the result of having just one row of rings near each outer edge. Instead of drawing up into neat folds, the fabric droops casually in the center, with a "tail" at each end. Beaded fringe trims the edge of the London shade at left, accentuating the graceful fall of the folds.

balloon shades feature deep inverted pleats, with or without tails on the ends. Like Roman shades, they pull up by means of rings and cords on the back, but when they're raised, gentle poufs instead of folds form at the lower edge. Balloon shades require more fabric than Roman or London shades. Here, neutral linen shades grace the windows in a child's bedroom. Contrasting fabric edges and vertical "popcorn" trim add a fanciful touch to what are usually "grown-up" shades.

roller shades, used alone or with stationary curtain panels or top treatments, provide privacy and block light when pulled down but are unobtrusive when rolled up. The operating mechanism is either a standard spring roller or a bead chain, which can stop the shade in any position. Basic roller shades are vinyl or a combination of vinyl and fiberglass; others feature cotton-poly or other blended fabric bonded to a vinyl backing for a softer effect. Fanciful pulls and decorative hems, like the scalloped edge pictured near right, increase the design possibilities. Roller shades can be mounted inside or outside the casing (see page 305), depending on the type of bracket you buy.

pleated and cellular shades, with their pleat and "honeycomb" structures, deliver both style and practicality. Pleats (shown far right) are typically 1 inch, while "cells" come in two sizes, $3/8$ or $3/4$ inch. Cellular shades may be single or double; the primary advantage of a double-cell shade is energy efficiency. Both pleated and cellular shades are available in sheer to opaque materials, some with room-darkening or reflective backings; both come in top-down or bottom-up versions. These treatments can be custom-fitted to arched and angle-top windows, and the simplicity of pleated shades makes them ideal for skylights.

hybrid shades are a cross between a sheer curtain and a horizontal blind. With opaque fabric slats enclosed between gossamer fabric in front and back, they tilt like blinds to control light and provide privacy—or reveal the view when you want it. This treatment can be mounted top-down or bottom-up on a headrail and can be custom-fitted to skylights and odd-shaped windows. Their simplicity makes hybrid shades well suited to contemporary settings, but they adapt nicely to more traditional rooms when paired with valances or side panels.

BALLOON SHADES

ROLLER SHADE

PLEATED SHADES

HYBRID SHADES

blinds, shutters, and screens

WINDOW TREATMENTS MADE OF WOOD, VINYL, OR ALUMINUM OFFER A SLEEK and highly practical alternative to fabric treatments. Blinds provide versatile light control: they can be closed completely; tilted to direct light up, down, or straight into the room; or raised to disappear behind a cornice or decorative headrail. Shutters have the same tilt function as blinds, but they fold to the sides when opened for maximum light.

Although highly functional, these treatments are not lacking in style. The natural beauty of stained wood blinds or shutters is incomparable, and both treatments add warmth and architectural character to a room. Horizontal blinds can be paired with curtain panels, valances, or simple cornices for softer effects; newer vertical blinds feature sheer fabric on either side of the vanes (the vertical slats). And shoji screens say "Asian elegance" as no other window covering can.

ALUMINUM BLINDS

WOOD BLINDS

horizontal blinds are ideal for windows that are taller than they are wide. Aluminum or vinyl slats range in size from ½ inch to 2 inches (1 inch is standard). Wider slats let in more light and stack more compactly; narrower slats are a better fit for smaller windows and shallower sills. Horizontal blinds come in various colors, finishes, and textures, from metallic to pearlescent to faux fabric. Lowe's will custom-cut blinds to fit your windows while you wait; be sure to carefully measure your windows before you shop.

wood blinds add warmth and beauty to any room. A handsome, tailored treatment on their own, they are just as effective paired with curtain panels or topped by a cornice or valance, as shown here. Wood blinds are available with 1-, 2-, or 2½-inch slats, with a coordinating valance and bottom rail, in finishes ranging from oak to maple to pine stains, as well as distressed and glazed finishes. Vertical cloth ladder tapes can coordinate with your room's color scheme. *Faux-wood blinds* made of polymer won't warp or fade, even in high-moisture or variable-temperature rooms. Cordless versions of either wood or faux-wood blinds are safest for kids and pets.

vertical blinds, especially useful for sliding glass doors and large picture windows, come in many textures, finishes, and colors, but the look is always contemporary. They create visual height, are excellent for blocking light and providing privacy, and collect less dust than their horizontal counterparts. The 3½-inch vinyl, aluminum, or fabric-faced vanes typically hang loosely from the top beneath a metal headrail. Vanes come 84 inches long but can be cut down to any length. "Soft" vertical blinds, shown here, sandwich the vanes between layers of sheer fabric, diffusing the light even when the vanes are tilted open.

traditional shutters, with 1¼-inch wood or vinyl louvers in frames hinged to the window casing, are light in scale and work best in smaller windows or as café-style treatments covering only a portion of the window, as shown near right. The narrow louvers restrict the light and block the view more than wider ones but provide greater privacy when tilted open.

plantation shutters, with 2½-inch or larger louvers made of wood (typically basswood, as shown far right) or vinyl (the best option for humid climates), contribute a strong architectural presence in traditional interiors. Typically mounted onto the window casing, they open up the view and let in more light than shutters with narrower louvers. The initial cost is quite high, but plantation shutters last a long time and add to a home's value (wood shutters eventually require fresh paint or refinishing). Arched shutters are available for uniquely shaped windows; they may tilt, but they will not open.

shoji screens are a staple of traditional Japanese homes, their translucent rice-paper panels bathing rooms in gentle, even light. In this country they are generally used over sliding glass doors and windows, either gliding in a track or folding back on hinges like shutters. Shojis have inspired innovative panels with solid inserts ranging from decorative glass or patterned acrylic to woven reeds.

VERTICAL BLINDS

TRADITIONAL SHUTTERS

PLANTATION SHUTTERS

SHOJI SCREENS

top treatments

VALANCES, CORNICES, AND SWAGS COMPLETE WINDOWS IN STYLE. IF PRIVACY AND light control aren't an issue—or if the windows are noteworthy on their own—top treatments can stand alone. More often, they are added to hide the mounting hardware of no-nonsense blinds and shades or to finish off curtains and draperies.

Top treatments are useful for visually altering a window's proportions. You can shorten too-tall windows by mounting a valance so that it extends well into the glass. Or you can create the illusion of a taller window by mounting a gently scalloped valance or shaped cornice above the frame, just skimming the upper area of the glass. (Be aware that undesired effects can occur, too: a deep valance overhanging a wide picture window will only accentuate its width, for example.) Top treatments can also unify windows—a single continuous valance or swag for windows separated just by moulding, for instance, or windows that meet in a corner.

Some treatments atop windows are simply shorter versions of curtains and shades, such as tab-top, rod-pocket, or London valances. Others—notably swags and cornices—are strictly top treatments. Because they are mounted high, covering the upper portion of the window, all valances lend themselves to hem embellishments and fancy trims.

BOARD-MOUNTED VALANCE

SWAGS AND CASCADES

fabric valances can be paired with matching panels for a traditional look, combined with blinds or shades in a casual setting, or used alone to add a dash of color and pattern at the window. The standard valance length is 12 to 18 inches at the center, though some styles—like the beige striped valance shown at left—taper to a longer length at the sides. (Note that this softly pleated treatment is mounted on a board rather than hung on hardware.) A rod-pocket valance, with or without a heading (see page 307), remains a classic top treatment. Box-pleated valances are a tailored option, tab-top valances a more casual look.

swags are lengths of fabric that have been pleated, gathered, or draped at the top of the window, usually over a rod or attached to a mounting board. Light- and medium-weight fabrics that drape well are most easily coaxed into swags and cascades (the fabric lengths that sometimes hang alongside swags). Although swags may appear to be casually arranged, creating them is both a skill and an art. Window-treatment books offer step-by-step instructions, or you may opt to have your swags fabricated and installed by a window-treatment workroom. The swags and cascades shown on the facing page (bottom) are made of a semisheer fabric for a light, airy effect; rod-pocket café curtains below balance the top treatment and afford a bit of daytime privacy. Abbreviated swags with fringe edging are well suited to the intricate leaded-glass windows pictured at right; mounting the swags inside the frames showcases finely crafted mouldings.

cornices can be either upholstered or made from stained or painted wood. Either way, they neatly hide the heading and hardware of any treatment underneath and—because they are closed at the top—also block drafts. Cornices are natural partners for blinds and shades, which can look unfinished on their own. Atop matching drapery or curtains, they lend a regal look to a formal room. Upholstered cornices require only a small amount of fabric, giving you the freedom to splurge on pricier material and embellishments. The lower edge of an upholstered cornice can be shaped or straight; same-fabric welting (see "Passementerie," page 315) or gimp (a scrolled trim) is the traditional finishing touch. Wood cornices can imitate the look of deep crown moulding or be shaped at the lower edge for a decorative effect; simple wood cornices can be stenciled, glazed, or covered with a wallpaper border. Cornices are typically mounted just outside and above the window frame; be sure to measure the depth required to accommodate any hardware that will be installed underneath. Lighting beneath a cornice casts a soft glow on the window and adds ambient light to a room; mount fixtures so they don't generate heat (fluorescent tubes are the safest option).

SWAG VALENCES

UPHOLSTERED CORNICE

WOOD CORNICE

hardware and trimmings

WINDOW-TREATMENT HARDWARE USED TO BE STRICTLY FUNCTIONAL, MEANT to do its job undercover. That's all changed, thanks to an influx of stylish rods, finials (decorative end pieces), and holdbacks. Traditional or contemporary, high-tech or arty, window-treatment hardware is available to suit any style and budget.

Rods fall into two general categories: those that are meant to be seen and those that, for the most part, are hidden. In the latter category are traversing drapery rods, flat curtain rods, and tension rods. These are suitable for treatments that cover the hardware—a stationary café curtain on a flat rod, for example. Much more fun is the decorative category, with rods in materials and finishes to complement any fabric treatment. Indeed, your biggest challenge may be choosing between brushed metal or painted wood, simple or intricate holdbacks and finials. The window-treatment department at Lowe's is the place to begin.

CONCEALED RODS

DECORATIVE RODS

concealed rods come in numerous configurations to handle various window treatments. A *traverse rod* (top in photo) allows draperies to be opened or closed with a wand or cord; carriers or slides hold the drapery hooks. When the draperies are closed, the rod is hidden; when they are open, it is visible unless covered by a top treatment. Traverse rods come in a two-way draw, as shown here, or a one-way draw, typically used for corner windows. A *swing-arm rod* (second from top) is hinged to pivot away from an open window or door and back again, covering the glass; it is most often used with sheers or other fabrics that look the same on both sides. A *flat curtain rod* (middle) is curved at the ends so the rod can be mounted away from the window; stationary rod-pocket curtains or valances cover the rod completely. *Tension rods* (second from bottom) come in white, silver, or gold finishes and may be round or slightly flattened; they fit into the window frame and are often paired with curtains on rings. At bottom, a *magnetic rod* is held in place by magnets mounted on the window frame or wall.

decorative rods, designed to go with ring-hung curtains and valances, come in many sizes, materials, and finishes. Among the most popular options are wood (either painted or stained), wrought iron, pewter, and brushed nickel rods, sold in fixed or adjustable lengths; mounting hardware is generally included. (For a rod longer than 5 feet, you will need a center bracket for extra support.) Finials typically come as part of the rod; those sold separately screw into the rod ends. The rods shown here illustrate the variety you'll find in finials, from classic designs to whimsical or naturalistic motifs.

wire rods can lend a high-tech, contemporary look to window treatments. The rod consists of a length of wire with end brackets; if your window is wider than 5 feet, there's also a center support. You attach the curtain (sheers and other lightweight fabrics are recommended) with decorative clips, rings, or cording.

rings are the simplest means of attaching flat panels to a rod. They come in various materials and finishes—including stained wood, hammered metal, and brushed metal—to coordinate with rods. Most rings attach to the fabric panels with clips; less common are rings with tiny "eyes" that are sewn to the panel heading. Clip-on rings, of course, make it easy to remove the curtain for cleaning and then rehang it. As you consider rings, think about how the clip or eye will fasten to your window treatment and which way it will turn the fabric when it's hanging from the rod.

pegs are a unique alternative to traditional rods. Panels hung on pegs are by nature stationary, though you can lift them to one side and secure them with a holdback for a different look, or to admit more light. Tied tabs work well with pegs. At right, both the generous ties and the curtain's upper edges have been sewn from an iridescent, copper-colored semisheer fabric.

holdbacks are decorative hardware for securing curtains and draperies to the sides of windows. Holdbacks usually jut out several inches to accommodate the folds of fabric; some are hook-shaped with decorative end pieces, and others have a medallion or other front piece to tuck the curtain behind.

passementerie is the term used for trimmings such as fringe, cord, and tassels—the finishing touches that give a window treatment a custom look and accent its edges. Welting, or piping, which consists of narrow cording encased in a strip of fabric, is the most basic kind of trim. More decorative trimmings include tassel, ball, beaded, and pleated fringe as well as "lipped" cording, which is sewn into a seam like welting. Trimmings range in price depending on the workmanship and fibers used, but they tend to be expensive—make sure you love whatever you choose. The most reasonably priced versions are found in home-decorating fabric stores; more lavish items are available through designer showrooms. As you shop, keep in mind the weight of your fabric and also the cleaning requirements of the trimmings you are considering.

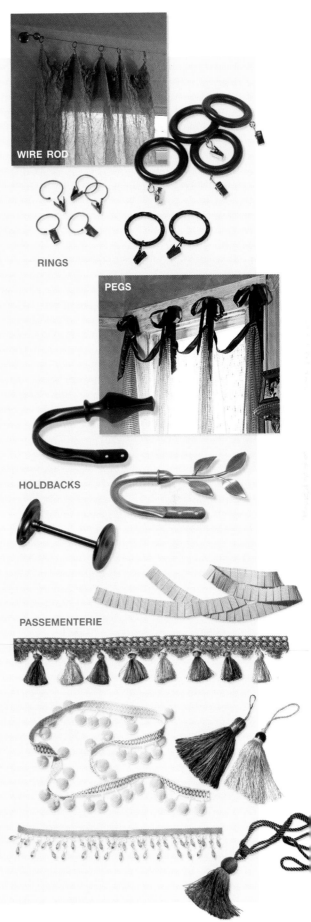

WIRE ROD

RINGS

PEGS

HOLDBACKS

PASSEMENTERIE

fabrics

GRACING FURNITURE, FRAMING WINDOWS, OR COVERING BEDS—WHEREVER YOU put them, fabrics add character to a room and help set its style. Their appearance, content, and cost vary widely, so it's useful to know how different fabrics perform.

fiber facts

Fabrics may be made of natural fibers, synthetic fibers, or a blend of the two. Natural fibers include cotton, linen, silk, wool, and mohair. Rayon, polyester, nylon, and acrylic are man-made fibers. Any fiber can be woven into a wide range of fabrics; cotton, for example, can be made into a sheer batiste or a medium-weight damask.

Fiber content is largely what determines whether or not a fabric will be practical for a particular purpose. Some fibers are more resistant to wear, stand up better to sunlight, and can be cleaned more easily than others. Often a blend of two or more fibers combines the best qualities of each: natural fibers gain durability, easier care, and a lower price tag when blended with

Cotton and cotton-linen fabrics are ideal for cottage-style decorating. A profusion of colors and patterns—florals, stripes, checks, and plaids—provides lots of opportunities to combine natural-fiber fabrics.

man-made fibers; synthetics become softer and more "breathable" when blended with natural fibers.

natural fibers Valued for their aesthetic appeal and comfort for millennia, natural fibers have a "breathability" that makes them easy to live with.

COTTON is the most widely used fiber for decorating fabrics because it is so versatile—it blends beautifully with other fibers, releases dirt easily, and is resistant to abrasion. However, cotton can eventually fade and rot in sunlight and will shrink when washed; washing will also remove any stain-repellant and decorative finishes that have been applied by the manufacturer, changing the durability and look of the fabric. Cotton fabrics generally fall into the moderate price range.

LINEN, woven from flax, wears well and resists fading. It breathes, but it also creases easily and shrinks when washed. Linen is often blended with cotton or rayon for easier care. Pure linen fabric is more expensive than cotton.

SILK is a luxury fabric that drapes exceptionally well and takes color beautifully. However, it fades and disintegrates over time in direct sun, and it stains easily (even water will stain it); like linen, it wrinkles. Silk carries a price tag to match its luxurious look.

WOOL is resilient, strong, and warm—and new processes have reduced its "itch" factor. In decorating, it is most commonly used in rugs, blankets, and upholstery. Unless treated by the manufacturer, all-wool fabric is susceptible to moth and other insect damage. Wool is more expensive than its synthetic counterparts.

MOHAIR, from the silky hair of Angora goats, is soft but strong, and very resilient. Professional cleaning is a must because of its pile (the yarn has been cut very short to create a velvety surface) and nap (the direction of the pile), but well-maintained, mothproofed mohair sofa upholstery will last for years. Mohair fabric is a high-end material, with a price to match.

synthetic fibers These modern inventions are known for their low cost and their practicality.

RAYON is the synthetic counterpart of cotton. It, too, drapes well and takes color beautifully, and it can have a remarkably natural appearance and feel. However, rayon shrinks and wrinkles; to compensate, it is usually blended with cotton or polyester for stability.

POLYESTER is durable and stable, holding its shape under pressure and changing conditions. It's colorfast, washable, and resistant to everything from rot, moths, and mildew to shrinking, stretching, and wrinkling. Polyester blends well and can take on the look of silk when woven into lightweight fabrics. It gives strength to natural fibers and will never go threadbare; many upholstery fabrics contain a significant percentage of polyester.

NYLON is stable, durable, strong, washable, and wrinkleproof; it's also resilient, easy to care for, and inexpensive. But nylon doesn't breathe: it can feel cold in winter, sticky in summer.

ACRYLIC often simulates wool: it shares wool's warmth and strength, though not its high price tag. Acrylic resists fading and is slower to show dirt than natural-fiber fabrics, qualities that make it suitable for blends. Alone, acrylic pills easily and is less breathable than natural fibers.

In a romantic sitting area, silk taffeta with narrow bands of satin graces a channel-back loveseat and a square ottoman. Cotton and cotton-blend fabrics covering the chair, bed, and window seat contrast with London shades made of shimmering silk.

LOWE'S QUICK TIP
Decorator fabrics, no matter what their fiber content, are *not* designed to be washed. The exceptions are cotton fabrics that you choose to prewash and preshrink before making them into either unlined curtain panels or casual slipcovers.

Provençal-style fabrics in butter yellow, soft green, and raspberry red suit pillows of various shapes and sizes on both the bed and the French-inspired daybed; ruffles and welting trim the pillow edges.

LOWE'S QUICK TIP
It's a good idea to buy several extra yards of upholstery fabric in case you need to make repairs down the road. Think of it as insurance against mishaps.

weave, weight, and hand Along with fiber content, three characteristics determine whether a fabric is right for a given job. Keep them in mind as you shop.

❖ Loosely woven fabrics are ideal for soft window treatments like curtains and casual swags; tight weaves, because they have little "give," are best for upholstery.

❖ Lightweight cotton and linen fabrics are suitable for pillows and other soft furnishings, but they won't hold up as covers for sofas or chairs that will get a lot of use. Midweight fabrics work well for pillows, Roman shades, and uphol-stered cornices, while seating pieces generally require mid- to heavyweight fabrics.

❖ For free-flowing curtain panels, you'll want a supple fabric that drapes well—that is, has a nice "hand." Fabric for sofas and chairs should be substantial and feel good to the touch.

buying tips Home-decorating fabrics are available from many sources. Most full-service fabric stores have departments dedicated to home decor, but you'll find an even larger selection at stores entirely devoted to home-decorating fabrics; there you'll also benefit from staff experienced in window treatments, pillows, slipcovers, and upholstery. The fabrics at these stores are often grouped to make selection easy for the do-it-yourself decorator, and prices tend to be moderate. Ask the salesperson if your chosen bolt is a "second"—that is, if it contains minor flaws that may or may not be noticeable. (Seconds can save you money if the flaws will not affect your intended use.) See "Ready, Set, Gather!" on page 224 for some tips on collecting fabric samples.

Try to buy all of your fabric from a single bolt, checking it for flaws such as color or pattern inconsistencies. If you must buy from more than one bolt, ask your salesperson to ensure that the dye lots match; with quality fabric, they almost always do. A chain fabric store may be able to locate another bolt from the same dye lot at another store.

Many retail furniture stores have their own collection of fabrics in a range of "grades." (In other words, the price of the sofa or chair depends on which grade of fabric you choose.) They may also sell you their upholstery fabric by the yard. Choose the best fabric you can afford—price does correlate closely with quality.

Finally, if you are buying cotton or cotton-linen fabric, consider whether you want to go against conventional wisdom and prewash it in order to preshrink and soften it. Being able to launder unlined curtains and small slipcovers is a big plus. But be aware that any stain-resistant finish will be compromised and that natural-fiber fabrics that have been prewashed will con-tinue to shrink a little—every time you wash them.

soft furnishings

Aside from the two main uses of fabric in the home—upholstery and window treat-ments—there are other settings in which textiles come into play. Pillows, slipcovers, and bed coverings all contribute significantly to the decorative mix.

pillows These accessories add spark and comfort to a room—and because they require relatively little yardage, you may be able to splurge on more expensive fabric, down filling, and gorgeous trimmings.

A pillow's size, shape, and fabric should be suggested by the sofa or chair on which it will rest, as well as your comfort preferences. If pillows are meant to make a sofa inviting, 16- or 18-inch square ones will do the job nicely. A round pillow can visually soften a boxy sofa; a rectangular pillow can provide lower-back support and enable a short person to sit more comfortably. And while many sofas come with matching "toss pillows," it's more interesting if pillows don't match—indeed, their modest size makes pillows perfect for introducing accent colors and contrasting patterns. Whatever pillows you choose, don't overdo it. Unless a sofa or chair is oversize or especially deep, extra pillows often end up on the floor, anyway.

Unattached seat cushions for chairs can be "knife-edge" (two pieces of fabric, top and bottom, stitched together around the edges) or "boxed" (with a panel between the top and bottom pieces, encircling the cushion). Welting or contrasting trim typically finishes the edges of seat cushions.

ABOVE: Knife-edge pillows can look casual or formal, depending on the fabric chosen and the furniture they grace. These simple pillows, made from silk fabrics, dress up a contemporary mohair sofa.

LEFT: Plain and patterned fabrics decorate a master bedroom in understated style. On the bench, a bolster and a seat cushion covered in a large-scale check reiterate the room's green-and-gold palette.

slipcovers Like a fresh change of clothes, slipcovers can effect a transformation, altering the look of a piece of furniture— or an entire room. A mohair sofa might cool off for the summer months with covers of white cotton duck (see page 325); velvet slipcovers can dress up folding chairs called into service for a winter dinner party. For dining chairs and ottomans in particular, slipcovers offer a great opportunity to introduce bold patterns without worrying that you're overdoing it, or committing to a look indefinitely.

Slipcovers are also enormously practical, protecting the furniture's original upholstery and extending its life. It's best to dry-clean slipcovers, but if you are determined to wash yours, keep in mind that even love-seat slipcovers are too voluminous to fit into many home washing machines—and the cost of commercial laundering adds up. (See "Buying Tips," page 318.)

Unless you are a confident and experienced seamstress, have your slipcovers sewn by a company that specializes in making them—and be sure you've seen examples of their work. Also recognize that, although there are many advantages to slipcovers, economy is not necessarily one of them: a properly made slipcover is likely to cost just as much as upholstery.

bed coverings Comforters, duvet covers, quilts, bedspreads, dust skirts, bed curtains, and pillows perform many tasks, but providing both comfort and style tops the list. As with sofas and chairs, the current fashion is for fewer pillows than in the past, perhaps as a matter of practicality: where do you put all of those pillows when you get into bed at night?

One formula for pillow placement is as easy as two plus two: for a queen-size bed, two European squares covered in an upholstery fabric against the headboard, then two sleeping pillows in decorative shams in front of them. An accent bolster can add a third fabric by day and provide under-the-knee support for a back sleeper at night. Another approach is to stack two layers of standard pillows. Some prefer to keep the sleeping pillows under the bed covering—a good option if the pillowcases don't contribute to the aesthetic mix.

Comforters or duvets have eclipsed traditional bedspreads as the bed covering of

FACING PAGE, TOP: European-square pillows covered in upholstery fabric and trimmed with brush fringe form the backdrop for white cotton pillowcases and patterned bolsters; underneath it all is a matelassé bedspread. Bed curtains and a matching dust skirt soften the painted headboard and frame.

BELOW: For the summer season, cotton and linen slipcovers tie together a casual mix of seating; antique quilts add a dash of color and pattern.

TRIMMINGS

TRIMMINGS

Known by design professionals as "passementerie" (French for "ornamental braid"), trimmings are the tassels, cords, fringes, and braids that complete soft furnishings. Gorgeous and tempting as they are, it is important to make sure these extras are in keeping with the weight, scale, and fabric of whatever they are paired with. Cost may figure into how many trimmings you use: the most sumptuous are very expensive. When you shop, bring samples of your fabrics with you, along with accurate measurements.

choice. Fabrics are generally light- to medium-weight, with washable cotton blends being the most popular. You can make your own duvet cover from two flat sheets, using a pillow-sham closure on the back: one part of the cover overlaps the other and is held in place by buttons or ties.

Dust skirts can inject color and pattern into a bedroom and keep the area under the bed cleaner. True dust "ruffles" have a feminine look, box pleats or flat panels a more tailored appearance.

Another use of textiles is for the traditional canopy bed, with its frame covered in fabric; a 12- to 14-inch valance typically drops down over the top railings. Formal canopies often feature floor-length curtains pulled back at each of the four posts.

In a small guest bedroom, flat trim finishes the leading edge of a curtain panel and encircles a bolster; ball fringe decorates the bolster ends. When fabric patterns and trimmings vary as much as these, a simple color scheme keeps the effect serene.

lightweight fabrics

MOST SHEER AND LIGHTWEIGHT FABRICS ARE MADE OF COTTON, LINEN, SILK, OR various synthetic fibers. Sheer, translucent fabrics are best as unlined curtains, draperies, and valances, or as loosely structured swags and London shades. Opaque lightweight fabrics can be used for the same applications and also for duvet covers, pillows, and lined window treatments. Think twice about using any lightweight fabric for upholstered seating—it may not wear well over time.

SHEER CURTAINS

COTTON PRINT

LINEN

sheer and semisheer fabrics—organdy, organza, lace, voile, casement, batiste, and others—typically are available in white, cream, or light colors, simply because darker colors are less transparent. Plain sheer curtains, once referred to as "glass curtains," and subtly patterned sheers are typically 100 percent polyester. Embroidered sheers made of cotton, cotton blends, or silk combine the gauzy look of a translucent fabric with a pleasing tactile quality. Because sheers and semisheers don't provide much privacy, particularly at night, they are often paired with curtains or draperies made of a heavier fabric. If privacy is not an issue, generous quantities of sheer fabric can be draped in holdbacks (see page 315) or tied to the side for an ethereal look.

cotton prints are plain-weave fabrics (with lengthwise and crosswise threads the same size) that come in every pattern style imaginable, from naturalistic florals to abstract, geometric, and stylized designs (see pages 232–233). Chintz is a glazed cotton fabric with a smooth, lustrous finish (which is lost through washing). In traditional and cottage-style decorating, it's common to mix a number of cotton prints in a room, using them on everything from upholstery to pillows to window treatments.

linen fabrics, plain or patterned, bestow a casual, shabby-chic look on windows and furniture. Because linen has a tendency to wrinkle and stretch, and even to shrink in humid climates, it is often blended with cotton or synthetic fibers for home-decorating fabrics. Although this midweight fabric will eventually become threadbare if used for seating, it holds up well and shows off its weave beautifully when it is made into tailored Roman shades, flat valances, and upholstered cornices.

taffeta has a close, plain weave that produces a crisp, smooth "hand," or feel, and a subtle sheen. It's typically used in elegant settings, in solids, stripes, and plaids; on this loveseat and ottoman, satin and metallic accents establish the pattern. Traditionally made of silk, taffeta is available in synthetics as well.

TAFFETA

shantung has elongated "slubs" (soft, thicker bits of texture) created by irregularities in the yarns; these imperfections give the fabric its natural, relaxed beauty. Found in traditional and contemporary settings alike, shantung is usually made of silk and comes in a full spectrum of intense colors, all with a lovely sheen. It's suitable for pillows, window treatments, and bed coverings, but when employed for upholstery it must have a fusible knit backing applied unless the furniture is rarely used.

SHANTUNG

moiré is a ribbed, plain-weave fabric made of cotton, silk, or rayon. Its distinctive "watermarked" appearance is the result of pressure from heated cylinders while the fabric is damp and folded; washing destroys the pattern. Among decorator fabrics, moiré is a classic usually reserved for very formal interiors.

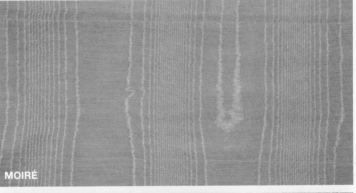

MOIRÉ

chambray, a light- to medium-weight cotton fabric, has a smooth, tight, plain weave; interwoven white threads give it a "frosted" appearance. Chambray conveys a casual, fresh feeling, making it especially appropriate for children's rooms and family rooms. Lightweight chambray is suitable for curtains and top treatments, midweight a better choice for slipcovers and upholstery.

CHAMBRAY

heavier fabrics

MEDIUM-WEIGHT FABRICS SUCH AS DAMASK, CHENILLE, CANVAS DUCK, AND MOHAIR are good choices for lined window treatments and upholstery; damask is also fine for slipcovers, bed coverings, pillows, and fabric screens. Fabrics of heavier weight, like mohair, guarantee the longest life for upholstery. Before you commit to any fabric, make sure you check its fiber content; synthetics and synthetic blends will be the most durable.

DAMASK

VELVET

CHENILLE

MOHAIR

damask is woven in a pattern of alternating matte (dull) and sheen threads, creating a positive-and-negative design. It is available in a variety of fibers, but cotton is the most common. Tone-on-tone color combinations of two closely related hues are typical of traditional damask table linens and upholstery fabrics; more prevalent today is damask printed in multicolored stylized or naturalistic patterns, like the dogwood design pictured here.

velvet is a luxurious cut-pile fabric usually made of cotton, acrylic, or polyester; it can be solid, striped, patterned, or crushed, as shown here. Most velvets have a lustrous finish that shimmers in the light, though some are matte. Light-weight versions are stunning as elegant draperies, slipcovers, pillows, and even bed coverings; heavier weaves are suitable for upholstery. The color of velvet will appear to change depending on the direction of the nap (see "Mohair," page 317), so be sure to look at the fabric with this in mind.

chenille is almost always a blend of fibers—typically rayon, cotton, and polyester. It has the plush feel and light-catching nap of velvet, but with a texture woven into its cut pile. Though durable, chenille is soft to the touch, giving informal furniture a casual elegance; its nubby texture makes solid colors more appealing. You'll also find chenille woven into traditional florals and paisleys, as well as retro and contemporary patterns.

mohair, made from the wool of Angora goats, is a cut-pile fabric (see page 317) renowned for its luxurious feel and its durability; it is sometimes blended with acrylic or rayon for stability. Like velvet, mohair has a definite nap that needs to be considered when it is used for upholstering furniture— the nap should run down on seat backs and toward the front on seat cushions. Mohair takes dye beautifully, so look for it in vivid hues. New treatments have largely eliminated the itchiness once associated with pure mohair.

duck is a broad term for cottons made in strong, plain, firm weaves; its heavier counterpart is canvas, the lighter version sailcloth. Once reserved for outdoor cushions and sails, duck has gained popularity as an interior fabric because of its casual look and practicality. "Natural" is the color most associated with this hard-working fabric, but duck and sailcloth also come in prints, checks, and stripes. At right, a plain cotton duck slipcover turns a dark sofa into summer seating.

COTTON DUCK

matelassé, a double-woven fabric made from two sets of warp and weft threads, has an embossed pattern that simulates quilting. You'll typically find it in white or cream, but you'll also see soft colors like lavender, pale blue, and willow green. Woven patterns range from old-fashioned floral or classical motifs to more contemporary geometric designs. Matelassé is a natural for bedspreads, pillows, and slipcovers.

MATELASSÉ

tapestry, woven on a special Jacquard loom, was originally intended to resemble tapestry wall hangings. Another Jacquard weave, *brocade*, displays raised motifs that resemble embroidery. Floating yarns on the back make it easy to identify. Tapestry is rougher and more substantial than its damask and brocade cousins but features the same kinds of floral and pictorial motifs. Most often used for accent pillows and small chair seats, it can be overwhelming on large pieces of furniture. In the photo at right, it is interpreted in a naturalistic design for a traditional setting.

TAPESTRY

indoor-outdoor fabrics are 100 percent acrylic or polyester that has been either printed or "solution dyed," meaning the fiber was dyed before being spun and woven into fabric. Most often used for outdoor cushions, these tough fabrics are also good choices for indoor upholstery that gets heavy use. Usually they can be machine-washed in cold water using mild soap; check the specific care requirements when you shop. To prolong the life of the fabric, remove outdoor cushions from the elements, including direct sunlight, when you're not using them. (If you see mildew on outdoor cushions, it's actually the soil on the surface or the cushion filling that has mildewed, not the fabric itself.)

INDOOR-OUTDOOR

furniture

PERHAPS MORE THAN ANY OTHER ELEMENT IN A ROOM, FURNITURE EMBODIES the marriage of form and function. So many daily activities rely on it—eating, sleeping, working, reading, socializing. Choose your furniture well and it will serve your patterns of living. Position sofas, chairs, and tables thoughtfully and they will organize spaces and direct foot traffic. Select carefully from among the infinite possible combinations of wood, upholstery, metal, and glass, and your furnishings will be a true expression of your personal style.

Designers generally recommend buying only essential pieces at first, of the finest quality you can afford, rather than compromising on quality and durability in order to furnish an entire room in one go. This approach leaves you the time and space to acquire pieces as you fall in love with them, giving your room an evolved, layered look.

Still, it's a good idea to start with a general plan for what pieces you eventually want, where you will put them, and how they will fit into your overall scheme. This forethought will help ensure that future purchases fit in with what you already have—and prevent impulse buys that you'll later regret.

Furniture comes in styles and materials to suit every taste and decorating plan. A mix of textures and finishes—from shiny to matte—adds to the allure of this contemporary attic room.

LOWE'S **QUICK TIPS**
Large furniture stores often will do a complimentary space plan for you. Ask about their design services, too.

❖

Blame human nature, but research shows that only two people sit comfortably on a sofa, no matter how long it is. Plan accordingly.

upholstered furniture

Once you've settled on the general style and scale of the piece you're looking for, it's time to investigate what's underneath it all.

value for cost Made-to-order sofas and chairs are available in mid- to high-end price ranges from furniture, home, and department stores as well as designer showrooms. Upholstered furniture is one purchase that justifies the saying, "You get what you pay for." Think hard about how long you want a piece to last, and what you are willing to spend. Consider these points:

❖ The highest-quality and longest-lasting seating will have a frame of kiln-dried hardwood (such as oak or alder) at least ¾ inch thick. Softwood frames cost less but are less durable.

❖ Joinery should be secure; look for a sofa with corner blocks to give the frame extra stability.

❖ Legs that are an integral extension of the frame are preferable to screwed-in legs, which may wobble over time.

❖ Eight-way, hand-tied springs allow the widest range of movement. Zigzag, or sinuous, springs only move up and down, but they are more than adequate if connected by tie wires; the clips that hold the springs to the frame should be insulated steel, not plastic.

❖ Most seat cushions are made of a high-resiliency foam core encased in a cotton or cotton-blend "jacket" filled with a mix of down, feathers, and fibers; the cushion is then inserted into the outer cover. It's important that cushions have the soft jacket on both sides, so they can be flipped. Down and down-blend back pillows offer maximum softness and durability—and thanks to their resilience, they can always be "fluffed" back into shape.

❖ Made-to-order upholstered pieces are built by hand from the frame out, so it can take anywhere from 10 to 16 weeks from the day you put down your deposit to their arrival at your door. If you want your furniture by a certain date, inquire about delivery time before you order.

Made-to-order furniture isn't within everyone's means, of course. Many retailers sell medium-priced lines of furniture in stores, online, and through catalogs; be sure to check the return policy and shipping charges. Another alternative is to frequent estate sales or consignment stores. Second-hand furniture with "good bones" can be reupholstered or even restyled— you might eliminate a skirt, redo seat cushions with high-quality foam, or even change the shape of an arm. And, of course, slipcovers can mask a multitude of furniture flaws.

In a small living room, modestly scaled loveseats supply the main seating, while two stools pair up to serve as a coffee table— or separate to provide casual seating. A side table topped with a small lamp cozies up the corner and adds display space.

LOWE'S QUICK TIP
On sofas, arms should be low enough that you can easily reach over to a side table or other convenient surface to set down a drink or switch on a lamp.

the comfort factor Whatever your price range, comfort is paramount. Sit on lots of sofas and chairs and ask about their construction and filling. Decide what quality is more important to you: softness or support?

Pay attention to a piece's dimensions. The overall measurements will help you determine if it will go well in your room. Seat height, seat depth, seat back height, and armrest height are often-overlooked "comfort" measurements. If your household members vary in height, choose seating that "splits the difference"— that is, allows the tallest person to sit reasonably comfortably, yet is not so deep or low that other family members have difficulty getting up. Ask yourself if the sofa or chair supports the arms, back, head, and neck, and if the angle of repose is pleasing.

In a room full of soft, flowing fabric, a painted wood writing desk and "lady's chair" introduce firm surfaces and crisp edges. Repeating fabric colors in the case goods keeps the look unified.

A carved four-poster bed with upholstered headboard is the epitome of today's traditional style. With their contrasting stains, the nightstand and armoire prove the design adage, "Woods never fight."

case goods

The term "case goods" refers to task-oriented furniture that is primarily made of wood, metal, or other rigid material rather than being upholstered. Dining sets, desks, chests, benches, armoires, side tables—these pieces, with their rich wood grains, varied finishes, carved details, or eye-catching shapes, give a room character. Some case goods evoke past eras, while others embody the simplicity of contemporary design.

Most styles are available in a wide range of prices, depending on the materials used and the quality of construction. You can choose from (roughly in order of decreasing cost) designer or handcrafted pieces, antiques and collectibles, reproductions, modular or mass-produced furniture, and unfinished or ready-to-assemble furniture (RTA, also known as "knock-down").

Wood is the material most often used in case goods. "Hardwood" is the wood of deciduous trees: cherry, maple, mahogany, and walnut are a few of the more popular types. Softwoods, from conifers such as pine and fir, are usually less expensive and more casual in style; they are more prone to nicks than hardwoods because the wood is softer. Still less expensive is medium-density fiberboard (MDF), which can be heavier than wood but is also more dimensionally stable—meaning it doesn't shrink or expand when exposed to moisture, heat, or pressure—and resistant to warping.

In reproduction and mass-produced furniture, solid wood is used for legs (because it can be carved), bases, and other visible parts; unseen portions are usually MDF, particleboard, or plywood. The disadvantage of solid wood is that it will warp, shrink, and swell; kiln-dried wood (dried by

the manufacturer at very high temperatures) performs most consistently. If furniture made entirely of solid wood is important to you, look for antique or custom-made pieces.

"Layered" wood is composed of different kinds of wood. Don't be put off by the term: plywood with a veneer of another wood is actually more dimensionally stable than solid wood. Veneers are far less prone to chipping and peeling than they were in the past, and increasingly they are becoming the only economically and environmentally sound option.

You will also find case goods made of wrought iron in combination with glass or wood, letting you bring a bit of the garden indoors. Other metals, such as aluminum, steel, copper, and chrome, lend a more modern look.

As you shop for your case goods, keep an eye out for all the following hallmarks of quality:

❖ Do the drawers have smooth glides and stops, and are there dust partitions between drawers? Are the interiors nicely finished?

❖ Are all the joints secure, including those in the drawers? Screwed joints are stronger than stapled or glued joints. Dovetail and tongue-in-groove construction is very strong, but the craftsmanship required to produce it adds significantly to cost. Weight-bearing joints should be reinforced with corner blocks.

❖ Do the doors fit well, opening and shutting freely?

❖ Is the piece free of any squeaks and wobbles?

❖ Do long shelves have center supports underneath?

❖ Is the hardware sturdy and securely mounted?

❖ Does the finish feel smooth and appear to be evenly applied?

A trestle table and a Welsh dresser (both new but made to look old) bring to mind European farmhouse styling; dining chairs with ornamental backs and upholstered seats are as comfortable as they are handsome.

sofas and loveseats

WHETHER YOU CALL IT A SOFA OR A COUCH, THIS ESSENTIAL FURNISHING IS LIKELY to get more use than any other piece in your main living area. For this reason alone, many designers suggest you treat it as an investment. Buy a sofa with simple, classic lines and solid construction, and it will last a lifetime—given an upholstery job or a set of slipcovers to revitalize it along the way.

Because it is usually the largest, most used, and most expensive piece of furniture in a living area, a good approach is to make it your first purchase, then build the room around it. To narrow your choices, answer a few simple questions:

❖ How long a sofa do you want or need? They generally come in 7- and 8-foot lengths, though measurements are not always precise; that is, a 7-foot sofa may not measure 84 inches. (Take a tape measure to the showroom to determine if a given sofa will fit your space.) Some people opt to go shorter altogether with a loveseat or pair of loveseats in the 5- to 6-foot range—easy to walk around, though too short for most adults to recline on.

❖ How many seat cushions would you like? Since it's rare that more than two people sit on a sofa at the same time, no matter how long it is, two cushions are fine unless you prefer the look of three.

❖ Do you want finished wood legs, bun feet (short, rounded legs), or a tailored skirt that hides the legs? Exposed legs make a room feel a bit more spacious, while a skirt blocks drafts and enhances a sofa's "cozy factor."

❖ Do you need seating that doubles as a bed? Your choices range from fully upholstered sofabeds to wood-framed futons, in sizes from twin to queen. Sofabeds come with innerspring or air mattresses; the latter make them lighter. The bed should lift up and out in a single motion; a lock-down bar ensures easier opening and proper closure. A futon—a collapsible frame with a high-density foam pad forming a continuous seat and back—tends to take up more space than a sofabed, depthwise.

❖ Will it be easy for older family members and guests to get up out of the sofa you are considering? A low, deep sofa makes standing up difficult for some people. Arms that come all the way to the front can be used for leverage.

There are innumerable variations on sofa styles; knowing a few sofa types and terms will help you communicate with sales associates and designers.

LAWSON SOFA

Lawson sofas are the most traditional style, with rounded arms that are lower than the back and cushions that are fitted but unattached or semi-attached. They may have either exposed legs or a skirt, and either two or three seat cushions. "T-deck" cushions, shown here, extend in front of the arms, making the sofa feel a bit roomier.

CAMELBACK SOFA

camelback sofas have a somewhat tailored look, with a tight (no separate cushions), bell-curved back, slightly rolled arms, and (usually) exposed legs. This classic style is at home in either contemporary or traditional settings, covered in solid or patterned fabrics. The brilliant upholstery on the sofa pictured at right is mohair.

LOVESEAT

loveseats are ideal for a bedroom, where their modest scale contributes to a sense of cozy intimacy. The skirted loveseat at right, upholstered in shimmering sateen, befits the seating area in an elegant master bedroom. In living spaces, a pair of loveseats provides versatile seating that's easier to move than a full-length sofa.

TUXEDO SOFA

tuxedo sofas are distinguished by straight or slightly flared rectangular arms that are as high as the tight seat back. This style is most often seen in sleek, sophisticated settings and retro-themed decors.

contemporary sofas have clean, squared-off lines, characterized by straight arms and a back that is lower than on a traditional sofa. Upholstery for both contemporary and tuxedo sofas leans toward solid and textured fabrics rather than patterned ones.

CONTEMPORARY SOFA

sectionals can be configured into just about any shape to suit your living space. The array of pieces—sofa (usually with one arm and a backrest), corner, ottoman, chaise—makes for limitless possibilities, a real plus if you like to entertain or enjoy rearranging your furniture with the changing seasons. Contrast welting on the slim sectional shown at right gives these pieces a trim, tailored look.

SECTIONAL SOFA

chairs

MOST OF US SPEND THE MAJORITY OF OUR WAKING HOURS SITTING DOWN—working, reading, relaxing, eating, studying. That makes chairs all-important. No one chair fits all tasks or all people, of course, but as a guideline, a chair is most comfortable when the seat height is a bit less than the seated person's lower leg length (letting the feet rest comfortably on the floor) and the seat depth is a little less than the upper leg length. Good back support is a must in any piece that is intended for a home office or a child's desk.

Chairs fall into two broad categories—those that are upholstered and those that aren't. Many of the principles that apply to selecting a sofa (see page 330) also come into play when buying upholstered chairs; as you shop, ask about a chair's construction and the content of the seat cushion. Dining and side chairs that aren't upholstered should move easily and have "scooped" seats for comfort. Chairs for dining should fit the dining table but don't necessarily have to match it.

CLUB CHAIR

"T-DECK" CLUB CHAIR

WING CHAIR

DINING CHAIR

club chairs are the most classic and enduring armchair choice, with their rounded or squared arms set at a comfortable height, generous seat cushions, and supportive back cushions. The seat cushion may be flush with the arms, as seen far left, or wrap around in front of the arms in "T-deck" style, as shown near left. You'll find club chairs in a variety of sizes and interpretations; because they are built for comfort, they tend to take up more space than other styles.

wingback chairs are highly traditional, with "wings" that make them feel snug and inviting. People who are tall and like to sit in an upright position find them comfortable because of the good head and neck support they provide, though the tight, straight back doesn't offer the lower-back support many people need.

dining chairs must be comfortable as well as good looking. When you're seated, your feet should rest naturally on the floor. If the seats and backs are lightly upholstered, make sure the fabric is sturdy and stain resistant; simple slipcovers can protect chairs with upholstered seats. Mixing and matching dining chairs imparts a less formal look to a room, helps accommodate people of various dimensions, and allows you to collect chairs you like over time. The updated dining chair at left pays homage to its Chippendale predecessors, with modified ball-foot back legs and a pierced "splat" (ornamental back).

a chaise (chaise longue), with an elongated seat to accommodate outstretched legs, works in either a bedroom or a living area. Sometimes this piece comes as part of a sectional. A chaise may have just one arm, making sitting and rising more graceful, or a back that wraps around on both sides, as seen at right in a chaise extension of a plush chair.

recliners have enjoyed a renaissance as their styling has been updated and expanded. Whether you prefer a wood-framed Arts and Crafts look (as shown here), a classic club chair, or a trim wingback, you can find it as a recliner. Of course, the cushy, channel-stitched style most associated with recliners is available in a wealth of materials and colors. You can customize a recliner at the time of ordering, specifying the back, arm, and seat style and whether or not the chair rocks, swivels, or glides. Modern mechanisms allow a chair to fully recline even when placed just inches from a wall.

armless chairs come in various styles and sizes, all of which generally take up less space in a room—both physically and visually—than their armed counterparts. Lacking supportive armrests, they encourage conversation with those seated on either side, but they are seldom as comfortable as armchairs; a lumbar pillow can supply additional support. Armless chairs are useful in a small space or where you need to sit for only a short time; a slipper chair in a foyer or at a vanity is a classic armless style.

ottomans aren't just for feet: this multipurpose piece can be deployed as extra seating or as a "soft" coffee table. Some open up to store blankets or toys. Ottomans come in various shapes—from long and narrow to square to round—and coverings. Ideally, an ottoman will be an inch or more lower than the chair or sofa with which it will be paired. However, if it is to be used primarily as a coffee table, it should be an inch or two higher than the seating. An ottoman that has exposed feet, like the leather-upholstered one pictured at right, will have a somewhat lighter look than one that extends to the floor.

CHAISE

RECLINER

ARMLESS CHAIR

OTTOMAN

mirrored surfaces

REFLECTIVE SURFACES OPEN UP SPACE, BOUNCE LIGHT, AND PLAY WITH OUR PERCEPTION OF REALITY.

BELOW: An oversize mirror over a blackened-steel fireplace reflects ambient light and makes a high-ceilinged, contemporary living room appear even airier. The mirror was built in place—that is, the contractor glued it to the wall before attaching the walnut frame.

ABOVE: In a cozy guest bath, a beveled mirror makes the most of limited wall space and complements an exotic scroll-armed bench.

ABOVE: A mirror in French colonial style with gilt detailing reflects the formal ambience of this entry area.

ABOVE RIGHT: The frame on this mirror is itself a mirror, created by sandblasting and etching in a style known as Venetian. Variations in the finishes throughout the room—reflective mirror, worn wood, and matte paneling—give the cottage-style atmosphere a pleasing air of unpredictability.

RIGHT: In a sophisticated take on the traditional medicine cabinet, this mirror is hinged on the right and opens up to reveal recessed shelving. A subtle crackle finish on the frame adds a bit of texture to a palette that includes neutral walls, nickel sconces, and off-white cabinetry.

case goods

IF IT'S NOT UPHOLSTERED, IT PROBABLY FITS INTO THE CATEGORY OF CASE GOODS. Tables, dressers, desks, beds—these are some of the hardest-working pieces of furniture in your house, so they deserve to be well-thought-out purchases.

Because so many case goods are made of wood, one of your biggest decisions will have to do with the type of wood and the stain—two aspects that are as important as a piece's lines in determining its look. For refinishing an existing piece or staining bare wood, you'll find a wide selection of products and tools at Lowe's.

It pays to measure the spaces you have before you shop; carry those figures—and a pocket tape measure—with you at all times. You may find the perfect piece when you least expect it.

DINING TABLE

COFFEE TABLE

dining table decisions should be based on how you will use the table—for everyday meals or for occasional formal dining?—and how many people it needs to seat. If you're considering a table with leaves, be sure they not only fit properly but also match the table's graining and finish. Generally a 6-foot-long rectangle will seat eight people comfortably. A narrower trestle- or refectory-style table affords greater intimacy but allows little space for serving dishes or tabletop arrangements. A circular dining table feels "egalitarian" and is conducive to conversation for groups of four to eight; some have leaves that extend the table into an oval.

Measure to be sure a table you're considering isn't too large for the room: allow at least 32 inches from the table to the walls on all sides. Each seated person needs a space 24 inches wide and 18 to 24 inches deep, from the table's edge. There should be at least 7 inches between the bottom of the "apron" (the trim piece along the edge of the table) and the chair seat.

coffee tables meet the need for low, horizontal surfaces within easy reach of seating. A rectangular shape is standard, but a coffee table may also be square or oval—or it may consist of a pair of square tables or cubes placed side by side. A relatively flat ottoman can also serve as a coffee table. Many coffee tables feature a shelf below for books and other items, leaving the top clear for entertaining. For ease of movement, allow 18 inches between a table and a sofa or nearby chair.

occasional tables are small conveniences that provide places to set beverages, reading material, and lamps. *End tables* are traditional companions to sofas and chairs. *Nesting tables*—two or more tables that descend in size and stack—can be separated and moved around as needed (see page 245). A *console table*, seen here, is a taller, longer, and shallower table that fits against a wall; a *sofa table* is similarly proportioned to stand behind a sofa. A general rule of thumb for an occasional table alongside a chair or sofa is that it be approximately the same height as the arm, making it easy for a seated person to reach the table.

CONSOLE TABLE

hutches and sideboards add character to a kitchen or dining room and provide storage and display space for tableware. A hutch (shown here) is a cabinet on legs, with open shelving above; a sideboard is a waist-high cabinet that has a buffet surface. If a sideboard is small, it can also go in an entry, perhaps accompanied by a wall-mounted mirror and a pair of sconces. A more formal *china cabinet* is usually large, with cupboards and drawers below and glass-enclosed shelving above; a mirrored interior will bounce light back into the room. A hutch or similar cabinet doesn't need to match the room's other case goods, but it should complement them in style and scale.

HUTCH

writing desks tend to be diminutive compared to their hardworking office counterparts. They may serve a largely decorative function, but placed near an entry they make a convenient drop-off for keys or mail; in a guest room or tucked into the corner of a living room, they are both ornamental and practical. A *secretary* is an old-fashioned writing desk with small drawers and compartments above the writing surface, which often folds up. The antique secretary shown here mixes easily with traditional and contemporary furnishings and accessories in a bedroom.

SECRETARY

feature continues >

case goods

WOOD SLEIGH BED

METAL BED FRAME

TRUNDLE BED

MURPHY BED, OPEN FOR USE

MURPHY BED, CONCEALED

bed frames can be as simple as a metal "Hollywood" frame without any headboard or footboard or as elaborate as a grand four-poster bed draped with fabric. A headboard makes a versatile middle-ground option, whether it's made of painted or stained wood or upholstered and tufted. (Even with upholstery, beds are considered case goods.) There may or may not be a matching footboard. A *sleigh bed* features a scrolled headboard and footboard reminiscent of an old-fashioned sleigh, usually wood (as shown top left) or metal. Decorative *metal bed frames* are open and airy, making them especially suited for warm or humid climates where upholstery might feel oppressive and wood too heavy.

trundle beds, with an extra mattress that pulls out from underneath, and *captain's beds,* with storage drawers below, are two useful options for guest and children's rooms. The contemporary trundle bed shown near left mixes industrial-look metal with opulent fabrics for the bed covering and pillows.

Murphy beds let you "recapture" floor space in a studio apartment or a room that occasionally serves as guest quarters, like the office at left. Decorative woodworking on this bed's "wall" makes what lies behind it that much more of a surprise. Be sure to inquire about what kind of mechanism raises, lowers, and locks the bed in place. Some manufacturers offer hardware kits and detailed plans for building your own Murphy bed.

nightstands don't need to match the bed, nor must they come in pairs—let individual needs guide your selection. Should there be space for a lamp, a clock, or reading material? Would concealed storage be a plus, or is an open look preferred? Any occasional table can be pressed into service as a nightstand— even a small chest or an antique trunk will do the job nicely. Whatever you choose, the nightstand's top should be at least as high as the mattress, its width in proportion to the bed's size; a nightstand approximately a third of the bed width is traditional.

chests of drawers were among the earliest movable pieces of furniture devoted to storage. Chests are ideal in an entry, as seen here, where their presence can serve both practical and aesthetic purposes. Dressers (usually with mirrors) are a must for bedrooms without sufficient built-in storage; for maximum storage in large rooms, they come 5 feet or more in width. A small chest or *lowboy* (a table with drawers) can double as a nightstand; a *highboy* (a tall chest of drawers on legs) fits a lot of storage into a modest footprint. For a chest or dresser that will be used daily, look for drawers that move freely on center-mounted glides with steel rollers and have stops to prevent the drawers from falling out. For socks and other small items, shallow drawers are convenient.

armoires are a versatile storage option for bedrooms as well as for great rooms and other living spaces. Useful for holding everything from clothing and linens to books and electronics, they take up relatively little floor area because they utilize vertical rather than horizontal space. The armoire shown here serves as a wardrobe in a contemporary bedroom; with shelving and cord cutouts, it might just as easily conceal a small TV.

NIGHTSTAND

CHEST OF DRAWERS

ARMOIRE

LOWE'S QUICK TIP
For clearance and ease of movement, allow 3 feet between a chest of drawers and a bed.

built-ins

BUILT-IN UNITS ARE A REAL PLUS IN A HOME—WHERE ELSE CAN WE STOW OUR "STUFF" so efficiently? Many of them, like window seats, banquettes, and hutches, are also architectural features that add character and charm to a home.

Having a cabinetmaker construct built-ins allows you to tailor storage to your precise needs. This is expensive, however, so consider custom built-ins a long-term investment in your home. To get the look and functionality of a built-in without the high price, many homeowners opt for the "custom modular" approach. Using standard components from a cabinet manufacturer, you can put together anything from a home office system to a media center or a wall of living room bookcases. (See "Cabinetry," page 288.) Your cabinets may be open, with interiors to match the face frame, shallower (or deeper) than the usual 12-inch shelf depth, or staggered in height for a more custom look. Refer to the cabinetry catalogs available at Lowe's, or talk to a sales associate to explore the possibilities.

Changes in technology have had an impact on the design of home-office furnishings. Many people now have laptops as their primary computers, so they have less need for enormous desks or keyboard trays. Flatter monitors for desktop computers take less surface space, too—sometimes making a smaller built-in desk, perhaps with an auxiliary counter, the best choice.

WALL UNIT

wall units are the most popular built-ins for general storage and display. Space flanking a living room fireplace is a natural location for open or closed shelving; in a bathroom, built-in cabinetry permits easy access to towels and grooming items. Of course, any child's room can use a wall unit for clutter control. An efficient and handsome approach for a bedroom, as shown here, is to install closed cabinetry to counter height, with shallower, open shelves extending up to the ceiling. A combination of drawers and doors supplies the greatest flexibility.

DESK

desks are among the most practical of built-in units, providing space for many and varied tasks, often for several family members. If you want a desk to serve for more than occasional use, it needs to pack plenty of practical storage—upper and base cabinets, drawers, open shelving—and provide space for the computer and peripheral equipment. A desktop of wood, laminate, solid surface, or Richlite (see page

295) will be warmer and more comfortable than stone. Lighting is crucial for a desk; what works in the kitchen for task lighting is equally suitable for an office. In the example on the facing page, undercabinet fixtures illuminate the work surface and dispel shadows.

hutches started out as movable cabinets on legs, with open or closed shelving above, but today's hutch is just as likely to be a built-in. On the custom-built hutch shown here, the face frame has been cut in a decorative pattern to give this piece a distinctive, furniturelike look; undercabinet lighting brightens the counter, while interior paneling adds old-fashioned charm.

niches and cubbies transform otherwise wasted space into practical storage. In the example at right, the area under the stairs in an entry has been converted into generous cubbies, keeping shoes and gear from accumulating on the hall floor. Painting cubbies and niches a light color keeps them from looking like "black holes." *Window seats* often include storage that is accessed by lifting the seat or opening cabinet doors and drawers in front. A window seat tucked into a landing might combine with shelving to turn an unused space into a cozy reading nook.

banquettes, built-in benches running along a wall or perpendicular to it, are favored for the intimate yet relaxed atmosphere they impart. Usually installed in kitchens and other casual eating areas, banquettes may or may not have upholstered seat cushions, with or without storage below. In the example pictured at right, a corner banquette with thick, tailored cushions provides seating for an eat-in kitchen; roomy drawers take advantage of the space below the bench.

CUSTOM-BUILT HUTCH

CUBBIES

BANQUETTE

"what shall we do with the TV?"

AS OFTEN AS NOT THESE DAYS, PEOPLE ARE CONTENT TO LEAVE THEIR TELEVISIONS out in the open—both for the sake of simplicity and because today's flat-panel TVs are so sleek and stylish. Options range from simple stands to hardware that mounts the TV on the wall. Freestanding console units offer storage for other components on either side of the TV. Media centers remain a popular way to go; custom cabinetry can turn technology into an integral part of a room's design.

Wall-mount brackets for flat-panel sets come in two basic types: flush (the panel hangs slightly away from the wall) and articulating (the panel can tilt, extend forward, or pivot). With either type, part of the hardware attaches to the back of the television, and the other part is anchored into the wall studs; the TV slides onto the

mount and locks in place. Brackets are defined by the weight they can support, so check the specs before you buy.

For stationary panels, you'll want to arrange the room's seating with comfortable viewing in mind. LCD sets typically

A maple storage and display unit holds the TV in a contemporary living space; when it's not in use, the panel slides down to conceal the TV. Underneath, a 12-foot run of cabinets houses other media components.

lose picture quality when viewed from the side; primary seating should be more front-and-center. Be careful not to position the panel too high, or you and others will quickly tire of looking up. In general, the best location is just above eye level when you are seated.

Think twice before installing a flat-screen TV above a fireplace. Damage is likely to occur unless the panel is set within a recess or above a projecting mantel so the heat is deflected. Check with the manufacturer and read your warranty carefully before proceeding. A TV installed above a fireplace may be too high for comfortable viewing, anyway.

With media centers and armoires, the main concern is proper clearance for ventilation—equipment must have enough room that heat buildup can dissipate. Look for adjustable shelving that will allow you to change components down the road.

ABOVE: This television mounted in a kitchen wall niche is easily viewed from both the cooking area and the fireplace seating.

LEFT: In an elegant breakfast room, a sleek wall-mounted TV does not interfere with furnishings.

BELOW: An articulating bracket allows this midsize wall-mounted TV to be tilted and angled to suit viewers' needs.

techniques
and projects

WHEN IT COMES TO DECORATING YOUR HOME, THERE IS NO GREATER FEELING than "I did it myself!" This chapter is devoted to helping you achieve that wonderful sense of accomplishment, with step-by-step instructions for a host of projects, large and small, using tools and materials stocked in every Lowe's store.

From laying a vinyl tile floor to installing crown moulding or applying a decorative paint finish, these are doable projects that will enhance your home.

Your nearby Lowe's store is a great place to begin any decorating project. Besides an inspiring array of products to bring decorating visions to life, these are some of the ways we can help you:

❖ kitchen and bathroom design services

❖ flooring and tilework consultation

❖ materials estimates

❖ in-store how-to clinics

❖ installation services, from flooring
    to lighting, with all work guaranteed

You'll find additional information and inspiration online in the Project Center at Lowes.com. Check out the Do-It-Together Videos and How-to Library for more projects, tips, and techniques. Explore the possibilities with Interactive Design Tools that will help you envision color, calculate flooring, or choose a style of trim.

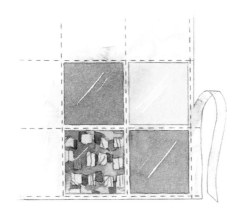

in this chapter

decorative painting basics

MATERIALS

MOST DECORATIVE PAINTING TECHNIQUES START with the same preliminary steps. You'll need to mask adjacent surfaces and then apply a base coat before proceeding with your decorative finish. These basic steps are explained here.

For "cutting in" edges at the corners, ceiling, and baseboards, invest in a good-quality 2- or 3-inch synthetic-bristle brush. Wear disposable gloves when painting; they protect your skin and allow greater flexibility than rubber gloves.

1 Wash the walls with trisodium phosphate. When they're dry, fill any cracks or holes with spackling compound, allow to dry, and sand smooth. Apply primer to the patches, or to the entire surface if necessary.

2 To mask an adjacent wall that will not be painted, start at the top, in the corner. Carefully apply the paper painter's tape to the wall you want to protect so that the sticky half is flush with the corner. Work your way down the wall, firmly pressing the tape in place. Cut the upper end flush with the ceiling. Mask the ceiling in the same manner. Apply tape along the upper edge of the baseboard on the wall that is to be painted, forming a ledge for catching drips. Tape the edges of the floor below the baseboards and then cover the floor with a drop cloth.

3 To cut in the edges for your base coat, pour some paint into the paint tray. Dip the paintbrush into the paint, coating about a third of the bristle length; brush off excess on the tray edge. Begin along the ceiling, followed by door and window trim, the wall corners, and finally the baseboards. At an adjacent wall, work upward by starting about two brush lengths down from the ceiling and brushing up to the corner, then moving down and brushing upward to join the wet edge, until you cut in from the baseboard to the wet edge above it.

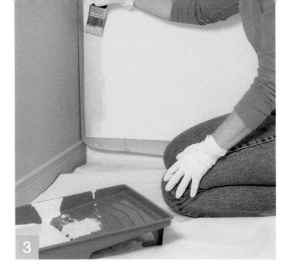

4 Attach the extension handle to your roller. Load the roller with paint by rolling it in the tray; roll off the excess. Starting a few feet from an upper corner, apply paint in an M shape to a 4-foot-square section. Work toward the adjacent wall, overlapping the cut-in edge at the corner.

5 Without reloading the roller, roll back over the same section to fill in unpainted areas. Still without adding paint, make a third pass to even out any marks left by the roller edge; apply more pressure this time. Continue in sections, loading the roller with paint, rolling in an M shape, and filling in, until you've covered the wall.

CLEANING UP

Cleanup is simple with latex paint. To limit the amount of paint that washes down the drain, first remove as much as you can. Scrape rollers with the curved edge of a 5-in-1 painter's tool; work paintbrush bristles back and forth on newspaper. Then wash out with warm water and a little detergent. Shake off excess water and allow tools to dry completely before storing them.

Between paint coats, simply cover tools and containers tightly with plastic—there's no need to rinse.

cloudy skies

MATERIALS

Basic painting supplies
(see page 346)

Mini-roller frame with
6-inch roller cover

Cheesecloth pom-pom
(see below)

3-inch chip brush for
stippling

2-inch chip brush for
applying navy glaze

Blender brush

Sky blue latex paint* for
base coat

1 quart white latex paint*
for glaze

1 quart navy blue latex
paint* for glaze

Latex glazing liquid (clear
mixing glaze)

Satin finish

A MIXTURE OF EQUAL PARTS WHITE PAINT AND CLEAR GLAZING LIQUID IS THE KEY to fluffy, fluttery clouds. Subtle shadows are the result of working navy blue glaze into the lower portion of some clouds.

MAKING A CHEESECLOTH POM-POM

Three of the decorative paint projects on the following pages call for a flat or slightly wrinkled pom-pom made of unbleached cheesecloth. A flat pom-pom yields a smoother finish, while a wrinkled one creates more texture. For either type, cut a length of prewashed cheesecloth equal to your "wingspan" (open arms). Gently pull out on the sides of the cloth to fluff it. Then form your pom-pom this way:

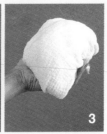

1 Drape the length of cheesecloth over your open hand, palm side up, so that the ends are approximately equal in length.

2 With your other hand, gather both loose ends and bring them up accordion-style toward your open hand.

3 Remove your open hand from under the cheesecloth and let the mounded cloth rest in your other hand. Tuck under the loose edges or "tails" to form a smooth, rounded pom-pom.

4 For a wrinkled pom-pom, let the folds of cloth gather when you remove your open hand, creating a slightly wrinkled surface.

1 Prepare your painting surface according to the instructions on pages 346–347. Using a paintbrush (for cutting in edges) and a standard roller, apply a base coat of sky blue paint to the walls and ceiling; allow to dry. Apply a second coat; allow to dry.

2 Mix the white glaze by combining 1 part paint with 1 part glazing liquid. Mix the navy glaze by combining 1 part paint with 3 parts glazing liquid.

3 Using the mini-roller, apply the white glaze generously in a loose pattern that approximates a cloud shape.

4 Using a slightly wrinkled cheesecloth pom-pom, "pounce" the cloud edges in a light tapping motion. Rotate your wrist to feather and blend the glaze. Leave the glaze heavier in the center.

5 Holding the 3-inch chip brush perpendicular to the surface, stipple the cloud interior in a quick tapping motion to soften the glaze. Using the corner of the brush, stipple outward to "grow" the edges. Leave a white highlight in the center.

6 With the 2-inch chip brush, apply the navy glaze at the lower edge of the cloud. The glaze will look dark at first, but it will lighten as you work it in.

7 Using a clean pom-pom, pounce the navy glaze to blend it into the white glaze.

8 With the 3-inch brush held perpendicular to the surface, stipple the glaze to further blend.

9 Using just the tips of the blender brush, sweep across the surface in a semicircular motion to soften the interior of the cloud and make the edges wispy. Working in a semicircular motion keeps the cloud rounded and creates the illusion that it is moving through the sky.

10 Repeat the same steps to create a smaller cloud to one side. If you make this cloud a bit lighter, it will appear more distant. Continue working in the same manner to complete the walls and ceiling.

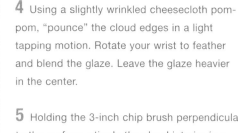

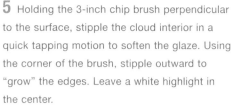

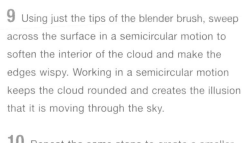

LOWE'S QUICK TIP
Add a little white glaze at the cloud edges, if needed, to fill out the shape. Use the pom-pom loaded with white glaze to create a delicate flutter at one end.

chamois walls

MIXING WATER AND GLAZING LIQUID WITH PAINT GIVES THIS TONE-ON-TONE paint treatment a matte finish. This is a good technique if you're on a budget, since you blend the glaze using knit rags and cheesecloth instead of the more costly blender brush. For a smooth effect, use all-cotton rags from good-quality T-shirts.

1 Prepare your surface according to the instructions on pages 346–347. Using a paintbrush (for edges) and a standard roller, apply a base coat of light tan paint to the walls; allow to dry. Apply a second coat; allow to dry.

2 Mix the medium tan glaze by combining 2 parts paint with 1 part water and 1 part glazing liquid.

3 Wet the rags and the cheesecloth, wring out excess water, and set aside.

4 Begin in the upper part of the wall, near a corner. Using the chip brush, apply glaze generously in a loose X pattern approximately 2 by 2 feet.

5 Use one of the rags to manipulate the glaze on the surface with a light scrubbing motion. Keep the edges soft and irregular. When the rag is loaded with glaze, switch to a fresh rag; rinse the rags as needed.

6 Using a slightly wrinkled cheesecloth pom-pom, pounce to refine the glaze. Rotate your wrist to feather and blend the glaze, keeping the edges soft and irregular and creating subtle areas of lighter and darker color. Rearrange your pom-pom to a clean portion of cheesecloth as soon as it becomes saturated with glaze.

7 Apply glaze to the adjacent area, making sure not to brush too close to the just-completed section. Manipulate the edges with the rag to feather the color toward the first section. Overlap only the lightest area of the previously created edge; if you stray too far, the color will be darker where the edges overlap. Pounce with the pom-pom to refine the glaze.

8 Continue working in the same manner, section by section, to complete the walls.

"denim" painted wall

IT TAKES ONLY A FEW INEXPENSIVE PAINT TOOLS, LIGHT AND DARK BLUE PAINT, and glazing liquid to create the look of patchwork denim squares. A slight overlapping of paint where the squares meet replicates seams. Because this effect is so striking, you'll probably want to limit it to one wall.

MATERIALS

Basic painting supplies
   (see page 346)

Steel tape measure

Plumb bob

Carpenter's level

Painter's tape

Trim roller frame with
   4-inch roller cover

9-inch texturing roller
   cover*

2-inch tapered paintbrush

Light blue latex paint**
   for base coat

Denim blue latex paint**
   for glaze

Latex glazing liquid
   (clear mixing glaze)

Nail or paint key

*Buy a texturing roller
cover (found near the
standard roller covers)
with small loops, rather
than a decorative texture
roller cover.

**Satin finish

1 Prepare your surface according to the instructions on pages 346–347. Using a paintbrush (for edges) and a standard roller, apply a base coat of light blue paint; allow to dry. Apply a second coat; allow to dry.

2 Measuring from one side to the other, find the wall's midpoint. With a helper, drop a plumb bob from the ceiling at that point. Mark the center line on the wall with a pencil.

3 Determine the size of square you want to use. If your wall has a window, use the measurement from the bottom of the windowsill to the top of the baseboard for your square size. Otherwise, choose a square size that divides evenly into the wall height. Using the steel tape and starting from the center line, measure and mark the wall for the vertical lines.

LOWE'S QUICK TIP
A texturing roller cover produces a definite directional pattern, or nap. Experiment to determine the correct way to snap the cover onto the roller.

4 Using the carpenter's level, draw the vertical lines, then measure, mark, and draw the horizontal lines.

5 Tape around every other square, placing the tape on the outside of the pencil lines and pressing it firmly against the lines. You will paint these squares first. Put pieces of tape in the alternate ones so you won't paint them by mistake.

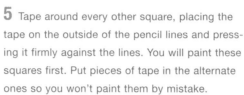

6 Mix 1 part denim blue paint with 1 part glazing liquid. Using the trim roller, apply the denim blue glaze to one or two taped-off squares at a time.

7 Using the standard roller with the texturing roller cover, go over the glaze vertically to create the brushed look of denim. Roll in one direction only—either up or down. Repeat the process on the remaining taped-off squares, applying glaze and going over it with the texturizing roller cover.

8 When the glaze is dry to the touch, carefully remove all the tape. On the remaining (light blue) squares, apply the denim blue glaze with the trim roller.

9 Where the squares meet, slightly overlap the edges to create the illusion of seams.

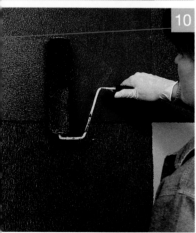

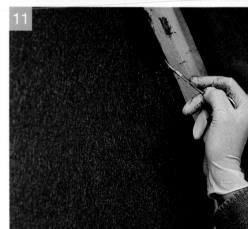

10 Using the standard roller with the texturing roller cover, go over the glaze horizontally, rolling in one direction only.

11 At the wall edges and the ceiling line, apply the denim blue glaze with a 2-inch tapered brush. Use a nail or a paint key on the wet glaze to mimic the effect of the texturing roller cover, moving it in the same direction as the paint grain, horizontally or vertically depending on which square you're in; allow to dry.

papier collé

INEXPENSIVE KRAFT PAPER, PASTED AND WRINKLED, GIVES A RICH TEXTURE TO this finish. Its French name, *papier collé*, literally translates as "pasted paper." You begin papering at the edges of each wall, then fill in the center areas. Glazing liquid seals the walls in preparation for three colors of glaze.

MATERIALS

Brown paper painter's tape

Kraft paper to total square footage of walls, plus 20 percent*

Drop cloth

Disposable gloves

Heavy-duty wallpaper paste

Paint tray with disposable liner

Mini-roller frame with 6-inch roller cover

6-inch foam brayer

1-inch chip brush

3-inch chip brush

2- or 3-inch synthetic-bristle paintbrush

Latex glazing liquid (clear mixing glaze)

Cream, tan, and green latex paint** for glaze

Cheesecloth pom-pom (see page 348)

Lightweight kraft paper is available at Lowe's. A heavier type producing more pronounced creases can be found at craft and framing stores.

**Satin finish*

1 Mask the ceiling and baseboards with brown paper painter's tape (see page 346). Tear the kraft paper lengthwise into several pieces approximately 14 inches wide and 3 to 4 feet long, maintaining one straight edge on each piece.

2 Spread the drop cloth on your work surface and lay down the first torn piece of paper. Pour wallpaper paste into the tray. Using the mini-roller, apply paste to the paper in a forward motion only, not back and forth. Roll paste beyond the edges to completely coat the paper.

3 Roll paste onto an upper area of the wall (adjacent to the ceiling or a corner) slightly larger than the piece of paper you have prepared.

LOWE'S QUICK TIP

To minimize seams, make the pieces as large as you can handle; a few big pieces will have greater impact than many small ones.

Overlap the paper pieces as little as possible to avoid bulk. It's all right to tear away a little paper, if necessary, while the paste is still wet.

4 Adhere the paper to the wall, with its straight edge neatly meeting the ceiling line or corner. Wrinkle the paper with both hands to create pronounced or subtle creases, depending on the look you want.

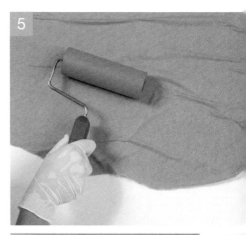

5 Using the brayer and working from the center out, roll firmly over the surface to flatten the creases and push the air out from under the paper. Roll a little beyond the edges of the paper to make sure they adhere to the surface; wipe any paste off the brayer with a damp rag. Use your fingers to work out any remaining air bubbles. Look over the piece carefully to make sure the edges and wrinkles lie flat.

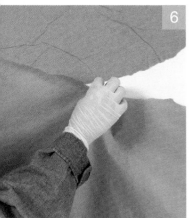

6 Continuing on the ceiling line or corner edge, tear the next piece of paper in an irregular shape to overlap the first piece. Apply paste to the back of the paper and to the wall. Adhere the piece to the wall, just overlapping the edge of the first piece.

7 Manipulate the paper to create creases.

8 If the edge of the second piece doesn't stick to the first piece, lift the edge and apply a small amount of paste with the 1-inch chip brush.

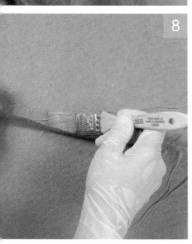

9 Roll over the surface with the brayer. Continue to tear, glue, and adhere pieces of paper to cover the wall. (Maintain a straight edge only where the wall meets another surface or edge, as at the ceiling, baseboard, or casings.) Repeat on the remaining walls; allow to dry overnight.

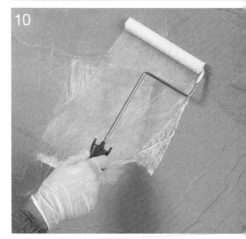

10 Using the mini-roller and a paintbrush (for the wall edges), apply clear glazing liquid over the paper to seal the surface; allow to dry.

11 Mix three glazes—cream, tan, and green— by combining 1 part paint with 3 parts glazing liquid. Using the 3-inch chip brush, apply some of each glaze to a section of the surface in a random, natural-looking pattern, brushing directly over the wrinkles.

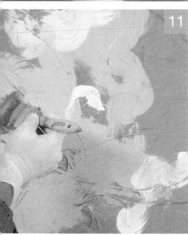

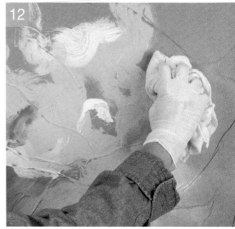

12 Using a slightly wrinkled cheesecloth pom-pom, rub over the surface. Rearrange the pom-pom to a clean area of cheesecloth as you continue to refine the glazes. Continue applying and rubbing the glazes to complete the room; allow to dry.

horizontal stripes

MATERIALS

Basic painting supplies
(see page 346)

Steel tape measure

Carpenter's level

2-inch painter's tape

Putty knife

Mini-roller frame with
6-inch roller cover

Trim roller with 3-inch
roller cover

Off-white latex paint* for
base coat

Navy blue, red, and pale
blue latex paint* for
stripes

*Satin finish

PAINTER'S TAPE IS THE SECRET TO CRISP, CLEAN STRIPES. THE STRIPES IN THIS room range from a 20-inch band of navy to a 1¼-inch ribbon of pale blue; you can use whatever widths suit your room. You'll probably need only 1 quart of each paint color, except for the base coat.

1 Prepare your surface according to the instructions on pages 346–347. Using a paintbrush (for edges) and the standard roller, apply a base coat of off-white paint to the walls; allow to dry. Apply a second coat; allow to dry.

2 Use the steel tape and carpenter's level to measure and lightly mark horizontal lines on the wall with a pencil. The stripes shown above measure as follows:

❖ Navy stripe—20 inches   ❖ Red stripe—12 inches

❖ Off-white space—2 inches   ❖ Pale blue stripe—1¼ inches

LOWE'S QUICK TIP

For the best coverage, always use the lightest color for the base coat and darker colors for the stripes.

❖

You don't need to apply a second base coat where the wall will be covered with dark stripes.

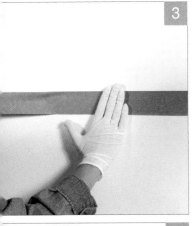

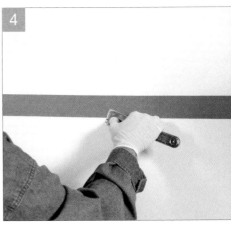

3 Tape the navy stripe first. Position the edge of the tape on the 20-inch line, with the tape itself *above* the line. (The baseboard edge will have been taped when you applied your base coat.)

4 Using the putty knife, burnish (rub firmly) the edge of the tape that you will paint—in this example, the lower edge. It's not necessary to burnish the top edge.

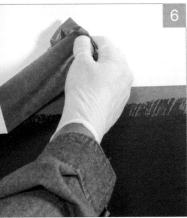

5 Apply the navy paint, cutting in along the baseboards and corners with a paintbrush and using the mini-roller elsewhere, rolling just over the burnished edge of the tape; allow to dry. Apply a second coat, if necessary; allow to dry completely.

6 Remove the tape gently at a 45-degree angle.

7 To tape the red stripe, position the edge of the tape just a hair below the edge of the navy paint line, with the tape itself in the navy stripe. Burnish the edge that you will be painting—in this case, the upper edge of the tape.

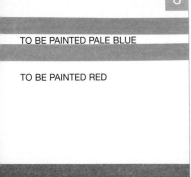

TO BE PAINTED PALE BLUE

TO BE PAINTED RED

8 Next apply tape over the 2-inch space between the red stripe and the pale blue stripe. Burnish both edges of this tape. Also tape the top of the pale blue stripe and burnish the lower edge of the tape.

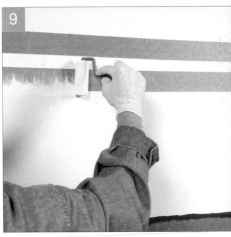

9 To prevent seepage of red or pale blue paint under the tape into the off-white areas, roll off-white base paint over the tape edges, using the trim roller (see page 358). Allow to dry. Leave the tape in place.

10 Using the trim roller, paint the pale blue stripe; allow to dry. Apply a second coat, if necessary; allow to dry completely.

11 Using the mini-roller, paint the red stripe; allow to dry. Apply a second coat, if necessary; allow to dry completely.

12 Gently remove the tape.

13 Tape and paint the remaining walls in the same manner to complete the room.

a tape trick

TO PREVENT PAINT FROM SEEPING UNDER THE TAPE WHEN PAINTING stripes, pros seal the edges with the paint that has been used for the base coat. Here the process is shown with vertical stripes.

1 Apply the base coat to the walls (yellow in this example); allow to dry completely. Apply a second coat; allow to dry.

2 With a carpenter's level and an acrylic ruler held horizontally, measure and mark the stripe widths across the wall.

3 Using the level and a long straight-edge held vertically at the marks you made in Step 2, draw lines from the ceiling to the floor.

4 Tape off the stripes on the drawn lines—the edge of the tape on the line, the tape itself in the area that will *not* be painted.

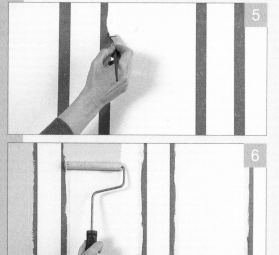

5 Before you paint the stripes, use a brush to paint the tape edges (the side next to the stripe you'll be painting) with the base-coat color. This seals the edge, and any paint that does seep under will be the same color as the base coat. In other words, you are painting the tape edges with the color you wish to protect underneath—yellow, in this example. Allow the paint to dry.

6 Roll on the stripe paint (blue in this case), rolling just over the painted edges of the tape; allow to dry. Apply a second coat; allow to dry completely.

7 Remove the tape gently at a 45-degree angle.

papering a room

MATERIALS

Trisodium phosphate
    (or no-rinse, premixed
    TSP substitute)

Spackling compound

200-grit sandpaper

Latex primer/sealer*

Paintbrush, standard
    paint roller frame with
    9-inch roller cover,
    and painter's tape*

Steel tape measure

4-foot carpenter's level

6-foot metal straightedge

Prepasted wallpaper

24-inch carpenter's
    square

Scissors

Standard paint roller
    frame with 9-inch foam
    roller cover

Paint tray with disposable
    liners

Paste for prepasted
    wallpaper

Medium or large plastic
    garbage bag

Smoothing brush

Wallpaper sponge

Single-edge razor knife

Broad knife

Wallpaper smoother

Seam roller

*As needed for Step 1.

SPECIALIZED TOOLS MAKE THE TASK OF HANGING WALLPAPER EASIER, BUT patience is perhaps the biggest component of success. This project uses paste designed especially for prepasted wallpaper. Before you begin, carefully review the manufacturer's instructions that come with your wallpaper.

project continues >

papering a room

1 Remove existing wall coverings and wash off any residue with trisodium phosphate. Fill any cracks or holes with spackling compound, allow to dry, and sand the surface smooth. Then cover the patches with a latex primer/ sealer formulated as a wall covering undercoat. If your walls are painted with latex paint or if they are new drywall, prime the entire surface (see pages 346–347). Alkyd (oil-based) paint doesn't require priming.

2 You can start papering in the middle of a wall, in a corner behind a door, or at a focal point in the room. The directions here are for starting in the middle of a wall. Measure and mark the wall's midpoint, then measure to the left a distance equal to *half* the wallpaper width. Mark this as the starting point for the first strip.

3 Using the carpenter's level, mark a vertical plumb line at the starting point as a placement guide for the first strip. (Never rely on wall edges or door casings to mark a vertical line; they are rarely plumb.) Continue the line down the wall using the 6-foot straightedge and checking with the level to keep the line plumb. Measure the height of the wall along the plumb line, from the ceiling to the top of the baseboard.

> **LOWE'S** **QUICK TIP**
> If you don't have a portable table to use as a work surface, invest in a sheet of plywood and two sawhorses. Be sure to protect the surface with a plastic tarp. Protect the floor with a canvas drop cloth; plastic is dangerous to walk on.

4 For a professional look, wallpaper strips should be cut so their motifs align at the ceiling all around the room. On the wallpaper roll, find the point in the pattern that you want to place at the ceiling and mark that starting point on the paper. With the carpenter's square, measure 2 inches *above* that point and mark a cutting line across the paper.

5 From the pattern starting point (not the cutting line), measure and mark a strip equal to the wall height plus 2 inches. Double-check that there are 2 inches above and 2 inches below the wall-height measurement. Using scissors, cut the strip on the marked lines.

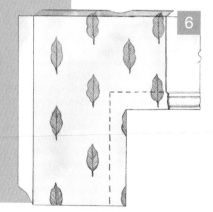

6 To accommodate a door or window opening, measure the distance from the vertical plumb line you made in Step 3 to the inner edge of the side casing. Also measure from the ceiling line to the inner edge of the top casing. Trim the strip accordingly.

7 Turn off the power to the room at the circuit breaker or fuse box while you remove the switch plates and receptacle covers. Lay the first length of wallpaper, right side down, on your work surface. Pour paste into the paint tray and use the paint roller with foam cover to apply an even coat of paste to the back of the strip.

8 To ensure even adhesion of the wallpaper, "book" the strip by folding both ends to the middle, pasted side in. After waiting the time recommended by the manufacturer (usually 5 to 15 minutes), loosely fold the booked strip over itself and enclose it in the plastic bag to keep it from drying out. You can book multiple strips and store them in the plastic bag.

9 Unfold the top portion of the first strip; allow the rest to drop down. Holding the strip by its upper corners, carefully align the edge of the strip with the plumb line and also align the pattern starting point (not the cut edge) with the ceiling line.

10 Use the smoothing brush to adhere the paper at the ceiling line and to coax out any air bubbles. Wet the wallpaper sponge, wring it nearly dry, and lightly wipe away excess paste at the ceiling line. Be gentle; wet wallpaper is fragile.

11 Working from the top down, use one hand to align the side of the strip with the marked line, being careful not to stretch the edge. With your other hand, smooth the paper, spreading your fingers broadly for even pressure. Once the strip is attached, coax out any air bubbles with the smoothing brush and wipe away excess paste at the edges with the sponge. Allow the wallpaper to rest for several minutes.

12 Around a door or a window, use scissors to cut a diagonal slit to the outer corner of the casing, as shown.

13 Holding down the wallpaper with the broad knife, use the razor knife to trim the excess paper flush with the edge of the casing. To avoid tears, make a continuous cut, keeping the razor blade in contact with the paper while you move the broad knife. Trim the paper above the casing the same way.

project continues >

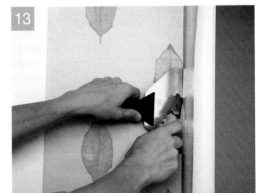

papering a room

14 If you've papered over a switch plate or receptacle, use the single-edge razor to slit an X in the wallpaper over the opening (make sure the power is turned off). Carefully fold back the cut pieces and trim them even with the edges of the opening. Restore power.

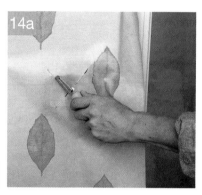

15 Wait 15 minutes, then use the wallpaper smoother held at a 30-degree angle to smooth the surface of the paper.

16 Trim the excess paper at the ceiling line and the baseboard, using the broad knife and razor knife.

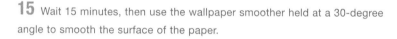

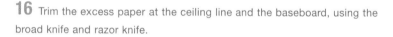

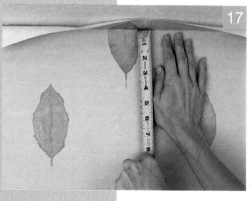

17 Measure, mark, cut, and paste the next strip. Adhere the strip at the ceiling line, checking to be sure the pattern is positioned properly.

18 Work the strip down the wall, aligning its edge with the edge of the first strip. Smooth, sponge, and trim as you did for the first strip, changing the razor blade often.

19 Use the seam roller to completely adhere the edges where the first and second strips meet (the strip in the photo falls above a door). Use a light touch to avoid squeezing adhesive from under the edges.

20 Continue hanging strips in the same manner. When you approach a corner, measure from the edge of the last strip to the corner in three places; add ¼ inch to the largest measurement. Mark and trim a new wallpaper strip to this width. Set aside the leftover piece.

21 Hang the trimmed strip. Smooth it with the brush and wipe it with the sponge. Snip ¼ inch into the extra paper at the ceiling and at the baseboard to make the strip lie flat around the corner.

22 Measure the width of the leftover piece. Starting in the corner, measure and mark that distance on the adjoining wall. Using the level and the straightedge, mark a plumb line down the length of the wall at that point.

23 Hang the piece, aligning one edge of the strip with the plumb line and butting the other edge into the corner (it will slightly overlap the previous strip).

24 Continue hanging wallpaper strips around the room, measuring and trimming the final one to butt against the starting plumb line.

PAPERING SWITCH PLATES AND RECEPTACLE COVERS

Once the walls are done, you can paper switch plates and receptacle covers for a seamless look. Instructions follow for a switch plate.

1 Cut a piece of wallpaper that roughly matches the pattern surrounding the opening. Hold it over the opening, line up the pattern, and draw lines on the sheet 1½ inches beyond the edges of the opening. Trim along these marks.

2 Position the plate over the opening and place the wallpaper sheet on top, matching the pattern to the pattern on the wall. At the upper edge, lightly fold the sheet around the back of the switch plate.

3 Fine-tune the pattern placement; then crease the paper around the outer edges of the switch plate.

4 Trim the sheet ¾ inch beyond the creases. Then trim the corners just to (but not into) the point where the creases intersect. Cut an X opening for the switch.

5 Apply wallpaper paste to the back of the sheet. Place the switch plate face down on the paper, aligning its edges with the creases. Fold the paper edges onto the back of the plate and secure with masking tape; secure the edges of the switch opening the same way. Allow to dry; pierce holes for the screws.

baseboard

REPLACING EXISTING BASEBOARDS WITH NEW MOULDING IS A RELATIVELY straightforward project, thanks to the availability of matching corner blocks that eliminate the need for traditional mitered joints. First you install the blocks in the corners, then you cut the moulding to fit in between.

MATERIALS

Utility knife

Putty knife

Wood shims

Small prybar

Nail puller

Baseboard moulding and corner blocks

Electric drill with appropriate bit (see Step 2)

Hammer

2-inch finishing nails

Nailset

Sliding T-bevel gauge

Steel tape measure

Adjustable miter box

Stud finder

Latex caulk

Caulking gun

Nonshrinking latex hole filler

200-grit sandpaper

1 Remove the existing baseboard. If it is fused to the wall by layers of paint, cut through the paint with a utility knife to open a gap large enough for the blade of a putty knife. Slip the putty knife in near one end of the baseboard and push a wood shim behind the blade to protect the wall. Use the small prybar to pry the baseboard ½ inch out from the wall. Continue along the wall with the prybar and shim until you can pull off the entire length of moulding. Use a nail puller to remove the nails.

2 An outside corner block will be nailed in place through its front corner. To drill pilot holes for the nails, clamp the corner block face down to your work surface on top of a scrap board. Fit the drill with a bit the same diameter as the nails. Drill two pilot holes straight through the block, back corner to front corner, about 1 inch from top and bottom. The bit should exit at the front corner of the block.

LOWE'S QUICK TIP
To keep new moulding from warping, apply a finish to the back face before you install it.

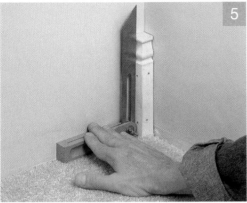

3 Hold the drilled block in position, making sure it is flat on the floor and flush with both wall surfaces. Drive a finishing nail into each hole to anchor it to the wall. To avoid marring the wood, leave the nails protruding slightly, then countersink the heads with the nailset.

4 For an inside corner, hold the block in position on your work surface and drill two pilot holes through each face of the block, locating them about 1 inch from top and bottom and offsetting them. Anchor the block to the wall by driving a finishing nail into each hole; countersink the nail heads with the nailset.

5 Most walls are not perfectly square, so check the angle of the corner blocks before cutting the baseboard to fit between them. Hold the handle of the sliding T-bevel gauge against the floor and adjust the blade to rest flush against the corner block. Then adjust the angle of your miter box to the angle set on the bevel gauge.

6 Measure the distance between two corner blocks. Transfer that measurement to a straight length of baseboard, marking two cutting lines. With the baseboard face up on the base of the miter box, align one cutting mark with the blade and cut at the angle established in Step 5. Measure the angle of the other corner block as shown in Step 5, adjust the saw accordingly, and cut the other end of the baseboard.

7 Using the stud finder, locate and mark the wall studs between corner blocks. At each stud and each end, nail the moulding to the wall with a pair of finishing nails, locating them 1½ inches from top and bottom baseboard edges. Countersink the nail heads.

8 Fill any gaps between the baseboard and the wall with latex caulk. Conceal the nail heads with nonshrinking latex hole filler. Allow the caulk and filler to dry according to the manufacturer's instructions. Then sand with 200-grit sandpaper and finish as desired.

MAKING A SCARF JOINT

When a wall is too long to be spanned by a single piece of moulding, use a scarf joint to join pieces. Center the joint over a stud, if possible, and direct it away from the most likely viewing angle. Cut the joining pieces at opposing angles (30 degrees is best if your saw allows; if not, cut at 45 degrees). Sand lightly to remove any roughness. Position the moulding against the wall, glue and nail the joint, then sand lightly.

peg rail and shelf

MATERIALS

Steel tape measure

Circular saw or handsaw

Adjustable miter box

3½-inch colonial base
    moulding* for peg
    railing

1 by 4 plain moulding*
    for shelf

1¼-inch lipped moulding*
    for shelf trim

Chalk line

Electric drill with combi-
    nation countersink–
    pilot hole drill bit, and
    bit the diameter of
    peg shank

Wood glue

Pegs (see tip, facing
    page)

Latex primer

2- or 3-inch synthetic-
    bristle paintbrush

100-grit sandpaper

Latex paint**

Stud finder

Painter's tape

Carpenter's level

Steel tape measure

2-inch wood screws

Paintable wood putty

Electric brad nailer with
    1¼-inch nails

*Lengths should total
the room's perimeter,
plus a few feet.

**Satin finish

A PEG RAIL IS USEFUL FOR HANGING CLOTHES AND OTHER BELONGINGS OUT of the way. A narrow shelf above the pegs provides a display area in a small room without gobbling up valuable floor space. Pegs and three kinds of standard moulding are all it takes for this simple project, designed to encircle the entire room.

1 Measure the width of the wall at the desired height of the peg rail; allow for door and window openings. Cut all moulding into lengths that correspond to each wall, mitering the ends as needed to fit in the corners. Decide on your peg spacing, making it consistent from wall to wall (the pegs on this rail are 9 inches apart). Do not place pegs in the corners.

2 On the front side of the colonial base moulding, snap a chalk line (see page 378) slightly above the midpoint. Mark your peg spacing on this line.

3 Place a scrap board underneath the base moulding and drill your peg holes, going all the way through the moulding.

4 Put a little glue in each hole and insert the pegs; allow the glue dry.

5 To make the shelf, glue lipped moulding to one long edge of each piece of plain moulding and to any exposed ends of plain moulding at window or door openings, butting the joints. After the glue has dried, use the brad nailer and 1¼-inch nails to further secure the lipped moulding. Set the nail heads, fill with wood putty, and allow to dry; sand smooth.

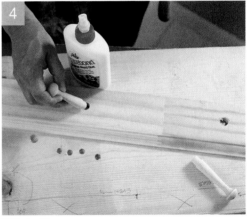

6 Prime the rail and shelf pieces; allow them to dry and then sand lightly with the 100-grit sandpaper. Paint all the pieces.

7 Using the carpenter's level, mark a horizontal placement line at the height determined in Step 1. Use the stud finder to locate the studs; mark with a bit of tape below where the rail will go. Drill pilot holes into the rail at intervals corresponding to the stud locations. Attach the rail to the wall with the 2-inch wood screws, screwing it into the studs. Fill the screw holes with wood putty; allow to dry and then sand. Touch up with the latex paint.

8 Position the shelf on top of the rail, its back edge flush with the wall and its lipped edge facing out. Brad-nail the shelf to the peg rail every 12 inches along the back edge.

LOWE'S QUICK TIP
Select pegs with a shank (the narrow projection at the back) no longer than the thickness of your base moulding.

beadboard

BEADBOARD PANELS MADE OF MDF (MEDIUM-DENSITY FIBERBOARD) ARE IDEALLY suited to high-moisture rooms such as bathrooms and kitchens. Acclimate panels and moulding by bringing them indoors, preferably into the room where they will be installed, 3 to 5 days before you begin.

Beadboard paneling can be installed only on flat walls; use a carpenter's level to make sure yours aren't bowed. Each panel has a "bead" on one edge and is smooth on the other edge, resulting in a seamless look once the panels are installed. Arrows on the back ensure that you orient the panels correctly.

1 The beadboard panels are 48 inches high, making it possible to cut two pieces from one 4- by 8-foot panel. Make a bird's-eye sketch of the room, noting dimensions, to determine how many full panels and how many feet of cap and base moulding you will need. Have the panels cut in half for you. Add 10 percent to the moulding footage to allow for cutting errors.

2 Remove the existing baseboards (see page 364).

3 If you are keeping the existing flooring, or if new flooring is already installed, skip to the next step. If you will be installing flooring later, make spacers the thickness of the planned flooring to raise the panels above the underlayment.

4 Start the beadboard at an inside corner. Place the first panel against the wall, orienting it according to the arrows on the back. With a carpenter's level, check for plumb along one vertical edge. To achieve plumb, you may need to trim the lower edge with the circular saw. You may also need to "scribe" the vertical edge that goes into the corner, cutting it with the circular saw to create an exact fit (see below).

With the panel in position, lightly draw a line on the wall at its upper edge. Using the level and straightedge, continue the line around the room.

5 If your beadboard panels didn't come preprimed, apply primer and allow to dry. Turn the first panel over so the wrong side is toward you. Using the caulking gun, apply a ¼-inch bead of the paneling and moulding adhesive in wavy lines. Do not apply within ½ inch of the edges.

6 When the adhesive is tacky (it usually takes several minutes), turn the panel over and set it in place, aligning the upper edge with the marked line on the wall. Press the panel against the wall firmly and evenly.

7 Using the brad nailer, shoot ⅝-inch nails through the beadboard and into the wall, spacing them approximately 10 inches apart along the upper, lower, and side edges.

project continues >

SCRIBING

A simple compass—the kind used to draw circles—will help you scribe an accurate cutting line for a corner that's uneven or not plumb. Hold your panel in plumb position up against the corner (if you don't have a helper, temporarily tack it in place). Set the compass at the widest gap between the panel and the corner with the pointed end of the compass against the corner and the pencil end on the panel. Pull the compass along the length of the panel; the pencil will "scribe" a vertical cutting line.

beadboard

CUTTING OPENINGS

To cut openings for light switches and receptacles that will fall within a beadboard panel, turn off the power to the room at the circuit breaker or fuse box while you remove the covers and screws; store them in a zip-top bag. Measure from the horizontal level line on the wall and from the side of the last-installed panel to determine the exact location of the opening. Measure and mark the opening shape on the beadboard and drill a starter hole. Put the blade of the jigsaw into the hole and cut the opening.

8 Install adjoining panels the same way, spacing them $\frac{1}{16}$ inch apart or according to the manufacturer's instructions. As you add panels, you may need to trim the lower edges with the circular saw to maintain plumb.

9 When you reach the next corner, measure, mark, and cut the panel to fit. (A 4-foot metal straightedge clamped to the panel makes a stable guide for the lengthwise cut.)

10 Return to the corner where you began. Position a new panel on the adjacent wall, butting its edge into the corner up against the first panel. Scribe the edge of the new panel if necessary for a precise fit; glue and nail the panel in place. Install the remaining panels on that wall, cutting the end panel to fit.

11 When you turn the next inside corner, cut the new panel so the beadboard design flows uninterrupted. For example, if the just-attached panel was cut in the middle of a bead, cut the new panel in the same spot so that it looks as if it continues around the corner in an unbroken line.

12 To turn an outside corner, see the bird's-eye-view drawing below left. Here a partial wall near the tub creates two closely placed outside corners. Measure and mark the panel $\frac{3}{16}$ inch (or the thickness of the beadboard) longer than the wall. Cut the piece, then glue and nail in place.

13 Measure, mark, and cut the next piece of beadboard so it fits against the previous one and extends $\frac{3}{16}$ inch beyond the second outside corner, as shown below right. Glue and nail. Glue and nail the next section, fitting it against the previous piece and continuing along the wall. Attach additional panels to complete the room.

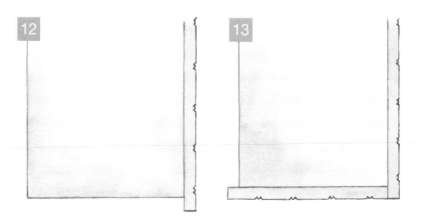

14 If you're not working with already-primed materials, prime your moulding using the 2½-inch paintbrush. You will install the moulding in this order: cap, base, and corner guard.

15 With the stud finder, locate the studs and lightly mark their location on the wall, just above the upper edge of the beadboard panels. Measure, mark, and cut the cap moulding, using the miter box to make 45-degree-angle cuts at the outside corners; cope one piece to fit at each inside corner (see below).

16 With the brad nailer and the 1½-inch nails, attach the cap moulding at its thickest part, nailing through the beadboard and into the studs.

17 If you are installing flooring, remove the spacers and install it now, before attaching the base moulding. Mark the stud locations on the beadboard just above the base moulding height.

18 Measure, mark, and cut the base moulding. Cope one piece at each inside corner. Attach the moulding to the beadboard with 1½-inch nails, nailing into the studs.

19 Measure, mark, and cut the corner guard moulding. Attach it to the outside corners using 1-inch nails. Attach quarter-round moulding to the inside corners using 1-inch nails, if desired.

20 Fill the nail holes with paintable wood putty. Use latex caulk to fill any gaps between the moulding and the wall; allow to dry. Sand with the 220-grit sandpaper.

21 With painter's tape, mask off the wall above the cap moulding and the floor below the base moulding. Also protect the floor with kraft paper. Using latex paint and the 2½-inch brush, paint the beadboard and the moulding. Allow the paint to dry. Sand lightly and apply a second coat of paint.

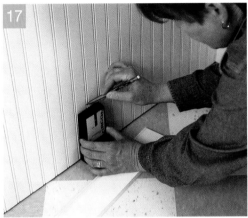

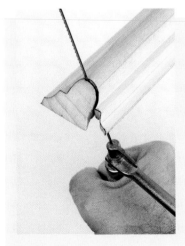

CUTTING A COPED JOINT

Coping is a way to create a gap-free joint in a complex moulding, or when corners are not square. It only works for inside corners.

Coped joints are asymmetrical. You butt one piece of moulding into the corner, then cut the joining piece with a coping saw to fit against it, as follows.

1 Miter-cut the piece you are coping at 45 degrees, so the back is longer than the front. Rub a pencil over the front edge of the cut to make the moulding profile easily visible.

2 Hold the coping saw over the moulding with the blade perpendicular to it (see photo). Cut from top to bottom following the curves you marked in pencil. In the middle of the cut, angle the blade inward; return to the perpendicular to complete the cut.

3 Test the fit of the joint; it will probably need adjustment. Use a small rasp or file to adjust the cut edge until you get a good, tight fit; be careful—thin edges can break easily. Nail the moulding in place on the wall.

island cabinets

MATERIALS

4- by 8-foot sheets of MDF (medium-density fiberboard) beadboard*

Steel tape measure

Circular saw

Spiral saw

Kraft paper

Masking tape

Latex primer, if needed (see Step 4)

100-grit sandpaper

White latex paint

Paint tray with disposable liner

2½-inch synthetic-bristle paintbrush

Furring strips

Wood glue

Electric brad nailer with ½-inch nails

Paintable wood putty

*See Step 1 for quantity.

BEADBOARD ADDED TO THE BACKS AND EXPOSED SIDES OF STOCK CABINETS (one 2 feet long, the other 3 feet long) gives this island a custom look. One edge of each beadboard sheet must be mitered; have a cabinet-maker make the cut for you. You can measure and cut the other edges at home.

LOWE'S QUICK TIP

For a finished look, you can trim the lower edges of the beadboard with primed and painted shoe base moulding, mitering the corners. If your floor is vinyl or tile (like the one pictured), consider instead running a bead of silicone acrylic caulk at the floor line.

1 Most islands will require two sheets of MDF beadboard. Have one edge of each sheet mitered at a 45-degree angle, as follows: with the sheets oriented the same way, miter the *left* edge on the first sheet (label it Sheet A) and the *right* edge on the second sheet (label it Sheet B).

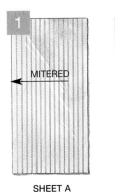

SHEET A   SHEET B

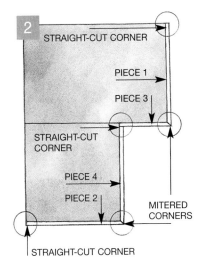

STRAIGHT-CUT CORNER

PIECE 1

PIECE 3

STRAIGHT-CUT CORNER

PIECE 4

PIECE 2

MITERED CORNERS

STRAIGHT-CUT CORNER

2 Before you start cutting the panels, it's important to understand which edges are mitered on this island. See the drawing at far right.

3 On Sheet A, measure and mark Piece 1, *making sure the mitered edge is on the left.* Cut the piece using the circular saw; cut out any openings (for electric receptacles, for example) with the spiral saw. Dry-fit the piece against the cabinet. Measure, cut, and dry-fit the remaining pieces, one at a time in the following order: Piece 2 from Sheet B, Piece 3 from Sheet B, and Piece 4 from Sheet A.

4 Prime the beadboard panels if yours didn't come preprimed; sand lightly with 100-grit sandpaper. Paint with white latex paint and allow to dry.

5 Tape kraft paper to the floor to protect the surface. Attach furring strips to the unfinished backs of the cabinets with wood glue.

6 Apply wood glue to the island where Piece 1 goes. Making sure the mitered edge is on the left, press the panel in place.

7 Using the brad nailer and ½-inch nails, nail Piece 1 to the side of the island, placing a nail approximately every 6 inches around the edges.

8 Glue Piece 2, with its mitered edge to the right; brad-nail in place. Glue Piece 3, with its mitered edge to the right, against Piece 1; brad-nail in place. Glue Piece 4, with its mitered edge to the left, against Piece 2; brad-nail in place.

9 Fill the nail holes with paintable wood putty; let dry and then sand. Apply a second coat of white paint to the beadboard.

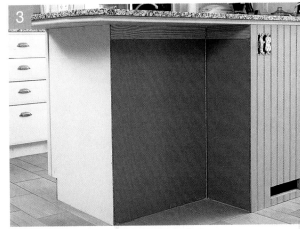

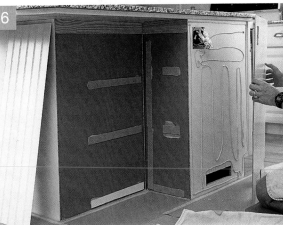

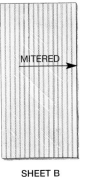

crown moulding

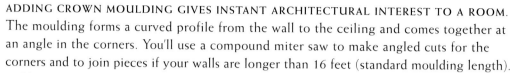

ADDING CROWN MOULDING GIVES INSTANT ARCHITECTURAL INTEREST TO A ROOM. The moulding forms a curved profile from the wall to the ceiling and comes together at an angle in the corners. You'll use a compound miter saw to make angled cuts for the corners and to join pieces if your walls are longer than 16 feet (standard moulding length).

It's easiest to paint or stain the moulding before installing it; you'll fill and touch up the nail holes once the crown is in place. If you stain the moulding, apply polyurethane before installation too.

The instructions that follow are for 90-degree inside corners—what you'd need to go around a room with four straight walls. For nonstandard inside corners, or for outside corners, you'll need to set different angles for your cuts.

MATERIALS

Stud finder

Painter's tape

Compound miter saw

1 by 1 lumber, or precut triangular pieces (see Step 2)

Steel tape measure

Crown moulding, painted or stained

Electric drill with combination countersink–pilot hole drill bit*

Hammer

Finishing nails*

Nailset

Sandable wood filler

Small putty knife

Cotton rag

200-grit sandpaper

Spackling compound, or wood putty to match stain

Latex caulk

Caulking gun

Paint, or stain and polyurethane

2- or 3-inch synthetic-bristle paintbrush

*Select size depending on your moulding.

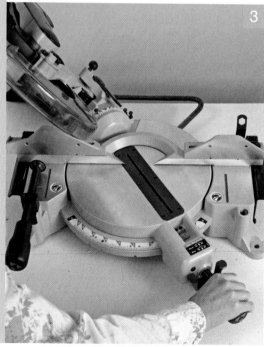

1 Go around the room with the stud finder and mark each wall stud with a piece of painter's tape just below the area the crown will cover.

2 Installing small wood blocks where the wall and ceiling meet provides something solid to nail the crown into. It also allows you to nail into the center of the moulding rather than the top and bottom, where the contours of the crown may leave little room. We used precut wood triangles that match this moulding; you can also cut blocks from 1 by 1 lumber. Nail one piece into each stud, using the tape from Step 1 as a location guide. Also nail a block into each corner.

3 Prepare the saw for a left-side, inside-corner cut (see Step 10 photo on page 376) by setting the miter table at the bottom of the saw to the right at 31.62 degrees. Set the bevel angle (the top of the saw that tilts left and right) to 33.85 degrees. Tighten both settings.

LOWE'S QUICK TIP
Before cutting your moulding, practice cutting left and right inside corners on scrap pieces to see how they fit together.

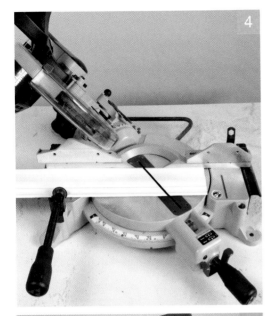

4 Stand facing a corner of the room. The wall on the left will need a length of crown with a left-side, inside-corner cut, and the wall on the right will need a length of crown with a right-side, inside-corner cut. First measure the wall on the left, then select a length of crown several inches longer. Place it face up on the saw table with the top edge (the one that will touch the ceiling) against the fence. You'll make this cut on the *right* end of the length of moulding, even though it's the cut for the *left* side. Cut the piece. (It will look like the left side of a V.)

5 Next cut the other end of the same piece of moulding. This will be a right-side, inside-corner cut (see the Step 10 photo); you'll be cutting what will be the left end of this length of crown. Starting the tape measure at the bottom of the V you've just cut, measure out to the wall length determined in Step 4. Add a little extra and then mark the spot on the piece of moulding with a pencil. It's better to make the piece a little long and have to shave it down than to cut it too short and waste the entire piece.

6 Place the bottom edge of the moulding against the saw fence. Move the miter table to the left at 31.62 degrees and tighten down the setting. Keep the bevel angle where it was at 33.85 degrees. Align the moulding under the blade so the blade will hit just past your mark. You'll cut off the excess to the right of the saw blade, making a cut that looks like the right side of a V.

7 Now that both ends are cut, lift the section into place. If it's too long, go back to the saw and shave off a little. You want the bottom "points" to fit snugly where the two walls meet. Once the piece is cut to the right length, have a helper hold it in place while you drill pilot holes through the crown into the underlying wood blocks. (The painter's tape is the guide for the block locations.) Also drill pilot holes about 1 inch in from each end.

8 While your helper holds the piece in place, drive finishing nails through the pilot holes. To avoid marring the moulding, leave each nail protruding a bit, to be countersunk later (see Step 12). It's also good to keep the pieces a little loose so you can adjust them to match neighboring pieces in the corners.

project continues >

crown moulding

9 For the next piece, measure from the bottom tip of the installed piece of crown across the adjoining wall. Set up the saw for the right- and left-side cuts (review Steps 3 and 6). Remember to cut each piece a little long and dry-fit it before making the final cut.

10 Once the second piece is cut, hold it in place and fit the ends of the pieces together as neatly as possible. Follow Steps 7 and 8 to drill pilot holes and drive nails.

11 Continue with the third and fourth walls. The fourth wall will be the most challenging, since its cuts will have to conform to the already-installed crown at both ends.

12 Once all the pieces are up, go back and countersink the nails with the nailset.

13 If there are gaps between pieces in the corners, fill them with sandable wood filler. Apply it with the small putty knife and then smooth it with a damp cotton rag. Once it's dry, sand it smooth.

14 Fill nail holes with spackling compound (or wood putty, if the moulding is stained). Allow to dry; sand any high spots.

15 Caulk the top and bottom edges, ideally with the same color as the paint or stain used on the moulding. If the pieces are painted, clean off any smudge marks with the rag; touch up the paint over the nail holes and in the corners. If the trim is stained, dab the filled nail holes with a little stain, let dry, and then touch up the polyurethane top coat.

vinyl tile floor

MATERIALS

Floor leveling compound

Drywall taping knife

100-grit sandpaper

Steel tape measure

Carpenter's square

Metal straightedge

Heavy string

Chalk line

Vinyl tiles

Kneepads

Rubber gloves

Adhesive comb*

Vinyl tile adhesive*

Rolling pin

Utility knife

Jamb saw or contour
    guide (see Steps 16–18)

Mineral spirits

Clean rags

Silicone acrylic caulk
    (optional)

Caulking gun (optional)

Buffable acrylic floor
    polish

Use the comb and adhesive recommended by the vinyl tile manufacturer.

COMMERCIAL-GRADE VINYL composition tile, known as VCT, can provide maximum impact at minimum expense. The tiles are 12 inches square and come in boxes of 45 same-color pieces. Buy the number of pieces equal to your room's square footage, plus 10 percent to allow for cutting errors. Before you commit to this project, evaluate your floor's underlayment. If it is not perfectly smooth, remove and replace it (see Steps 2–5 on page 381).

1 Vacuum the underlayment thoroughly. Mix the floor leveling compound according to the manufacturer's instructions. Using the drywall taping knife, apply the compound to the underlayment seams; allow to dry.

2 Using the 100-grit sandpaper, sand the areas that were covered by the compound. Thoroughly vacuum the surface again.

3 Make a sketch of the area to be tiled, with measurements, to help you plan the tile layout. A good approach is to start in the most visible part of the room and work outward, toward the walls. On your sketch, draw reference lines that intersect at right angles where you wish to begin tiling. In this example, full tiles were centered down the length of the galley, aligned with the midpoint of the French doors.

project continues >

MIDPOINT OF FRENCH DOORS

REFERENCE LINE

GALLEY

REFERENCE LINE

DINING AREA

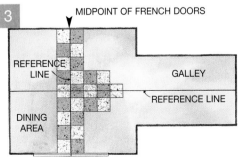

vinyl tile floor

4 Use the steel tape measure, carpenter's square, and metal straightedge to locate and mark intersecting reference lines on the floor, according to your sketch. Measure from the most visible wall (or the base of the most visible cabinets), checking at several points to ensure that each line will be parallel to the wall or cabinets.

5 Tape pieces of heavy string over the reference marks temporarily, using a carpenter's square to make sure the strings intersect at precise 90-degree angles. Adjust the marks as needed; then remove the string. Snap chalk lines as placement guides (see "How to Use a Chalk Line," right).

6 You'll lay tile in four-tile sections. Start with a tile at one of the right angles formed by your chalk lines. Wearing kneepads and gloves, use the adhesive comb to spread adhesive evenly over the four-tile area; allow it to set up according to the manufacturer's instructions.

7 Set the first tile, lining it up with the chalk lines. Apply light, downward pressure without shifting the tile.

8 Set the second tile so that it is snug against the edge of the first tile, aligning it with the chalk line; press.

9 Set the third and fourth tiles, fitting the tiles together snugly.

10 Continue working in one direction at a time until you reach a point where you need to cut tiles. Go over the laid tiles with the rolling pin to set them. Lay the remaining full tiles the same way.

HOW TO USE A CHALK LINE

A chalk line is a chalk-coated length of string stored inside a casing. It's released and retracted like fishing-reel line. With the aid of a helper, stretch the string between two points and set it flat on the surface. With the string pulled taut, grab it from directly above (not to the side) and let go quickly to "snap" a line of chalk on the surface.

LOWE'S QUICK TIP

As you apply the adhesive, use a utility knife or other sharp tool to remove blobs or bits on the surface. Imperfections in the adhesive can cause noticeable bumps once the tile is set.

11 Align the tile to be cut on top of the last full tile in the row. (The drawing at near right shows a white tile on top of a green tile.)

12 Lay a full tile (green in the drawing) flush with the wall, overlapping the stacked tiles. Using the flush tile as a straightedge, mark a cutting line on the tile to be cut.

13 Cut the tile on the marked line using the carpenter's square and the utility knife.

14 Set the cut tile in place to check the fit.

15 Cut the rest of the tiles the same way and check their fit. Place each tile on top of the row it will complete while you apply adhesive to the underlayment. Set the tiles and go over them with the rolling pin.

16 You can trim a door casing to accommodate tile by placing a scrap tile up against the casing on the underlayment and using a jamb saw to cut the casing flush with the tile. Or you can fit the tile around the casing, as shown here, by using a contour guide. Press the guide against the casing, creating a contour of the shape to be cut out.

17 Move the tile to be trimmed away from the door. Without disturbing the pins in the guide, set the edge of the guide against the edge of the tile. Mark around the protruding shape.

18 Using the carpenter's square and a utility knife, cut out the marked shape.

19 Apply adhesive to the floor and set the tile in place around the casing.

20 Clean up any adhesive on the tile surface with mineral spirits and a rag. Lightly wash the tile with mild soap to remove the residue.

21 Run a bead of silicone acrylic caulk along the edge where the tile meets the baseboards, if desired. Apply acrylic floor polish according to the manufacturer's instructions.

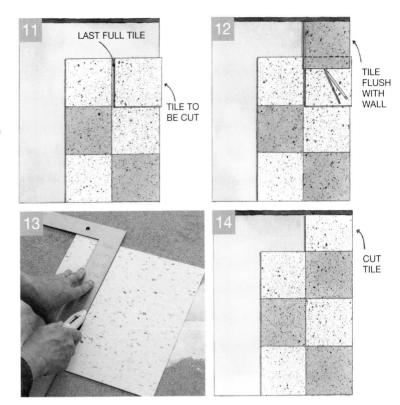

11 — LAST FULL TILE — TILE TO BE CUT

12 — TILE FLUSH WITH WALL

13

14 — CUT TILE

16 17 18 19

sheet vinyl floor

INSTALLING SHEET VINYL IS WITHIN REACH OF THE DO-IT-YOURSELFER IF THE room is small enough to allow a seam-free installation. (See tip, facing page.) Before starting this project, evaluate your floor's underlayment. If it is not consistently smooth, or if it shows signs of water damage, you will need to remove and replace it; materials and basic instructions are given here.

MATERIALS

Kneepads

Steel tape measure

3/8-inch particleboard underlayment or 1/4-inch underlayment-grade plywood*

Circular saw*

Jamb saw

Staple gun and 18-gauge staples, 1 1/4 inches long*

Floor leveling compound

100-grit sandpaper

6-inch putty knife

Builder's paper or rosin paper

Utility knife with fresh blades

Masking tape

Carpenter's square with 2-inch-wide legs

Sheet vinyl

Washable marker

Wide brush for cleaning vinyl underside

Vinyl adhesive trowel**

Vinyl adhesive**

Clean rags

Rented floor roller

Mineral spirits

* If needed; see Steps 1–5.

**Use products recommended by the vinyl manufacturer.

1 Remove the baseboards (see page 364), the existing flooring, and the underlayment if it is being replaced. (If not, skip to Step 6.) Carefully remove any debris or old adhesive from the surface of the subfloor.

2 Put on the kneepads. Using the steel tape, measure the room. Make a sketch showing the dimensions.

LOWE'S QUICK TIP
Plan to run vinyl in the direction that will make seams unnecessary. In the small bathroom shown here, standard 6-foot-wide vinyl was run the length of the room for a seamless fit.

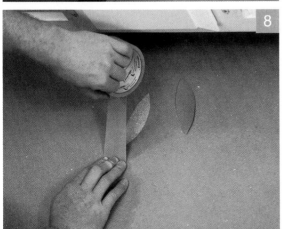

3 Based on your sketch, determine how to install the underlayment with the fewest possible cuts. Plan to leave gaps of $\frac{1}{32}$ inch between panels and $\frac{1}{8}$ inch at the walls to allow for expansion. Measure and mark the pieces; cut using the circular saw.

4 If necessary, trim door casings with a jamb saw to accommodate the underlayment.

5 With the staple gun and $1\frac{1}{4}$-inch staples, attach the underlayment to the subfloor. Space the staples every 3 inches along the outer edges and the seams, every 6 inches in the panel interiors.

6 Mix the floor leveling compound according to the manufacturer's instructions. Using the 6-inch putty knife, fill the small depressions at the underlayment seams and any gaps at the edges. Allow to dry; sand smooth.

7 You will probably need to overlap long pieces of pattern material (the builder's paper or rosin paper) to get the width you need. Do not tape the pieces together; just overlap them down the length of the room. If your heating/cooling register is in the floor, remove it before covering it with the pattern. Using the utility knife, cut the paper around the perimeter to within 2 inches of the edges (this distance need not be exact, as long as it's less than 2 inches).

8 To keep the pattern from slipping, make small cutouts in the paper every 4 feet and anchor the paper to the underlayment through the cutouts, using masking tape.

project continues >

sheet vinyl floor

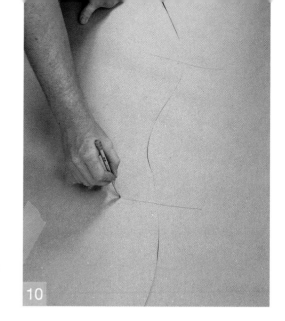

9 Where the pattern pieces overlap down the center, cut a long, wavy line through both layers at once. Lift the layers carefully and remove the scraps. Lay the pattern pieces down again so they fit together perfectly.

10 Mark a pencil line across the wavy cut every 18 inches so you will be able to align the pieces on the vinyl for cutting.

11 Check that the pattern is firmly anchored to the floor through the cutouts. With one leg of the carpenter's square against the wall (a shower enclosure is shown in this photo), draw along the *inner* edge of the leg onto the pattern, as shown. Work your way around the room to mark the entire pattern, making sure it does not shift. If there is a heating/cooling register in the floor, carefully mark the opening on the pattern. Remove the pattern and roll it up.

12 Lay the vinyl face up on a clean, hard surface, such as a smooth patio, deck, or garage floor. (An outdoor surface must be shaded; never lay vinyl in the sun to cut it.) Position your pattern on the vinyl, making sure the wavy edges and the marks you made in Step 10 line up; anchor the pattern to the vinyl using tape over the cutouts. With the carpenter's square positioned as shown in the photo and drawing, align its *outer* edge precisely on the line marked in Step 11. Using a washable marker, mark the vinyl along the *inner* edge of the carpenter's square to create an accurate cutting line. Double-check to make sure you are marking the cutting line correctly—otherwise the entire sheet of vinyl will be ruined.

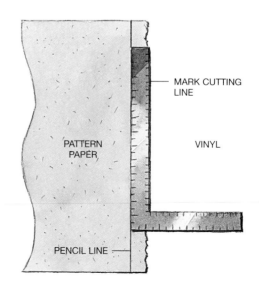

MARK CUTTING LINE

VINYL

PATTERN PAPER

PENCIL LINE

13 Using the carpenter's square and the utility knife, cut along the lines you have marked on the vinyl, including lines for the heating/cooling register, if any. Be careful not to ruin the blade by cutting into the surface underneath.

14 With the aid of a helper, turn the vinyl over and clean the underside thoroughly with the wide brush.

LOWE'S QUICK TIP
Be sure not to cut the vinyl on the pencil lines you drew at the edge of your pattern paper. Draw the actual cutting line on the vinyl 2 inches outside those lines.

15 Place a scrap of vinyl on the underlayment, up against each door casing. If the vinyl doesn't slide underneath easily, trim the casing with the jamb saw.

16 Vacuum the underlayment thoroughly. Lay out the vinyl on the underlayment to make sure it fits perfectly; trim if needed.

17 Lift up about half of the vinyl and loosely fold it over on itself. Do *not* crease the vinyl. Using the adhesive trowel and following the manufacturer's instructions, apply a thin layer of adhesive to the exposed underlayment. Be conservative: the most common mistake is to apply too much adhesive. Use a clean, wet rag to clean up any excess adhesive on the floor or adjacent surfaces.

18 Allow the adhesive to set up according to the manufacturer's instructions. When it is ready, carefully unfold the vinyl over the adhesive, making sure it is perfectly positioned.

19 Fold back the rest of the vinyl onto the just-laid portion and apply adhesive to the underlayment. Let the adhesive set up and then adhere the remainder of the vinyl.

20 Use the hand roller to work out any air bubbles. Clean up any dried adhesive with mineral spirits and a rag. Avoid walking on the vinyl for 24 hours. Reinstall the baseboards.

ceramic tile floor

THIS PROJECT INVOLVES TWO PHASES: FIRST INSTALLING CEMENT BACKERBOARD underlayment, then laying the tile. Backerboard comes in 3- by 5-foot sheets that weigh approximately 50 pounds each, so you'll want help moving them. For most tile, ½-inch-thick backerboard is adequate.

To ensure the sturdiest tile installation, lay the backerboard in the same direction as the floor joists. Dry-fit and cut all the sheets before mixing the thinset.

Layout is the key to a successful tiling project. Plan to use full-size tiles in the most visible area of the room, with the cut pieces at the perimeter. Keep your plan simple, especially if this is your first tile project. Lay the tiles square with the walls, rather than on the diagonal.

1 Use a stud finder to locate the floor joists and snap a chalk line (see page 378) over each joist to mark its location. Plan so that none of the backerboard seams will fall directly over a joist.

2 Do a rough sketch to plan the layout of the backerboard sheets, staggering them as in a brick-laying pattern. Leave a ¼-inch gap at the walls, ⅛ inch between sheets.

3 Measure and mark where each sheet must be cut. Place the carpenter's square securely on the cutting line; use the utility knife to score the line several times, making sure the blade penetrates the material.

4 Kneel on the backerboard with your knees at the scored line and lift the edge until the piece snaps. Use the utility knife to complete the cut on the back side. Repeat to cut the other sheets to size.

5 Carefully sweep the subfloor to remove all debris.

6 Wearing disposable gloves, mix mortar in a bucket. Use the notched trowel to spread it on a section of the subfloor where a whole piece of backerboard will go.

7 Carefully lay the backerboard in the mortar bed. Use the level to make sure the board is flat, checking in several places in each direction. If it's low in one corner, shore it up with a little more mortar.

8 Screw the sheet into the subfloor, following the backerboard manufacturer's recommendation for spacing the backerboard screws and countersinking the screw heads.

9 Once all the pieces have been installed, tape the seams with fiberglass mesh tape. Go over the seams with mortar, using the flat edge of the notched trowel to skim the surface as smooth as possible.

10 Allow the mortar to dry completely, 24 to 48 hours.

11 Using a vacuum cleaner or broom and dustpan, thoroughly clean the underlayment and your work area.

project continues >

LOWE'S QUICK TIP

You can lay other types of rigid tile—such as cut stone—by the method shown here. A wet saw will cut all types of tile, or ask your Lowe's sales associate for the right kind of cutter for your tile. If you rent a wet saw from an equipment-rental store, take the time you need to learn to use it. When you buy your tile, ask for some broken pieces on which to practice making cuts.

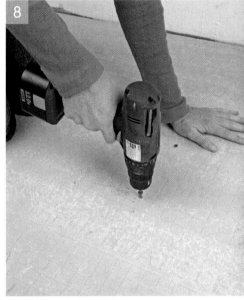

ceramic tile floor

ADDITIONAL TILING MATERIALS

Ceramic tiles*

Spacers**

1 by 2 wood strip with one factory-cut edge, to use as starter strip

Cement screws

Safety glasses

Margin trowel

Rubber mallet

Wax pencil

Tile snap cutter or wet saw (see tip, page 385)

Clean rags

Grout saw

Premixed sanded grout with latex additive

Buckets

Drill paddle attachment

Grout float

Tile sponge

Grout sealer

Silicone acrylic caulk

Caulking gun

*Bring your floor dimensions to Lowe's to have a sales associate help you estimate the amount you need.

**Use the size that gives you the grout width you want.

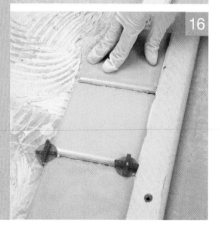

12 To find the center of the room, divide width and length measurements by 2 and mark the midpoint on each of the four walls. Snap two chalk lines (see page 378) connecting the corresponding midpoints across the room; where they intersect is the center of the room. The intersecting lines should form perfect 90-degree angles.

13 Dry-fit an entire row of tiles, including spacers, working in both directions from the center of the room to the walls. Ideally, the tile will fit perfectly; in reality, you'll probably need to cut tiles to fit at the edges. Adjust the layout as necessary so the cut tiles will be at least half the width of a full tile and about the same width on each end of the row; you may need to use one less tile and shift your center point to the left or right. Measure how far the tiles have to shift and snap a new chalk line for the starting point.

14 Align the factory-cut edge of your starter strip with the chalk line at the starting point in the center of the room. Temporarily screw the strip into the underlayment using the drill and cement screws. This strip becomes your guideline; butting the tiles against it will make your first row even, which should ensure that the whole floor will be in alignment.

15 Wearing disposable gloves and using the margin trowel, spread mortar over a 3-foot-square section of underlayment, beginning at the starter strip. Comb the mortar with the notched trowel, holding it at a 45-degree angle and combing in swoops and curves. Comb out any globs.

16 Once the section is completely combed out, set the first tile in the mortar and press it in place with a slight jiggling motion, butting it against the starter strip and aligning the adjacent edge with the chalk line. Set the neighboring tile in the same manner, using spacers along all edges to keep the tiles aligned and the eventual grout lines consistent.

LOWE'S | QUICK TIP
As you set the tile, mortar will ooze out between the joints. Use the blade of a utility knife to clean out these joints. Wipe off any mortar that gets on the face of the tile with a damp rag.

17 Continue setting tiles. Regularly check with the level to make sure the surfaces are even. If a tile sits too high, gently tap it down with the rubber mallet.

18 For edge tiles that need to be cut, measure the distance from the last full tile to the wall. Factor in the spacer width and mark the cutting line on the tile with a wax pencil.

19 Cut the tiles on the wet saw, or use the snap cutter by aligning the marked line under the blade, scoring the tile several times, and then pressing down on the handle to make the snap.

20 If mortar doesn't extend all the way to the wall, you'll need to "butter" the backs of cut tiles. Apply and comb out the mortar on the tile back just as you would on the floor. Set the tile with the cut edge against the wall.

21 Remove the starter strip. Continue setting tile, using spacers to keep the tiles aligned and checking frequently for level. Once all tile has been set, let it dry overnight without walking on it. Then remove the spacers and inspect the joints between the tiles. If mortar has oozed up to the level of the tile surface and dried, remove it with a hand-held grout saw; simply pull the serrated edge of the saw along the grout lines. Vacuum up the debris.

22 Using the drill with paddle attachment, mix the grout according to the manufacturer's instructions. It should be the consistency of smooth peanut butter and should not slide off the trowel.

23 Scoop out some grout with the float and, holding the float at a slight angle, push the grout into the joints. Work across the surface in several directions, packing the grout as firmly as possible until it is flush with the tile surface.

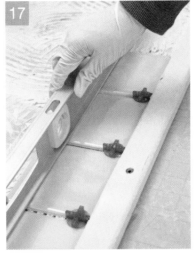

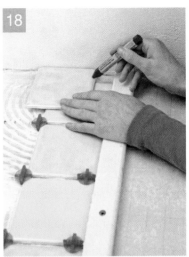

24 Moisten the tile sponge in a bucket of water and wring it nearly dry. Wipe away excess grout from the tile surface in a circular motion, being careful not to disturb the grout in the joints. Continue wiping the surface until the haze is gone, rinsing the sponge as needed. Allow the grout to cure at least 48 hours.

25 Apply the grout sealer after waiting as long as recommended by the manufacturer.

26 Caulk the edges of the floor with the silicone acrylic caulk.

painted-squares floor

MATERIALS

Trisodium phosphate
(or no-rinse, premixed
TSP substitute)

Painter's tape

Latex primer

2- or 3-inch synthetic-
bristle paintbrush

Standard paint roller
frame with 9-inch,
low-nap roller cover*

Roller extension handle

Latex paint for base
coat**

12-inch vinyl floor tiles
for templates

180-grit sandpaper

4-inch paint roller frame
with low-nap roller
cover*

Latex paint in several
colors**

Polyurethane

*¹⁄₄ or ³⁄₈ inch

**Satin finish

YOU CAN PAINT this floor on either plywood or oriented strand board subflooring. If the joints are uneven, use floor leveling compound to smooth them. Be sure to sand the surface before you prime it, and countersink nails or screws, if needed.

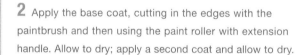

1 Wash the floor with trisodium phosphate. Tape off the baseboards with painter's tape. To prime the floor, cut in the edges with the paintbrush and then use the roller with extension handle, starting at one end of the room.

2 Apply the base coat, cutting in the edges with the paintbrush and then using the paint roller with extension handle. Allow to dry; apply a second coat and allow to dry.

3 Scatter tiles on the floor to create the pattern you want, varying their angles and the spacing between them.

4 Tape around each tile to form a square. Remove the tiles.

5 Lightly sand inside each taped-off square; wipe clean. Using the 4-inch roller and varying the colors, paint each square; allow to dry. Apply a second coat; allow to dry. Lighter colors may require a third coat.

6 When the paint is dry to the touch, remove the tape around the squares. Apply a coat of polyurethane over the entire surface; allow to dry. Apply a second coat; allow to dry. Remove the tape from the baseboards.

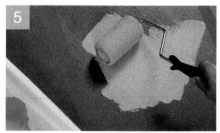

tumbled stone vanity

TILE

MATERIALS

- Thinset mortar
- Square-notched trowel
- Notched margin trowel
- Kraft paper
- Blue painter's tape
- Brown paper painter's tape
- Trisodium phosphate (or no-rinse, premixed TSP substitute)
- 60-grit sandpaper
- Steel tape measure
- 1 by 2 strip equal in length to the vanity width
- 4-inch tumbled stone tiles and 4- by 12-inch mosaic trim pieces
- Wedge spacers
- Metal straightedge
- 2-foot carpenter's square
- Small carpenter's square
- Eye and ear protection
- Heavyweight rubber gloves
- Wet saw
- Tile nippers
- Carpenter's level
- Grit rubbing stone
- Sanded grout
- Grout float
- Tile sponge
- Stone sealer
- Grout sealer

TILING OVER EXISTING TILE IS A REAL TIME-SAVER; SEE STEP 3 TO DETERMINE if you must rough up the surface so that it will accept new tile. Because "nipped" tiles have uneven edges, this project is suitable only for a vanity with self-rimming sinks. You'll need to rent a wet saw to make the cuts; be sure to ask for instructions for using it. For the backsplash, you will probably need to cut the mosaic trim pieces to turn each corner; check your measurements carefully before cutting.

1 Remove sinks and fixtures. If pieces of tile come loose or break off, mix a small batch of mortar and, using the straight edge of the square-notched trowel, fill the voids to the level of the existing tile. Allow to dry overnight.

2 Attach kraft paper to the front of the cabinets below the area you plan to cover with tile, using painter's tape.

3 Wash the existing surface with trisodium phosphate; allow to dry. Mix a small batch of mortar and comb on a little bit using the square-notched trowel; allow to dry overnight.

If the mortar adheres to the surface, you can proceed (chip off the test mortar). If the mortar comes off easily, use sandpaper to roughen the entire surface.

4 Using the steel tape and a pencil or marker, measure and mark the midpoint along the front of the vanity.

5 Determine whether to center a tile on the midpoint or to set tiles on either side of it, as was done here. The goal is to have the cut pieces at each end be as large as possible.

project continues >

tumbled stone vanity

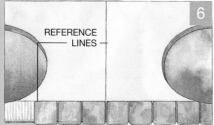

REFERENCE LINES →

MIDPOINT ▲

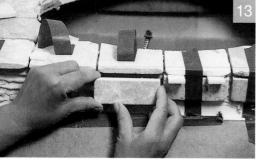

6 The first row of counter tile must overhang the front edge a distance equal to the thickness of the tile. To mark a horizontal reference line, hold a tile against the face of the cabinet, its top edge even with the upper edge of the counter. Lay another tile on the counter so its front edge is flush with the surface of the face tile. Mark the counter at the back edge of the top tile; measure from this point to the front edge of the vanity and use this measurement to draw a reference line on the counter parallel to the front edge. With the carpenter's square, also draw a reference line from the midpoint marked in Step 4 to the back of the countertop.

7 Using the two reference lines as guides, lay out as many full tiles as possible on the counter, adding wedge spacers (thin edge down) between tiles. Where a tile extends into a sink opening, mark the curve.

8 Wearing eye and ear protection and gloves, use the wet saw to cut the tiles that go around the sinks, making straight cuts ⅛ inch apart toward the marked curve. Using the tile nippers, break off the slivers of stone. Nip away at the remaining stone all the way to the marked curve. Don't be concerned about perfect edges; the sink rim will cover the cuts.

9 With the tiles arranged as desired on the countertop, number the back of each tile and make a numbered sketch of your layout. Load the square-notched trowel with mortar and turn it upside down. If the mortar adheres to the trowel and does not sag, it's ready to spread. Holding the straight edge of the trowel at a 30-degree angle, spread mortar for the first row, starting at the midpoint and working toward one end. Use the narrow notched edge of the trowel to comb the mortar toward the front.

10 Set the first row of tile according to your layout plan, starting at the midpoint and working toward the ends. Align the back edges of the tiles with the reference line and place spacers between the tiles. Use the carpenter's level to check the surface; if it's not level, pry up the offending tiles, scrape off or add a little mortar, and reset. Measure, mark, and cut the last piece at each end to fit. Set in place.

11 Set the remaining rows from front to back, using wedge spacers between tiles and rows and cutting pieces to fit as needed at the ends and at the back edge.

12 Determine the ideal measurement for the face tiles, based on the design of your cabinet front. Measure, mark, and cut the tiles. Smooth the just-cut edges with the grit rubbing stone, rounding them to match the tumbled edges.

13 Using the 60-grit sandpaper, roughen the cabinet front where the face tile will be set. Spread and comb mortar horizontally using the margin trowel. Set the face tiles directly under the counter tiles, cut edges down. Insert spacers between counter and face tiles as shown; use painter's tape to keep the pieces from sagging. Cut end pieces to fit; set. Use a level to make sure the face tiles are straight up and down, not tilted in or out; adjust while the mortar is still wet.

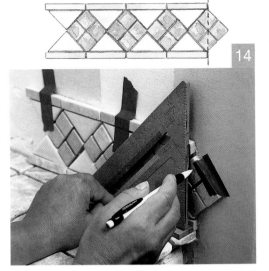

14 Start the mosaic trim at the most conspicuous end of the vanity. With these trim pieces, you need to cut off the projecting portion of the first piece. Rest a trim piece on the counter tile against the wall, aligning the lower edge of the trim with the outer edge of the counter tile. Insert a spacer under the trim piece near each end. Tape the upper edge to the wall to secure. Using the small carpenter's square, mark a cutting line as shown at left; cut the trim piece with the wet saw.

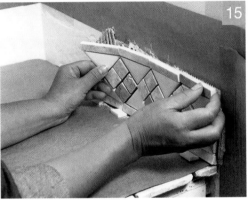

15 Lightly pencil a line on the wall at the upper edge of the trim piece, using the carpenter's level. Lay kraft paper on the counter and fasten brown paper painter's tape to the wall above the line. Comb mortar vertically onto the wall; set the first trim piece, with spacers underneath. Check the upper edge with the level. Insert spacers as needed to keep the mosaic pieces from sagging.

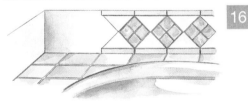

16 To make the backsplash design flow smoothly around a corner, measure from the end of the last complete trim piece to the corner. Subtract the width of the grout line and the thickness of a trim piece to arrive at the cut length needed for the next piece. Measure and mark the piece for cutting; double-check your measurement to avoid a cutting error. Cut the piece on the wet saw; set the leftover portion aside.

17 Comb mortar onto the wall and set the cut piece with spacers underneath; check for level along the upper edge. Set the leftover portion on the adjoining wall, positioning it away from the corner the same distance as the previous piece.

18 Finish setting the backsplash, cutting the final piece as needed.

19 Remove the tape supporting the tiles on the front of the cabinet. Mix the grout according to the manufacturer's instructions. It should be the consistency of smooth peanut butter and should not slide off the trowel.

20 Scoop out some grout with the float and, holding the float at a slight angle, push grout into the joints on the counter and backsplash. Work in several directions, packing the grout as firmly as possible until it's flush with the tile surface. Use a gloved fingertip to work grout into and between the trim pieces.

21 Moisten the tile sponge and wring it nearly dry. Wipe away any grout on the tile surface, working in a circular motion and being careful not to disturb the grout in the joints. Continue wiping until the haze is gone, rinsing your sponge as needed. Allow the grout to cure at least 48 hours.

22 Apply stone and grout sealers according to the manufacturer's instructions. Allow to dry; remove the remaining tape and kraft paper.

LOWE'S QUICK TIP

Before setting mosaic trim pieces, cut away the backing mesh $1/16$ inch in from the edges. It's next to impossible to cut it away once the piece is mortared in place.

ceramic tile backsplash

MATERIALS

80-grit sandpaper

Standard, surface
   bullnose, and radius
   bullnose ceramic
   wall tiles

Tile spacers*

Carpenter's level

Steel tape measure

Tile snap cutter

Kraft paper

Masking tape

Notched trowel

Mastic

Rubber gloves

Grout

Grout float

Tile sponge

Grout sealer

*Use the size that gives
you the grout width you
want.

THIS SIMPLE BACKSPLASH CONSISTS OF TWO ROWS OF 4- BY 4-INCH CERAMIC TILES.
The bottom row is made up of standard glazed wall tile. The tile in the top row, which
has one rounded edge, is known as surface bullnose tile. A surface bullnose tile also
finishes each end of the bottom row, while a radius bullnose tile, with adjacent rounded
edges, goes at each end of the top row.

1 Ceramic tiles do not bond well with paint. If
your wall is painted, sand the paint off the area
you plan to tile.

2 Set a pair of tile spacers on the countertop
against the wall to be tiled and place a standard
tile on them. Place another pair of spacers on
top of the tile, followed by a bullnose tile with its
rounded edge up. Mark a pencil line on the wall
along the bullnose edge.

3 Using the carpenter's level, extend the pencil
line for the entire length to be tiled. Measure and
mark its midpoint with a vertical line across the
level line.

4 Starting at the midpoint mark, lay out a row of
tiles horizontally along the wall, placing a spacer
between each pair of tiles. The space at each end
of the row should be at least half the width of a
tile; if it's less, adjust the starting point so the end
tiles will be at least one-half a tile's width (you'll
use one less whole tile in the row).

5 Once you're satisfied with your layout, mark
cutting lines on the bullnose tiles for the row ends.

6 When you cut the surface bullnose tiles, pay
careful attention that you keep the rounded edge
on the *outside* and cut off the opposite edge. On
the radius bullnose tiles, the rounded edges go
on the *top* and *outside*. Position a tile on the
base of the tile cutter so the cutting line is directly
under the scoring wheel. Pull the scoring wheel
across the tile and then push down on the handle
to snap the tile.

> **LOWE'S QUICK TIP**
> Take the time to plan
> your layout carefully.
> It's much easier to make
> adjustments during a
> dry run than it is after
> pressing your tiles into
> fresh mastic.

7 With masking tape, tape a sheet of kraft paper to the countertop to protect it from mastic. Using the notched trowel and working from the midpoint to one end, spread mastic on the wall between the countertop and up to, but not covering, the level line for the tile tops. Apply the adhesive carefully so that the level line remains visible. Angle the trowel at 45 degrees and sweep it across the wall to create ridges of adhesive.

8 Starting at the midpoint, set a pair of tile spacers on the countertop. Wearing rubber gloves, set a standard tile in place on the spacers, aligning one edge with the midpoint line. Use spacers to install the remaining tiles for half of the first row, ending with the surface bullnose tile you cut in Step 6.

9 In the same way, install surface bullnose tiles in the second row, inserting spacers between tiles and aligning the bullnose edges with the level line. At the end, set the radius bullnose tile cut in Step 6 with its rounded edges at the top and the outside.

10 Spread adhesive on the other side of the midpoint line and install the rest of the tiles. Allow the adhesive to set up for the length of time recommended by the manufacturer.

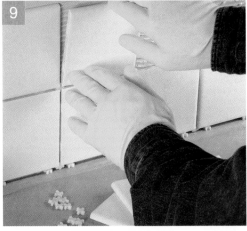

11 Remove spacers. Mix the grout according to the manufacturer's instructions. Using the grout float, spread grout across the tile, holding the float at a slight angle to push grout into the joints. Work in several directions, packing the grout as firmly as possible until it's flush with the tile surface. Scrape off excess grout with the straight edge of the float.

12 Moisten the tile sponge and wring it nearly dry. Wipe away grout from the tile faces in a circular motion, being careful not to disturb the grout in the joints. Continue wiping until the haze is gone, rinsing your sponge as needed. Allow the grout to cure for at least 48 hours.

13 Brush grout sealer onto the joints.

tile counter

MATERIALS

Eye and ear protection

⅝-inch chisel

Hammer

Nailset

Electric sander with 80-grit sandpaper

Utility knife

Metal straightedge

Ceramic tile backerboard and screws

Electric drill with combination countersink–pilot hole drill bit

Thinset mortar

¼- by ⅜-inch square-notched trowel

Disposable and heavyweight rubber gloves

Graph paper

Granite tiles, 12 by 12 inches

Painter's tape

Wet saw

Steel tape measure

Tile spacers*

Carpenter's level

Silicone sealant

Polyurethane

Grout and sanded caulk (see "Grout Basics," facing page)

Caulking gun

Grout float

Tile sponge

Granite sealer

Grout sealer

*Use the size that gives you the grout width you want.

SETTING TILE IS A GREAT DO-IT-YOURSELF PROJECT. HERE WE SHOW GRANITE TILE, a less expensive alternive to granite slab, but the technique can be used for any rigid tile, including smaller sizes. The steps that follow are for a kitchen island; you can use the same method for a sink counter and a backsplash (do the backsplash last).

To cut tiles to fit your counter, rent a wet saw from an equipment-rental store. Take the time you need to learn to use it. When you buy your tile, ask for some chipped or broken pieces on which to practice making cuts.

For a counter with a sink or drop-in stove, remove the sink or stovetop before planning your layout and installing the tile.

1 Wearing eye protection, use the chisel and hammer to crack the existing tile surface, starting in the center of a tile.

2 Slide the chisel under the tile, lifting the pieces and removing the adhesive down to the underlayment. Remove all tiles in this manner.

3 To remove wood trim, place a scrap of wood at one inside corner and tap with the hammer to loosen the joint. Tap the trim piece at 1-foot increments, easing it away from the counter at a consistent distance to prevent splitting. Label each piece for reinstallation later.

4 With the electric sander and 80-grit sandpaper, remove the remaining adhesive to level the underlayment surface.

5 Using the metal straightedge and utility knife, measure and cut the backerboard to fit the counter. Predrill holes in the backerboard where marked by the manufacturer, using the combination countersink–pilot hole drill bit.

6 Prepare the mortar according to the manufacturer's instructions. Holding the wide-notched side of the trowel at a 30-degree angle, spread the mortar, creating ridges approximately two-thirds the depth of the notches.

7 With a helper, set the backerboard in place, pushing it down with medium pressure.

8 Screw the backerboard in place through the predrilled holes and into the counter, countersinking the screws.

GROUT BASICS

For grout lines up to $\frac{1}{8}$ inch wide, use unsanded grout; for grout lines wider than that, use sanded grout. (Sand adds stability, but in narrow joints sanded grout does not pack as well as unsanded grout.) Where tile meets a different surface, such as the wood trim on this island, use sanded caulk in the joints.

To minimize small differences in the width of grout lines, choose a grout color that matches your granite.

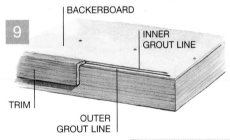

BACKERBOARD

INNER GROUT LINE

TRIM

OUTER GROUT LINE

9 With a trim piece held against the counter, draw a line on the backerboard to indicate an outer grout line. Set the trim piece aside. At the desired grout width ($\frac{1}{8}$ inch on this project), draw the inner grout line.

10 A standard approach to setting tile on a rectangular counter that's not interrupted by a sink or a stovetop is to use a whole tile in each corner, then adjust the sizes of the remaining tiles. On graph paper, draw the countertop to scale and sketch your tile layout, allowing for the grout lines between tiles and around the edges. Number the tiles in your drawing and include directional arrows for grain line or pattern, if your tile has either. Label each tile to be cut with a piece of painter's tape marked with its number and a directional arrow.

Whole tiles are shaded; the others were cut to fit.

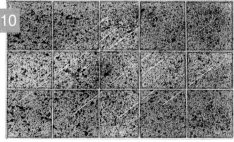

project continues >

tile counter

11 Gather the tools you need to cut the tile with the wet saw: heavyweight gloves, eye and ear protection, and a steel tape measure. Set the wet saw's fence (the piece that guides the tile during cutting) to the desired tile width, as indicated on the measurement bar. Use the steel tape to check the bar's accuracy; if the measurement on the bar is not correct, you'll need to adjust the fence.

12 Remove the tape label from your first tile. With the finished side of the granite facing up, cut the tile. (Cutting on this side minimizes chipping.) Don't force the tile; if sparks fly, you are pushing too hard. Use a gentle touch and allow the blade to grind through the tile.

13 When you're finished cutting the tile, reposition the tape with the arrow correctly oriented. Cut the remaining tiles, returning their labels immediately after cutting.

14 Before you begin the actual installation, dry-fit the tiles on the counter, using tile spacers where corners meet to ensure right angles. Check the tile locations against your drawing. Recut tiles if necessary for an accurate fit. Remove the tiles.

15 Apply mortar to the backerboard as you did to the counter underlayment, stopping at the inner grout line you marked in Step 9. As before, the ridges should be two-thirds the depth of the trowel notches.

16 Place an end tile along the inner grout line. Set the tile straight down, parallel to the surface. Place spacers at the corners.

ANGLED CUTS

You can make angled cuts for mitered corners by tilting the blade on the wet saw; hold the tile against the fence as you would for any other cut.

17 Set the next tile, aligning it with the first one and fitting it snugly against the spacers. Check the surface with a carpenter's level and adjust the tiles if necessary.

18 Continue laying the tiles in your prearranged pattern, adding spacers between tiles and checking your work with the carpenter's level. Allow the mortar to set up for 24 hours.

19 Refinish the counter trim as desired, sanding it and resealing it with several coats of polyurethane to protect it from moisture. Allow to dry after each coat.

20 Attach the trim. If it was originally secured with finishing nails, nail through the existing holes, countersinking the nails with the nailset. Before you apply grout, tape off the trim with painter's tape.

21 Mix the grout according to the manufacturer's instructions. (Remember to use sanded caulk instead of grout where tile meets wood trim.) The grout should be the consistency of smooth peanut butter and should not slide off the trowel.

LOWE'S QUICK TIP
Tiles come with a tiny bevel on their edges. When you trim tiles, the cut edges won't have these bevels. As a result, you'll see that the grout lines between cut tiles appear narrower than those between uncut tiles—but these differences won't be noticeable once all the tile is set and grouted.

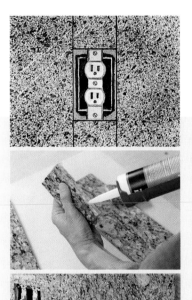

TILING AROUND A RECEPTACLE

Turn off the power to the room at the circuit breaker or fuse box while you remove the receptacle cover or switch plate. Carefully measure to determine the dimensions of the tile pieces to be cut. The pieces plus the opening must add up to the dimensions of one tile. Cut the tile.

Working on a slick surface such as a sheet of plastic, apply silicone sealant to the cut edges. Press the pieces together and attach the entire unit to the wall with mortar, just as you would attach a whole tile.

22 Scoop out some grout with the float and, holding the float at a slight angle, push the grout into the joints. Work in several directions, packing the grout as firmly as possible until it is flush with the tile surface.

23 Moisten the tile sponge and wring it nearly dry. Wipe away any grout from the tile surface, working in a circular motion and being careful not to disturb the grout in the joints. Wipe until the haze is gone, rinsing your sponge as needed. Allow the grout to cure at least 48 hours.

24 Apply granite and grout sealer according to the manufacturer's instructions. Allow to dry; remove the tape.

color-block curtain

MATERIALS

Steel tape measure

Scissors

Transparent tape

Tear-away stabilizer,*
   equal to the finished
   curtain size plus
   2 inches on each edge

Cardboard cutting board
   with 1-inch grid*

6- by 24-inch acrylic
   rotary ruler, rotary
   cutter, and cutting mat*

Cotton fabrics

Thread to blend with
   the fabrics

4-ml clear vinyl, 54 inches
   wide, twice the length
   of the curtain plus
   ¼ yard*

Clear-drying fabric glue

Pins

Sewing machine

Walking foot for sewing
   machine (optional)

Size 16 jeans needle for
   sewing machine

Clip-on curtain rings, one
   more than the number
   of squares across

Tension curtain rod

*Available at craft and
fabric stores. Stabilizer is
only 22 inches wide, so
you'll need to tape pieces
together.*

THIS EASY-TO-MAKE CURTAIN PANEL SANDWICHES COLORFUL SQUARES OF FABRIC between two layers of clear, lightweight vinyl. A walking foot for your sewing machine is helpful but not necessary. Use a shorter-than-average stitch length to make it easier to tear away the stabilizer foundation material and to keep the threads from raveling at the edges.

1 Measure the width of your window opening with the steel tape. Decide how many squares you want across and divide the window width by that number to determine the size of the grid squares. Decide how many squares long you want the curtain to be.

2 Cut and tape together pieces of stabilizer to equal the finished curtain size plus 2 inches on each edge. Tape the stabilizer to your cardboard cutting board. Directly on the stabilizer, using the rotary ruler, measure and draw a grid with the desired number of squares across and down (use the grid-square size from Step 1).

3 Using the rotary ruler, cutter, and cutting mat, cut your fabrics into the number of squares you need, making each one ¼ inch smaller than the grid squares drawn on the stabilizer. For example, if the grid squares are 5¼ inches, the fabric squares should be 5 inches. (The squares in the photo are 5 inches.)

4 Using scissors, cut the vinyl into two equal pieces, each several inches larger than the grid you drew in Step 2. Lay one of the pieces on top of the grid so its edges extend beyond the grid's outer lines. Tape the vinyl to the cutting board at each corner.

5 Arrange the fabric squares in a pleasing pattern on top of the vinyl on the grid. Put a tiny dot of fabric glue on the wrong side of each square at each top corner; center the fabric square in its grid square and apply a little pressure to attach it.

6 Carefully lay the second piece of vinyl on top of the fabric squares. Pin through the layers at each grid-line intersection.

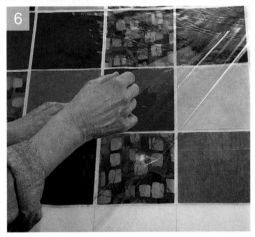

7 Attach the walking foot, if you have one, and install the jeans needle. Carefully remove the pinned unit from the cutting board and stitch on the vertical grid lines. Be sure you're stitching through all layers (stabilizer and both vinyl pieces); remove pins just before you reach them. Start and stop ¼ inch beyond the outermost grid lines. Repeat on the horizontal grid lines.

8 Working from the back, cut a slit in each stabilizer square, *being careful not to cut into the vinyl;* gently tear away the stabilizer, square by square.

9 Using the rotary equipment, carefully trim the curtain ⅛ inch *beyond* the outer stitching lines, cutting through both layers of vinyl.

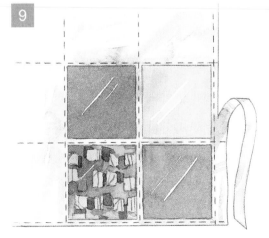

10 Attach a clip-on ring at each vertical line of stitching. Slip the rings onto the tension rod and fit it into the window opening.

curtain panels

MATERIALS

Curtain rod with mounting
   hardware

Clip-on rings to match
   curtain rod, 7 rings
   per panel

Steel tape measure

Home decorating fabric,
   54 inches wide*

Curtain lining fabric, at
   least 48 inches wide*

Fabric scissors

Pins

Thread to blend with
   curtain fabric

Straight yardstick or 6-foot
   metal straightedge

Rotary ruler, mat, and
   cutter**

Fabric marker

Carpenter's level

*You'll need yardage
equal to twice the desired
finished length of your
curtain panels (see Step 1),
plus 1 yard.

**Available at craft and
fabric stores.

LOWE'S QUICK TIP
Choose "home dec"
fabrics, sold at home
decorating stores and
most fabric stores. These
have a looser weave than
garment fabrics, allowing
you to press crisp folds
and stitch flat hems for
your curtains.

LINED, FLAT CURTAIN PANELS ARE A STYLISH WINDOW TREATMENT THAT'S functional too—they provide both privacy and insulation. Making a pair of panels is a
straightforward project, requiring only basic sewing skills. Decorator fabrics are not
meant to be washed, so plan to dry clean your curtains.

1 To determine the desired finished
length of your panels, decide where
you want to mount the rod. (Do not
actually install the hardware at this
point.) Slide several rings onto the rod
and have two helpers hold the rod up
where you want it. (In this room, the
rod was installed near the ceiling, but
you could position it just above the
window casing, or anywhere in between.) Then measure from the middle
of a clip (not a ring) to the floor; add
½ inch, as the fabric may draw up
slightly when folded and stitched.
This is your finished curtain length.

2 Cut a length of curtain fabric equal
to the finished length plus 18 inches;
cut an equal length of lining fabric. Set
aside the remaining fabric and lining
for the second curtain panel.

3 To ensure that the lower edge is
straight, the pros "pull a thread" on
the curtain fabric. Clip into the selvage where you want to begin cutting
across the fabric. Find a crosswise
thread and gently pull it across the
width of the fabric, creating a visible
guideline. Cut along the line.

4 Trim the selvages off both sides, being careful not to stretch the fabric. Along the bottom, measure up 6 inches and mark with pins placed parallel to the lower edge. Turn the fabric up at the pins and press; remove pins. Turn in the raw edge to meet the pressed fold; pin in place.

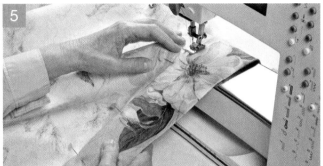

5 With your sewing machine set on a medium-long straight stitch, sew close to the pinned fold, removing the pins as you come to them.

6 Using the yardstick or metal straightedge and rotary equipment, trim the lower edge of the lining straight across, square with the side edges. Measure up 4 inches from the lower edge; make a hem the same way you did on the curtain fabric.

7 Place the curtain panel, right side *down,* on your work surface. Lay the lining, right side *up,* on top, with its lower edge 2 inches above the curtain's lower edge. (At the upper edges, the lining will extend beyond the curtain fabric; you'll trim it later.) Trim the lining so it is 2 inches narrower than the curtain fabric on each side.

8 On one side, fold the curtain fabric in 2 inches and press the fold. Turn the raw edge under ½ inch and pin through all layers, encasing the lining; stitch. Repeat on the other side. Press the side hems.

9 Lay the curtain panel right side up on your work surface. Measure up from the lower edge your desired finished length and mark with pins across the width of the fabric. Measure 6 inches beyond that point and use the fabric marker and yardstick or metal straightedge to mark a line across the fabric. Cut on the line, through both layers.

10 Turn the upper edges down at the pins and press a fold; remove the pins. Turn in the raw edges to meet the pressed fold and pin as you did for the lower hem. Stitch close to the pinned fold, through all layers, removing the pins as you come to them. Press the entire curtain panel. Repeat the steps to make the second panel.

11 Attach the hanging rings to the curtain panels and slide them onto the rod. Place the rod in the brackets and have two helpers hold the rod and brackets in place against the wall so that the lower hem just skims the floor. Use the carpenter's level to ensure that the rod is straight, and mark the hardware placement on the wall through the screw holes. Install the hardware according to the manufacturer's instructions and set the rod in place.

color-block pillow

MATERIALS

20-inch pillow form

¾ yard of muslin for foundation

⅛ yard each of 10 different fabrics, at least 42 inches wide (you'll have enough strips for two pillow fronts)

⅝ yard of coordinating fabric, at least 42 inches wide, for pillow back

Rotary ruler, mat, and cutter*

Scissors

Fine, sharp pins

Invisible monofilament thread

Regular thread in a neutral color for the bobbin

Variegated yarn, approximately 4 yards

*Available at craft and fabric stores. A 6- by 24-inch ruler and a 24- by 36-inch rotary mat are ideal.

LOWE'S QUICK TIP

To keep the fabrics' crisp finish (and to make the strips easy to weave), it is best not to preshrink them and not to wash the finished pillow top.

STRIPS OF BRIGHT FABRIC WEAVE OVER AND UNDER TO FORM THE FRONT OF THIS casual, colorful, easy-to-make pillow. There's no need to finish the raw edges; once woven, the strips are zigzag-stitched to a muslin foundation using invisible thread. Variegated yarn stitched over the vertical seams adds pizzazz; a simple pillowcase opening in back eliminates the need for a zipper or hand-stitched closure.

1 Cut the muslin to a 27-inch square. Use a pencil to draw a 21-inch square centered on the fabric, making sure the corners are true right angles. Measure and mark grid lines as shown in the diagram at right to create placement lines for the strips, continuing the lines an inch or so beyond the square you have drawn. (The strips around the perimeter are wider because they include seam allowances.)

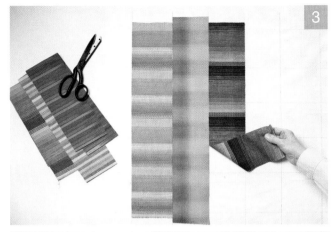

2 Decide which four fabrics you want to place along the edges of the pillow; set the others aside. Lay the first ⅛-yard piece (folded at the center, as it was on the bolt) on your rotary mat. Using the rotary cutter and ruler, carefully cut a 4½-inch-wide strip, cutting from the fold to the selvage. Repeat for the other edge fabrics. Cut 4-inch-wide strips from the remaining fabrics. Using scissors, cut across each strip at the fold to make two strips. Set aside one strip of each fabric for another pillow top.

3 Starting at one side of the square, place a 4½-inch-wide strip on the grid with its ends extending beyond the top and bottom grid lines. Next lay down three 4-inch-wide strips, aligning their edges with the guidelines and the adjoining strips. End with a 4½-inch strip.

4 Pin the strips to the foundation at their upper edges. Fold back the second and fourth strips just above the upper grid line. Place the first horizontal strip (4½ inches wide) as shown at left, aligning its edges with the guidelines.

5 Fold the second and fourth vertical strips back into place on top of the horizontal strip.

LOWE'S QUICK TIP
As you place the horizontal strips, make sure their raw edges touch, leaving no gaps for the muslin to show through.

6 Fold up the first, third, and fifth vertical strips and lay a 4-inch horizontal strip in place, aligning its edges with the guidelines. Bring the vertical strips back down, as in Step 5.

project continues >

color-block pillow

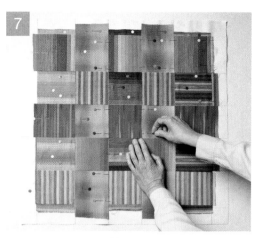

7 Continue to "weave" the strips, ending with a 4½-inch strip at the lower edge. Pin the edges of the vertical strips, placing the pins perpendicular to the raw edges and pinning through all the layers.

8 Thread your sewing machine with the monofilament thread on top and the regular thread in the bobbin. Set the machine to a medium-wide, medium-long zigzag stitch. Stitch the vertical seams, just catching the raw edges and removing the pins as you come to them. Zigzag-stitch the outer edges as well.

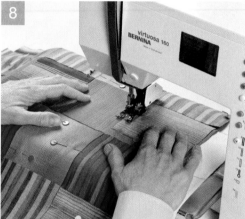

9 Zigzag-stitch the horizontal edges so that all raw edges are anchored. Press the pillow top from the back side.

10 Lay a piece of yarn over the vertical edges where the first two strips meet; zigzag-stitch the yarn to the pillow top. Repeat on the remaining vertical edges (but not the horizontal or outer edges). Trim the pillow top along the 21-inch square you originally marked.

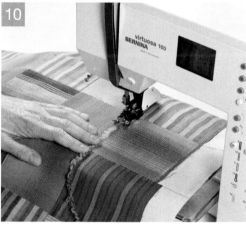

11 Cut two back pieces, each 21 inches by 14 inches. On each piece, turn under one 21-inch edge 1 inch and press. Turn the raw edge in to meet the pressed fold; pin and then stitch. Lay the pillow top, right side up, on your work surface. Lay the two backing pieces, right sides down as shown, with the hemmed edges overlapping. Pin through all layers at the outer edges. Stitch together along the edges using a ⅝-inch seam allowance. Trim the excess fabric from the corners, taking care not to cut into the stitching. Turn the pillow cover right side out and insert the pillow form through the pillowcase opening.

refurbished chair

PAINT, FABRIC, AND A FEW BASIC supplies are all you need to transform a thrift-store chair into a stylish accent piece. Choose a chair with interesting features or frame details—and no missing screws or loose legs. Home decorating fabric is the ideal weight for this project.

MATERIALS

Screwdriver

200-grit sandpaper

Tack cloth or rag

Mini-roller frame with
    4-inch roller cover

2-inch synthetic-bristle
    paintbrush

Latex primer

Latex paint*

Fabric**

Scissors

Staple gun

*Satin finish

**If your fabric has a
dominant pattern,
buy enough to center
major motifs.

1 Unscrew the seat from the chair frame. Set aside the seat and screws.

2 Sand the frame. Wipe up the dust with a tack cloth or damp rag.

3 Use the mini-roller and paintbrush to prime the frame. Allow to dry at least 2 hours and then apply a second coat of primer. Once the primer is dry, sand and wipe again to create a smooth finish for painting.

4 Apply a base coat of paint with the roller and paintbrush. Smooth all surfaces with the paintbrush, using long, straight strokes in one direction. Allow to dry and then apply a second coat (don't sand between coats).

5 Pull the old cover off the chair seat. With the seat resting upside down on the wrong side of your new fabric, mark the outline of the seat with chalk or pencil. (If the fabric has stripes, like the example shown here, make sure they run parallel to an edge; center dominant stripes or, for patterned fabric, any major motifs.) Measure and cut the fabric approximately 2 inches larger than the outline on each edge.

6 Wrap the fabric over one seat edge and secure with a staple. On the opposite edge, pull the fabric taut and staple to secure. Repeat on the remaining two sides, then staple all around the edges, pulling the fabric taut and stopping 2 inches from the corners.

7 Fold the fabric at one corner into a neat finish, smoothing it taut and tucking under the excess. Secure with three or four staples, keeping the folds flat and even; avoid stapling over the screw holes. Repeat for each corner. Once the frame is dry, screw the seat back on.

appliqué lampshade

MATERIALS

Pattern (facing page)

White or off-white lamp-
    shade

Rotary cutting mat or
    thick cardboard

Medium-weight white
    rice paper*

Craft knife

Repositionable spray
    adhesive*

*Available at art and craft
stores

A PLAIN LAMPSHADE TAKES ON A CUSTOM LOOK WITH THE ADDITION OF A STYLIZED rice-paper appliqué that shows up when the lamp is turned on. Before cutting out the design, test a swatch of your rice paper against your lampshade. It should be opaque enough to leave a visible shadow.

1 Enlarge the pattern on a copying machine to a size that will fit your shade. It's all right to trim the tip from a top or bottom petal—a little cropping adds sophistication.

2 Place a sheet of rice paper on the cutting mat or piece of cardboard. Tape the template to the rice paper. Using the craft knife, cut out the flower.

3 Cut out a strip from the middle of every other petal, following the pattern. Turn over the cutout strips, spray with adhesive, and adhere to the uncut petals.

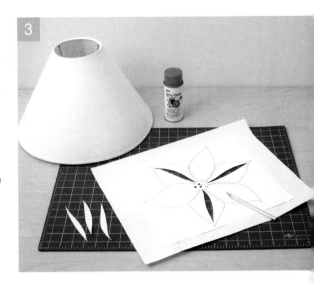

4 Decide where you want to place the flower, avoiding the lampshade seam. Spray adhesive on the flower, covering the entire surface. If the rice paper curls while you are spraying it, hold it down with a chopstick or pencil.

5 Lift the adhesive-coated flower and place it, sticky side down, on the inside of the lampshade liner. (It may help to hold the lampshade upside down on your lap.) Position the center of the flower first, followed by each petal; adjust as needed to avoid overlaps.

6 When the flower is positioned to your liking, press it firmly against the shade to remove air bubbles or wrinkles. Attach the shade to the lamp base.

dollhouse bookcase

MATERIALS

Unfinished wood
  bookcase

Metal straightedge

Spiral saw

Latex primer

2-inch synthetic-bristle
  paintbrush

100-grit sandpaper

White and yellow latex
  paint (satin finish)

Paint tray with disposable
  liners

Wood clamps

Two 1 by 12 pine pieces,
  each equal in length to
  your bookcase width

Circular saw

One sheet of door skin,
  36 by 84 inches

Circle template with
  3- and 2¼-inch circles

30 feet of 2¼- by ⅜-inch
  pine moulding

Electric brad nailer with
  ¾-inch nails

Two decorative wood
  brackets

30 feet of ¾-inch corner
  guard trim*

Four corner brackets
  with screws

Screwdriver

Adjustable miter box

Wood glue

*Have an 18-inch section
cut, then have one edge
of the remaining trim
ripped to ⅜ inch.

SCALLOPED ROOF SLATS AND DECORATIVE BRACKETS DRESS UP THESE SIDE-BY-SIDE bookcases. The yellow one at left features shingles made from door skin (a thin veneer). Wood appliqués decorate the blue-gabled bookcase in the center, while the one at right has a gable covered with pink-painted veneer strips. Instructions follow for the yellow bookcase, purchased unfinished and measuring 30 inches wide, 12 inches deep, and 60 inches tall.

1 Window openings on the side walls (more clearly visible on the blue bookcase) are 3 by 5 inches; doors on each side are 5 by 12 inches. Measure and mark the openings, then cut with the spiral saw.

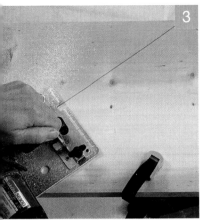

2 Brush primer onto the bookcase; allow to dry and then sand lightly with 100-grit sandpaper. Paint with white latex paint.

3 To make a gable, clamp one of the 1 by 12 pine pieces to your work surface. Measure and mark the midpoint along the upper edge. Mark a line from each lower corner to the upper midpoint, creating a triangle. Using the circular saw, cut on each line, beginning at the corner (discard the two leftover pieces or save for scrap purposes). Repeat to cut the second gable.

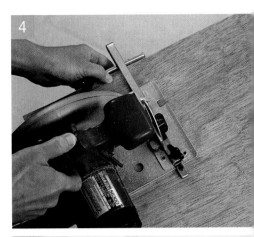

4 On the sheet of door skin, measure and mark three strips 3 inches wide by 84 inches long. Cut along the lines with the circular saw.

5 Mark across each strip every 5 inches to make the gable shingles. Using the circle template, mark a 3-inch semicircle approximately ⅜ inch from one end of each shingle.

6 Clamp a door skin strip to a scrap of wood. (The scrap supports the strip and gives the saw more to cut into.) Cut the first curve with the spiral saw, cutting through both the door skin and the scrap. Unclamp the strip and shift it so the next marked curve extends just beyond the newly cut curve in the scrap. (The curved scrap will support the strip on subsequent cuts.) Cut the next curve, releasing the first shingle. Continue, cutting 38 shingles and a few extras.

7 Clamp a shingle to a scrap of wood that has a straight edge, positioning it so the straight marked line on the shingle is just beyond the straight edge of the wood. Cut on the marked line, creating a shingle with one curved edge and one straight edge. Cut the remaining shingles the same way.

LOWE'S QUICK TIP
To cut out a window opening, tip the spiral saw blade into the delineated area, with the saw blade running. Work your way toward a corner and cut along the marked lines.

8 On the 2¼-inch-wide pieces of moulding, mark 14-inch-long strips for the roof slats (this bookcase required 18 slats). Mark a 2¼-inch semicircle on one end of each strip. Cut the curved lines with the spiral saw and the straight lines with the circular saw.

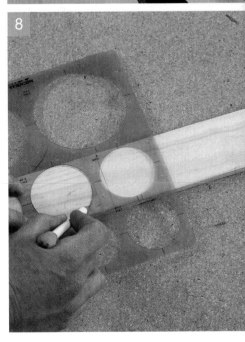

project continues >

dollhouse bookcase

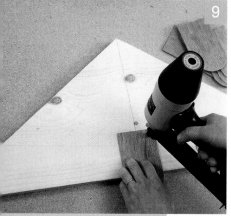

9 Lay one gable on your work surface. Mark a vertical line from the peak to the midpoint on the lower edge. Center a shingle on the line, with its curve overlapping the gable the appropriate distance (see tip at right). Using the brad nailer and ¾-inch nails, attach the shingle to the gable.

LOWE'S QUICK TIP

To keep the curves of the shingles from extending into the bookcase opening, hold the gable on top of the case and position a shingle so it overlaps just far enough to meet the edge of the opening (see photo on page 408). Mark the gable at the upper edge of the shingle and draw a horizontal guideline at that point.

❖

Before you begin nailing the second row, experiment with positioning the rows to determine how much they should overlap.

10 Add shingles to the left of the center and then to the right, overlapping the gable ends.

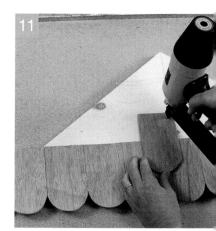

11 Position the first shingle for the second row, placing its right edge at the center line so its curved end is centered over the two shingles below, overlapping their tops. Nail the shingle to the gable. Work to the left, then to the right, as you did on the first row.

12 Position the first shingle for the third row over the center line; nail in place. Work to the left, then to the right.

13 Attach the shingles for the fourth row. Add the top shingle.

14 Turn the gable right side down and clamp it to your work surface so the shingles on one sloped side extend over the edge of the surface. Using the circular saw, trim the shingles flush with the gable side. Do the same thing on the other sloped side.

15 Prime the front of the shingled gable, one side of the plain gable, the roof slats (both faces and all edges), the wood brackets, and the corner guard trim. Let dry, then paint with the yellow latex paint. Allow to dry.

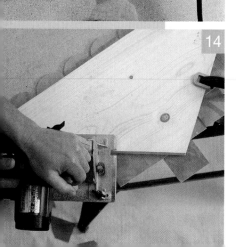

16 On the wrong side of each gable, measure and mark the lower edge into thirds. Attach one arm of a corner bracket at each of the two marks, as shown.

17 Place the plain gable on top of the bookcase, flush with the back edge. Screw the free arm of each corner bracket into the top of the bookcase. Then attach the shingled gable to the front of the case the same way.

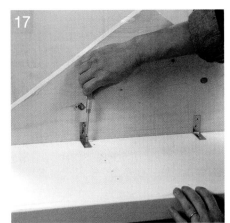

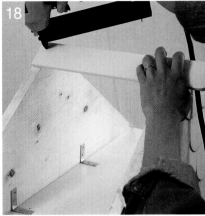

18 Lay a roof slat at the peak of the gables so its straight end is flush with the back gable. Using the brad nailer and ¾-inch nails, attach the slat to both gables.

19 Continue nailing slats to the roof, allowing the last one on each side to hang over the edge.

20 For each window you'll need four ripped trim pieces for the outside and four for the inside. Position a trim piece in the adjustable miter box so the narrower (ripped) edge is standing up, as shown; make the first 45-degree-angle cut. Make the next cut at a distance corresponding to the window measurement.

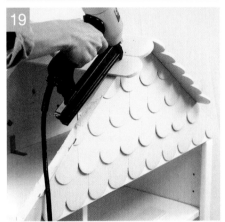

21 Cut a complete set of inside pieces, as shown. Repeat to cut an identical set of outside trim pieces.

22 Run a thin bead of wood glue on the wider edge of one trim piece and attach it to the inside of one of the window openings.

23 Glue the remaining inside trim pieces.

24 Glue the outside trim pieces.

25 Cut inside and outside door trim so the lower ends of the vertical pieces are straight across and flush with the bottom of the door opening; miter the upper ends of these pieces, as well as both ends of the cross pieces. Cut a threshold piece from the trim that hasn't been ripped, cutting each end straight across. Glue in place.

26 Glue the decorative wood brackets to the upper corners of the bookcase.

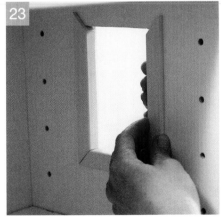

console table

MATERIALS

Two 36-inch table legs

Two 1 by 8 pine pieces, 4 feet long, for tabletop

1 by 4 pine piece, 4 feet long, for hidden support

Two 1 by 2 scraps of wood or medium-density fiberboard (MDF), approximately 12 inches long, for braces

5-inch crown moulding, 8 feet long

Wood glue

Two bar clamps

Steel tape measure

Ten 1½-inch wood screws

Compound miter saw

Electric brad nailer with 1½-inch nails

Electric drill with combination countersink–pilot hole drill bit

Four 3-inch wood screws

Paintable wood putty

2- or 3-inch synthetic-bristle paintbrush

Latex primer

Black latex spray paint*

Sanding sponge

Two 1-inch angle irons

2- or 3-inch chip brush

Antique walnut polyurethane stain

Two ¼-inch drywall hollow wall anchors

Two #8 screws

*Satin finish

THIS STYLISH console table can double as a breakfast bar or a desk in a room where space is at a premium. You need just two legs, for the front; the back of the table attaches to the wall. Standard crown moulding forms the decorative profile. Distressed edges stained a deep walnut color lend an antique look to the piece.

1 Decide which side of each 1 by 8 pine piece will be the top. Apply wood glue to one long edge of one piece; press it against the corresponding edge of the other piece. Use the bar clamps to hold the pieces together tightly.

2 To brace the tabletop, position the 1 by 2 scraps on the underside across the glued seam, making sure they are no closer to the tabletop edges than 1½ inches. Attach them with the 1½-inch wood screws.

3 Mark the underside of the tabletop ¾ inch from the front edge and ½ inch from each side edge as a guide for attaching the crown moulding.

4 The front piece of crown moulding fits between the marks you made along the side edges in Step 3; for this table, that measurement is 47 inches (48−½−½=47). To be safe, measure your tabletop from mark to mark to double-check the exact length.

5 Set the miter table at the bottom of the saw to the right at 31.6 degrees. Set the bevel angle (the top of the saw that tilts left and right) to 33.9 degrees. Tighten down the settings. Place the moulding on the saw with its top edge nearest to you, as shown at right; leave several inches extending beyond the blade. Make the first cut.

6 Measuring from the just-cut end, along *the same (top) edge,* mark the length determined in Step 4. (To make sure to cut in the correct direction, draw the angle on the moulding.)

7 Move the miter table to the left 31.6 degrees; keep the bevel angle set at 33.9 degrees. Tighten down the settings. Position the moulding so the blade will hit just beyond your cut mark; make the cut.

8 With the underside of the table facing up, position the moulding between the ½-inch marks on the side edges, with its front edge on the ¾-inch marks. Brad-nail the edge of the moulding to the underside of the table near each corner and about every 8 inches in between.

9 Measure, mark, and cut the side pieces of moulding, paying careful attention to the angles of your cuts on the front edges (the back edges are straight cuts). Position a side piece on the ½-inch marks with the miter snug against the front piece; check the fit. Remove the side piece and apply glue to the mitered edge; reposition and brad-nail to the tabletop. Repeat on the other side.

10 With the underside of the tabletop still facing up, position one of the legs in a front corner, its outer edges butted against the front and side moulding. Mark the outline of the leg on the tabletop.

11 Remove the leg. Make X marks for the placement of two screws as shown (avoiding knotholes, if any). Repeat at the other front corner.

project continues >

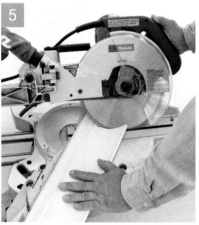

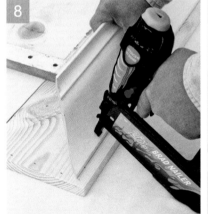

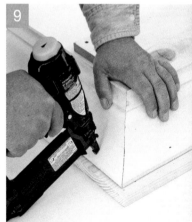

console table

12 Using the combination countersink–pilot hole bit, drill through the tabletop at the screw marks in each front corner.

13 Turn the table right side up and drill countersink holes for the screws, making sure the bit goes all the way through the lumber.

14 Turn the tabletop upside down again and position a leg in one corner, butted against the front and side moulding. Brad-nail the moulding to the leg as shown; repeat for the other corner.

15 Bracing the table with one hand, screw through the top and into the leg using the 3-inch wood screws. Repeat on the other leg. Fill the screw holes with putty; allow to dry. Sand smooth.

16 To make the hidden support that fits between the side pieces of moulding, cut the 1 by 4 pine piece to the inside measurement from one side moulding to the other. Brad-nail the side mouldings to the support as shown.

17 Using the 2- or 3-inch paintbrush, apply latex primer to all visible surfaces of the table and the legs. Allow to dry.

18 Working outdoors on a tarp, spray-paint the table black. Allow to dry completely; apply a second coat.

19 Using the sanding sponge, rub the edges of the table to distress the finish.

20 With the table turned upside down, attach an angle iron to the back edge of the support piece near each corner, using the screws provided with the angle irons.

21 Using the chip brush, apply walnut stain to the distressed edges. Allow to dry completely.

22 Place the table against the wall. Attach the other half of each angle iron to the wall with the hollow wall anchors and #8 screws.

floating shelves

MATERIALS

1 by 6 pine piece,
    3 feet long

1 by 6 pine piece,
    2 feet long

1 by 4 pine piece,
    6 feet long

3⅝-inch colonial base
    moulding, 8 feet long

Steel tape measure

Compound miter saw

Wood glue

C-clamp

Electric brad nailer with
    1½-inch nails

Four small sawtooth
    leveling hangers for
    up to 20 pounds

1-inch by 16-gauge nails

Hammer

2- or 3-inch synthetic-
    bristle paintbrush

2-inch chip brush

Latex primer

1 quart Nantucket Fog
    latex paint* (Valspar)

1 quart Atlantic Gray
    latex paint* (Valspar)

1 quart white latex paint*

Porcelain Crackle Glaze
    (Valspar)

Sanding sponge

*Satin finish

LOWE'S QUICK TIP

The most important cuts
are for the brace that
runs along the back of
the shelf; it must be the
same length as the short
(lower) edge of the front
moulding.

SIMPLE SHELVES WITH HIDDEN SUPPORTS ARE A SPACE-SAVING WAY TO DISPLAY
treasures in a hallway or an entry. The shelves pictured here were painted a cool
seaside green, then finished with a porcelain crackle glaze and pale blue paint for a
gently weathered look. The materials listed are for a pair of shelves—one 2 feet
long, the other 3 feet long.

1 For each shelf, measure, mark, and cut the front piece of moulding as instructed in Steps 3
through 7 of "Console Table," page 413, with the following differences. On the 3-foot shelf, the
top (longer) edge of the front moulding should measure 35 inches (36–½–½=35). On the 2-foot
shelf, the top edge of the front moulding should measure 23 inches (24–½–½=23). To be safe,
measure your shelf piece from mark to mark to find the exact length you need.

2 Measure the bottom (shorter) edge of the cut
moulding. Use that measurement to cut the 1 by 4
pine lumber straight across at each end to make a
brace for the back of the shelf.

3 Position the brace on the underside of the shelf
along one long edge, centering it lengthwise; mark the
placement. Glue the brace to the shelf, holding it in
place with the C-clamp as shown; allow to dry. Brad-
nail the brace to the shelf using the 1½-inch nails.

project continues >

floating shelves

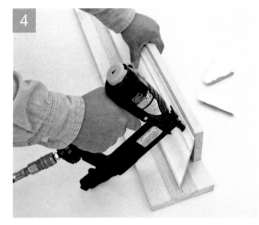

4 With the shelf upside down and the brace facing up, position the front moulding so that its lower edge aligns with the brace ends. Brad-nail the moulding to the inside of the brace, as shown. Then brad-nail the *upper* edge of the moulding to the underside of the shelf, placing a nail near each end and approximately every 8 inches in between. Measure, mark, and cut the moulding end pieces, paying careful attention to the direction of the miters and cutting the back edges straight.

LOWE'S QUICK TIP
The bottom (shorter) edge of each moulding end piece should match the thickness of the brace, approximately ¾ inch on this shelf.

5 Glue the end pieces to the sides of the brace. Once the glue has dried, brad-nail the pieces to the brace and the shelf.

6 Attach the sawtooth hangers to the back of the shelf, one near each end, using the 1-inch nails (not the nails that come with the hangers).

7 Using the 2- or 3-inch paintbrush, apply latex primer to all exposed sides of the shelf unit. Allow to dry.

8 Brush on a base coat of green (Nantucket Fog) paint to all exposed sides of the shelf unit. Allow to dry. Apply a second coat; allow to dry.

9 Dip your clean brush an inch or so into the white paint and then work some of the paint off by brushing back and forth on newspaper or a scrap of wood. Paint the shelf in lengthwise strokes, feathering the ends of each stroke so that the green base coat is not completely covered. Allow to dry.

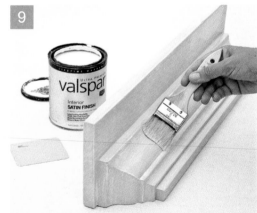

10 Use the sanding sponge to distress the edges, revealing a bit of the wood.

11 Using the 2-inch chip brush, apply the porcelain crackle glaze according to the manufacturer's instructions. (The glaze goes on milky white but dries clear.) Allow to dry the recommended time.

LOWE'S QUICK TIP
A uniform application of the crackle medium yields an even pattern, while brushing it on thick and thin creates an irregular design.

12 Dip the chip brush into a container of clean water, then into the blue (Atlantic Gray) paint. Apply this mixture to all painted surfaces of the shelf unit, working it into the cracks.

13 Quickly wipe off most of the mixture with a paper towel. Allow to dry. Use the 1-inch nails to hang the shelves, following the directions that come with the sawtooth hangers.

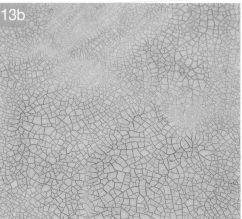

blackboard message center

A FULL-LENGTH MESSAGE CENTER MADE OF MEDIUM-DENSITY FIBERBOARD (MDF) coated with blackboard paint hides the side of the refrigerator in an open-plan kitchen. Decorative wood moulding finishes the edges.

MATERIALS

Latex primer

Mini-roller frame with 6-inch foam roller cover

Paint tray with disposable liners

2-inch synthetic-bristle paintbrush

¾-inch MDF, cut to size (see Step 1)

2-inch moulding, enough to frame the edges of the MDF plus at least 6 inches on each side

Adjustable miter box

Latex paint*

Latex blackboard paint

Wood glue

Ten all-purpose clamps

Painter's tape

Tinted furniture finish wax

Clean rags

One or two L-brackets with screws (see Step 10)

*Satin finish

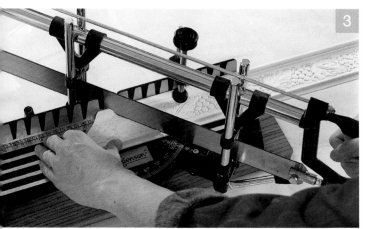

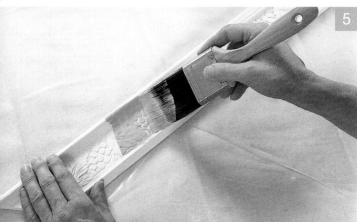

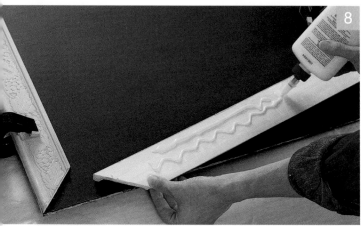

1 To determine how wide your MDF piece needs to be, measure from the baseboard of the wall to where the refrigerator doors begin (the doors must be free to swing open). The piece should be tall enough to hide the top of the refrigerator, or to come just below overhead cabinets.

2 Prime the MDF and the moulding, using the roller with foam cover on the MDF and the brush on the moulding. Allow to dry.

3 Using the adjustable miter box, make the first 45-degree-angle cut on one piece of moulding.

4 Hold the just-cut piece of moulding against the corresponding edge of the MDF and mark for the second miter cut; make the cut. Cut the remaining pieces the same way.

5 Paint the moulding with the latex paint.

6 Using the roller with foam cover, paint the MDF with three coats of the blackboard paint, allowing the paint to dry between coats.

7 Carefully paint the edges of the MDF with the same paint you used on the moulding.

8 Apply wood glue to the back of each moulding piece. Set each piece in place and secure with clamps, protecting the moulding with clean rags if needed. Allow the glue to dry.

9 Protect the edge of the blackboard surface with painter's tape, as shown. Apply tinted wax to the moulding with a clean rag, wiping off the excess and buffing the surface.

10 Screw an L-bracket to the underside of the overhead cabinets at their front edge. Position the blackboard against the baseboard with its lower edge about 1 inch out from the refrigerator so the board tilts back slightly. Screw the other end of the L-bracket to the back of the board. Gently kick in the lower edge of the board for a snug fit.

If you don't have overhead cabinets, attach the board to the wall with two L-brackets, one at the top and one at the baseboard. (The brackets will be partially visible when viewed from the front.)

guide to lowe's color palettes

THE COLOR PALETTES IN THIS BOOK ARE BASED ON THE VALSPAR PAINT COLLECTIONS you'll find at Lowe's. Because of the limitations of the printing process, the colors on the book pages may not be exact representations of specified paints. Check the paint chips at Lowe's for a true color rendition. If you like the color on the book page better than the paint chip, a Lowe's paint sales specialist can mix a paint to match.

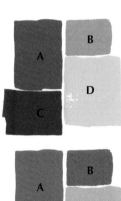

page 175

A. 34015 Baked Clay (WV)
B. 34010 Olive Tree (WV)
C. 41010 Classic Blue (WV)
D. 31010 Golden Rod (WV)

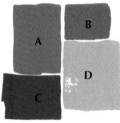

page 177

A. 10-1 Dune Grass (EB)
B. 4002-6B Merlin (VC)
C. 28-2 Claret (EB)
D. 905 Pale Cowslip 5 (LA)

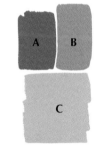

page 179

A. 4001-4B Classical Violet (VC)
B. 3009-4 Bamboo Leaves (VC)
C. 3008-6A Carolina Inn Crossroads Gold (VC)

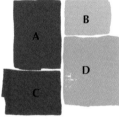

page 181

A. 31-2 Ballard Blue (EB)
B. 103 Olive Oil (MS)
C. 28-2 Claret (EB)
D. 21-3 Lettuce (EB)

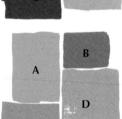

Page 183

A. 710 Lake Marsh (SR)
B. 26-1 Molasses (EB)
C. 714 Earthy Sage (SR)
D. 5005-3C Jekyll Grand Dining Sea Mist (VC)

ABBREVIATION KEY

EB = Eddie Bauer Home

LA = Laura Ashley Home Colour Collection

MS = Martha Stewart Colors

SR = Seaside Retreat

VC = Valspar Colors

WV = Waverly Home Classics

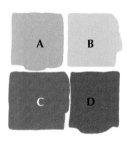

page 185
A. 4004-3B Courtyard Shadow (VC)
B. 1008 Heath Green 2 (LA)
C. 5005-4B Green Peppercorn (VC)
D. 4004-4A Window Screen (VC)

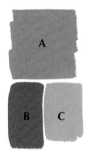

page 193
A. 6008-4B Caraway Shield (VC)
B. 28-2 Claret (EB)
C. 37-4 Burnt Brick (EB)

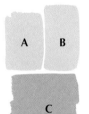

page 187
A. 308 Sand Between Your Toes (SR)
B. 706 Garden Fairy (SR)
C. 1403 Violet Whimsy (SR)

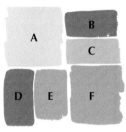

page 195
A. 6005-1A Asiago (VC)
B. 5002-2A Beguile (VC)
C. 204 Seaside Villa (SR)
D. 2002-5B La Fonda Tile Red (VC)
E. 6006-6A Homestead Resort Moss (VC)
F. 202 Dolphin Cove (SR)

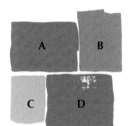

page 189
A. 5001-6B Sky Space (VC)
B. 3005-7C Woodlawn Lewis Gold (VC)
C. 3005-8A Cloudy Sunset (VC)
D. 1001-5B Purple Hills (VC)

page 197
A. 6006-6B La Fonda Olive (VC)
B. 34014 Sweet Tomato (WV)
C. 6005-2A Coastal Villa (VC)

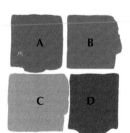

page 191
A. 41014 Pansy Purple (WV)
B. 39013 Bitter Rose (WV)
C. 35010 Irish Moss (WV)
D. 41012 Paris Blue (WV)

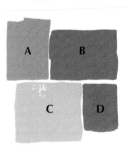

page 199
A. 056 Terrace Tile (MS)
B. 200 Tadpole (MS)
C. 082 Peach Marmalade (MS)
D. 053 Brick Hearth (MS)

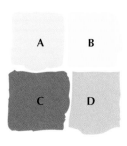

page 204 top

A. 2004-8C Warm Cappuccino (VC)
B. 7003-17 Churchill Hotel Lace (VC)
C. 1004-9C Irish Tea (VC)
D. 6006-1B Oatbran (VC)

page 206 top

A. 6008-1B Shoreline Haze (VC)
B. 1002-7B Plum Legacy (VC)
C. 5001-1C Blue Twilight (VC)
D. 3003-8A Fairmont Suite Gold (VC)
E. 6007-2A Arid Plains (VC)
F. 2006-8A Lyndhurst Estate Peach (VC)

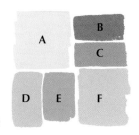

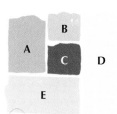

page 204 bottom

A. 6004-1B Woodlawn Colonial Gray (VC)
B. 6004-3B Willow Wind (VC)
C. 1004-9B Lincoln Cottage Brown (VC)
D. 6004-3A Summer Mist (VC)
E. 3007-10C Cincinnatian Hotel Hannaford (VC)

page 206 bottom

A. 1417 Deep Sapphire (LA)
B. 1418 Forget Me Not (LA)
C. 309 Dark Burgundy 3 (LA)
D. 701 Deep Cowslip 1 (LA)
E. 1002 Pale Apple 2 (LA)

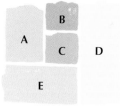

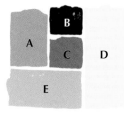

page 205 top

A. 6008-2A Jekyll Club Cherokee Tan (VC)
B. 6011-1 Fired Earth (VC)
C. 5003-2A Lincoln Cottage Lattice Green (VC)
D. 7003-18 Homestead Resort Antique Lace (VC)
E. 3006-10A Prairie Dance (VC)

page 207 top

A. 193 Fondant (MS)
B. 309 Boathouse Blue (MS)
C. 150 Tintype (MS)
D. 221 Spring Bluegrass (MS)
E. 308 Blue Eucalyptus (MS)
F. 195 White Grape (MS)

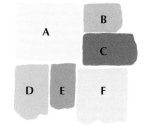

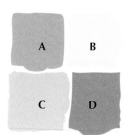

page 205 bottom

A. 6006-1C Ivory Brown (VC)
B. 7002-10 Bermuda Sand (VC)
C. 4008-1A Bay Waves (VC)
D. 6004-2A Aspen Gray (VC)

page 207 bottom

A. 703 Deep Cowslip 3 (LA)
B. 417 Cameo (LA)
C. 1410 Navy 4 (LA)
D. 1202 Pale Jade 2 (LA)
E. 1408 Navy 2 (LA)

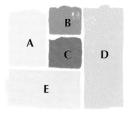

page 208 top

A. 2002-5C Jekyll Clubhouse
   Terra Cotta (VC)
B. 6003-4B Prairie Brush (VC)
C. 2005-9A Boston Legacy (VC)
D. 2005-10B Dust Bunny (VC)
E. 5002-4A Secluded Garden (VC)

page 210 top

A. 2006-1C Orange Cream (VC)
B. 6007-6A New Avocado (VC)
C. 2003-5B Florentine Clay (VC)
D. 3004-4B Homestead Resort Tea
   Room Yellow (VC)
E. 5007-9B Aqua Glow (VC)

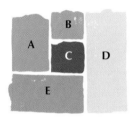

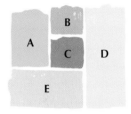

page 208 bottom

A. 2006-10C Vanilla Steam (VC)
B. 2007-7C New Haven Clay (VC)
C. 6006-4C City Arboretum (VC)
D. 6006-3C Bayou Shade (VC)
E. 2006-9B Hubbell House Clayo (VC)
F. 2007-8B Sahara Sands (VC)

page 210 bottom

A. 4005-7C Promise (VC)
B. 2005-2B Sand Swept (VC)
C. 4001-10B Berries Galore (VC)
D. 4004-10B Simply Purple (VC)

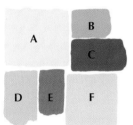

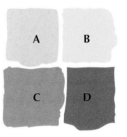

page 209 top

A. 36006 Smooth Pebble (WV)
B. 40014 Grape Purple (WV)
C. 33006 Smoke (WV)
D. 34005 Purple Drop (WV)
E. 32015 Pompei Orange (WV)
F. 36008 Rainforest (WV)

page 211 top

A. 007-7C Gentle Wave (VC)
B. 2003-4A Brushed Rose (VC)
C. 6005-7C Crocodile Smile (VC)
D. 4003-6A Bliss (VC)

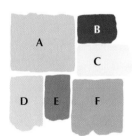

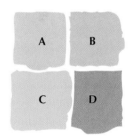

page 209 bottom

A. 28-3 Crimson (EB)
B. 34-3 Palm (EB)
C. 31-1 Night Sky (EB)
D. 11-3 Coir (EB)
E. 32-2 Mercer Blue (EB)

page 211 bottom

A. 6008-8B Parsley Sprig (VC)
B. 5003-7C Fresh Basin (VC)
C. 1005-3A Deep Sunset (VC)
D. 1006-1B Passion Pink (VC)
E. 6008-7B Gleeful (VC)

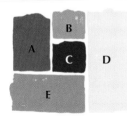

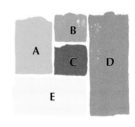

design

front matter

1 *ARCHITECT:* Neal Schwartz, Schwartz and Architecture, www.schwartzandarchitecture.com **2–3** *INTERIOR DESIGN:* Carol Corcoran, ONE Interiors, www.oneinteriors.com; *ARCHITECT:* Mark Donohue, Visible Research Office, www.visibleresearch.com **5** *DESIGN:* Emma Star Jensen **6** *INTERIOR DESIGN:* Lovelace Interiors, www.lovelaceinteriors.com; *ARCHITECT:* Folck West + Savage **7** *INTERIOR DESIGN:* Steven Gambrel, www.srgambrel.com; *ARCHITECT:* Historical Concepts, www.historicalconcepts.com **8–9** Carol Corcoran, ONE Interiors, www.oneinteriors.com; *ARCHITECT:* Mark Donohue, Visible Research Office, www.visibleresearch.com **10–11** *ARCHITECT/INTERIOR DESIGN:* John Lum Architecture, www.johnlumarchitecture.com **12–13** *INTERIOR DESIGN:* Linda Woodrum; *ARCHITECT:* Summerour and Associates Architects

room-by-room design

14 TOP *ARCHITECT:* Peter Brock (principal) and Marina Rubina (project architect), Peter Brock, Architect, www.peter-brock.com **14 TOP MIDDLE AND RIGHT** *ARCHITECT:* Ana Williamson, www.awarchitect.com **14 BOTTOM** *INTERIOR DESIGN:* Bethe Cohen Design Associates, www.bethecohen.com **16–17** *INTERIOR DESIGN:* Artistic Environments; *ARCHITECT:* David George & Associates, Architopia **18 TOP** *INTERIOR DESIGN:* McDonald & Moore, www.mcdonaldmoore.com; *ARCHITECT:* Dahlin Group Architecture/Planning, www.dahlingroup.com **18 BOTTOM** *INTERIOR DESIGN:* Gail Lesley Diehl Interiors **19** *INTERIOR DESIGN:* Bethe Cohen Design Associates, www.bethecohen.com **20** *DESIGN:* Kevin Price, J.A.S. Design-Build, www.jasdesignbuild.com **21 LEFT** *INTERIOR DESIGN:* CGA Interiors; *ARCHITECT:* Cornerstone Group Architects **21 RIGHT** *INTERIOR DESIGN:* Shirley Jensen, Forget-Me-Nots Designs **22 LEFT** *INTERIOR DESIGN:* Cathy Nason and Katherine Elkins, Spirit Interior Design, www.cathynasoninterior.com; *ARCHITECT:* Faulkner Architects, www.faulknerarchitects.com **22 RIGHT** *DESIGN:* Anna Labbee and Kevin Price, J.A.S. Design-Build, www.jasdesignbuild.com **23** *ARCHITECT:* Lindy Small Architecture, www.lindysmall architecture.com **24–25** *INTERIOR DESIGN:* Phillip Sides Interior Design; *ARCHITECT:* Harrison Design Associates, www.harrisondesignassociates.com **26–27** *INTERIOR DESIGN:* Jennifer Hershon and JoAnn Hartley, Hershon Hartley Design, Inc., www.hershonhartley.com **28** *ARCHITECT:* Safdie Rabines Architects, www.safdierabines.com **29 TOP** *INTERIOR DESIGN:* Kimberley Nunn, Shopworks Design, www.shopworksdesign.com **29 BOTTOM** *INTERIOR DESIGN:* McDonald & Moore, www.mcdonaldmoore.com; *ARCHITECT:* Dahlin Group Architecture/Planning, www.dahlingroup.com **30–33** *INTERIOR DESIGN:* Tres McKinney Design, www.tresmckinneydesign.com; *DECORATIVE PAINT:* Peggy Del Rosario, www.peggydelrosario.com **34–35** *INTERIOR DESIGN:* Tres McKinney, www.tresmckinneydesign.com, and Karen Graham Interiors **36 TOP** *INTERIOR DESIGN:* David H. Mitchell Interior Design, www.davidmitchellinteriordesign.com; *ARCHITECT:* Harrison Design Associates, www.harrisondesign associates.com **36 BOTTOM** *INTERIOR DESIGN:* Gordon Phaby, Sechrist Design Associates, Inc., www.sechrist design.com **37** *INTERIOR DESIGN:* Sunrise Home, www.sunrisehome.com; *ARCHITECT:* Dahlin Group Architecture/Planning, www.dahlingroup.com; *BUILDER:* Monahan Pacific **38 LEFT** *INTERIOR DESIGN:* Annie Speck Interior Designs, www.anniespeck.com; *ARCHITECT:* Eric Trabert & Associates, www.etadesign.com **38 TOP RIGHT** *ARCHITECT:* Cary Bernstein Architect, www.cbstudio.com **39 TOP** *INTERIOR DESIGN:* Steven R. Gambrel, www.srgambrel.com; *ARCHITECT:* Historical Concepts, www.historicalconcepts.com **39 BOTTOM** *INTERIOR DESIGN:* Sunrise Home, www.sunrisehome.com; *ARCHITECT:* Dahlin Group Architecture/Planning, www.dahlin group.com; *BUILDER:* Monahan Pacific **40** *ARCHITECT:* Lloyd Architects, www.lloyd-arch.com **41 TOP** *ARCHITECT:* Ana Williamson, www.awarchitect.com; *INTERIOR DESIGN:* Surrina Plemans, By Design Interiors **41 BOTTOM** *DESIGN:* Kevin Price, J.A.S. Design-Build, www.jasdesignbuild.com **42–43** *ARCHITECT:* Jo Landerfeld Architect **44–45** *INTERIOR DESIGN:* Bethe Cohen Design Associates, www.bethecohen.com **46–47** *INTERIOR DESIGN:* T.S. Hudson Interiors; *ARCHITECT:* George Graves **48–49** *ARCHITECT:* Ana Williamson, www.awarchitect.com; *INTERIOR DESIGN:* Surrina Plemans, By Design Interiors **50 TOP** *INTERIOR DESIGN:* Kathryne Designs, www.kathryne designs.com **50–51 BOTTOM** *INTERIOR DESIGN:* Sunrise Home, www.sunrisehome.com; *ARCHITECT:* Dahlin Group Architecture/Planning, www.dahlingroup.com; *BUILDER:* Monahan Pacific **51 TOP, 52–53** *ARCHITECT:* J. Allen Sayles, www.jasarch.net **54–57** *INTERIOR DESIGN:* David Ramey, David Ramey Interior Design, www.davidramey interiordesign.com **58–59** *INTERIOR DESIGN:* Sunrise Home, www.sunrisehome.com; *ARCHITECT:* Dahlin Group Architecture/Planning, www.dahlingroup.com; *BUILDER:* Monahan Pacific **60** *INTERIOR DESIGN:* Lovelace Interiors, www.lovelaceinteriors.com; *ARCHITECT:* Folck West + Savage **61** *KITCHEN DESIGN:* Ken Burghardt, Studio Mehler, www.studiomehler.com **62 TOP** *ARCHITECT:* Grey Design Studio, www.greydesignstudio.com **62 BOTTOM** *ARCHITECT:* Lane Williams Architects, www.lanewilliams.com **63 TOP** *DESIGN:* Lara C. Dutto, D-Cubed

63 BOTTOM *INTERIOR DESIGN:* Marcy Voyevod Interior Design, www.marcyvoyevod.com **64 BOTTOM** *KITCHEN DESIGN:* Katharine Fisher, Lamperti Contracting & Design Inc., www.lampertikitchens.com **65** *KITCHEN DESIGN:* Annette Starkey, Living Environment Design **66–67** *ARCHITECT:* David S. Gast & Associates, Architects, www.dsga.com; *DESIGN:* Cydney Posner **68–71** *KITCHEN DESIGN:* Carmen Mateo, Brand Kitchens & Design, Inc., www.brandkitchens.com; *CABINETS:* Neil Kelly, www.neilkellycabinets.com **72–73** *INTERIOR DESIGN:* Lovelace Interiors, www.lovelaceinteriors.com; *ARCHITECT:* Folck West + Savage **74** *INTERIOR DESIGN:* Steven R. Gambrel, www.srgambrel.com; *ARCHITECT:* Historical Concepts, www.historicalconcepts.com **75** *INTERIOR DESIGN:* Mary Evelyn McKee Interiors; *ARCHITECT:* Henry Sprott Long & Associates **76 LEFT** *ARCHITECT/ INTERIOR DESIGN:* John Lum Architecture, www.johnlumarchitecture.com **77 TOP** *INTERIOR DESIGN:* Woodvale Interiors; *ARCHITECT:* Ben Patterson **77 BOTTOM** *INTERIOR DESIGN:* Sunrise Home, www.sunrisehome.com; *ARCHITECT:* Dahlin Group Architecture/Planning, www.dahlingroup.com; *BUILDER:* Monahan Pacific **78** *INTERIOR DESIGN:* Phillip Sides Interior Design; *ARCHITECT:* Arc Design Atlanta, Inc. **79 TOP** *ARCHITECT:* Ana Williamson, www.awarchitect.com; *INTERIOR DESIGN:* Surrina Plemans, By Design Interiors **79 BOTTOM** *INTERIOR DESIGN:* McDonald & Moore, www.mcdonaldmoore.com; *ARCHITECT:* Dahlin Group Architecture/Planning, www.dahlingroup.com **80–81** *INTERIOR DESIGN:* Tres McKinney, www.tresmckinneydesign.com; *DECORATIVE PAINT:* Peggy Del Rosario, www.peggydelrosario.com **82–83** *DESIGN:* Anna Labbee, J.A.S. Design-Build, www.jasdesignbuild.com **84** *ARCHITECT:* David S. Gast & Associates, Architects, www.dsga.com **85** *ARCHITECT:* Ana Williamson, www.aw architect.com **86** *BATHROOM DESIGN:* Ken Burghardt, Studio Mehler, www.studiomehler.com **87 TOP** *INTERIOR DESIGN:* Jeanese Rowell Design, Inc., www.jrdesign.com **87 BOTTOM** *INTERIOR DESIGN:* Sunrise Home, www.sunrisehome.com; *ARCHITECT:* Dahlin Group Architecture/Planning, www.dahlingroup.com; *BUILDER:* Monahan Pacific **88–89** *DESIGN:* JoAnn Van Atta; *BUILDER:* De Mattei Construction, Inc.; *TILEWORK:* Phillip Knowles, Ceramic & Stone Design **90–93** *ARCHITECT:* Peter Brock (principal) and Marina Rubina (project architect), Peter Brock, Architect, www.peter-brock.com **94–95** *INTERIOR DESIGN:* Suzanne and Robert Chestnut **96 BOTTOM** *INTERIOR DESIGN:* Ann Jones Interiors, www.annjonesinteriors.com **97–98** *INTERIOR DESIGN:* David H. Mitchell Interior Design, www.davidmitchellinteriordesign.com; *ARCHITECT:* Harrison Design Associates, www.harrison designassociates.com **99 TOP** *DESIGN:* Maison d'Etre **99 BOTTOM** *ARCHITECT:* Ana Williamson, www.aw architect.com **100–101** *INTERIOR DESIGN:* Cathy Nason and Katherine Elkins, Spirit Interior Design, www.cathy nasoninterior.com; *ARCHITECT:* Faulkner Architects, www.faulknerarchitects.com **104–105** *ARCHITECT:* Ana Williamson, www.awarchitect.com **106 TOP** *ARCHITECT:* J. Allen Sayles, www.jasarch.net **106 BOTTOM** *INTERIOR DESIGN:* Lamperti Contracting & Design Inc., www.lampertikitchens.com **107** *ARCHITECT:* J. Allen Sayles, www.jasarch.net **108** *INTERIOR DESIGN:* Kathy Coomer, Art Pie, and Daniel Daniloff, Design Changes **109 TOP** *INTERIOR DESIGN:* Sunrise Home, www.sunrisehome.com; *ARCHITECT:* Dahlin Group Architecture/Planning, www.dahlingroup.com **109 BOTTOM** *ARCHITECT:* Ana Williamson, www.awarchitect.com **110–111** *INTERIOR DESIGN:* Paris Renfroe Design, www.parisrenfroedesign.com **112 TOP** *INTERIOR DESIGN:* McDonald & Moore, www.mcdonaldmoore.com; *ARCHITECT:* Dahlin Group Architecture/Planning, www.dahlingroup.com **112 BOTTOM, 113–114** *ARCHITECT:* J. Allen Sayles, www.jasarch.net **115** *ARCHITECT:* Ana Williamson, www.aw architect.com **116** *INTERIOR DESIGN:* G. Kelly Interiors; *ARCHITECT:* Looney Ricks Kiss Architects, www.lrk.com **117 TOP** *INTERIOR DESIGN:* Brooks Interior Design; *ARCHITECT:* Looney Ricks Kiss Architects, www.lrk.com **117 BOTTOM** *INTERIOR DESIGN:* McDonald & Moore, www.mcdonaldmoore.com; *ARCHITECT:* Dahlin Group Architecture/Planning, www.dahlingroup.com **118–119** *INTERIOR DESIGN:* Annie Speck Interior Designs, www.anniespeck.com; *ARCHITECT:* Eric Trabert & Associates, www.etadesign.com **120 BOTH** *INTERIOR DESIGN:* Tamm Jasper Interiors; *ARCHITECT:* Dale Gordon Design **121 RIGHT** *INTERIOR DESIGN:* Steven R. Gambrel, www.srgambrel.com; *ARCHITECT:* Historical Concepts, www.historicalconcepts.com **122** *INTERIOR DESIGN:* Ken Burghardt, Studio Mehler, www.studiomehler.com **123** *INTERIOR DESIGN:* Carol Corcoran, ONE Interiors, www.oneinteriors.com; *ARCHITECT:* Mark Donohue, Visible Research Office, www.visibleresearch.com **124–125** *INTERIOR DESIGN:* Annie Speck Interior Designs, www.anniespeck.com; *ARCHITECT:* Eric Trabert & Associates, www.etadesign.com **126 TOP** *DESIGN:* Nick Williams Designs, www.nickwilliamsdesigns.com **126 BOTTOM** *DESIGN:* Linda Applewhite & Associates, www.lindaapplewhite.com **127** *LANDSCAPE ARCHITECT:* Arterra, www.arterrallp.com; *ARCHITECT/INTERIOR DESIGN:* John Lum Architecture, www.johnlumarchitecture.com **128** *INTERIOR DESIGN:* De Witt Residential Design and Interiors, www.dewittvision.com; *ARCHITECT:* Siegel & Strain Architects, www.siegelstrain.com **129 TOP** *INTERIOR DESIGN:* Phillip Sides Interior Design; *ARCHITECT:* Arc Design Atlanta, Inc. **129 BOTTOM** *INTERIOR DESIGN:* Nevin Interior Design; *ARCHITECT:* Historical Concepts, www.historicalconcepts.com **130 TOP** *DESIGN:* Karen and Shaun Burk, Bravura Finishes Decorative Painting **130 BOTTOM** *LANDSCAPE ARCHITECT:* The Berger Partnership, www.bergerpartnership.com **131** *INTERIOR DESIGN:* Tish Key Interior Design, www.tishkey.com **132–137** *ARCHITECT:* Ana Williamson, www.awarchitect.com **138–139** *INTERIOR DESIGN:* Francesca Quagliata, 4th Street Design, www.4thstreetdesign.com **140–143** *INTERIOR DESIGN:* Cathy Nason and Katherine Elkins, Spirit Interior Design, www.cathynasoninterior.com; *ARCHITECT:* Faulkner Architects, www.faulknerarchitects.com **144–145** *KITCHEN DESIGN:* Ken Burghardt, Studio Mehler,

design

www.studiomehler.com; *BUILDER:* Hazel Construction, Inc. **146–149** *INTERIOR DESIGN:* Robie Livingstone; *ARCHITECT:* Ana Williamson, www.awarchitect.com **150–151** *INTERIOR DESIGN:* Lara C. Dutto, D-Cubed **152–153** *INTERIOR DESIGN:* Lovelace Interiors, www.lovelaceinteriors.com; *ARCHITECT:* Folck West + Savage **154–157** *INTERIOR DESIGN:* Carol Corcoran, ONE Interiors, www.oneinteriors.com; *ARCHITECT:* Mark Donohue, Visible Research Office, www.visibleresearch.com **158–159** *INTERIOR DESIGN:* Molly English, Camps and Cottages

all about color

162 TOP LEFT *INTERIOR DESIGN:* Nancy Bostwick, Nancy's Maison et Jardin Antiques **162 TOP CENTER** *INTERIOR DESIGN:* Kendall Wilkinson, www.kendallwilkinsondesign.com **162 BOTTOM** *ARCHITECT:* SHKS Architects, www.shksarchitects.com **164** *INTERIOR DESIGN:* Susan Federman and Marie Johnston Interior Design **165 TOP** *KITCHEN DESIGN:* Cee and Pat Michael; *COLOR:* Sherry Glommen, Stylings by Sherry **165 BOTTOM** *INTERIOR DESIGN:* CGA Interiors; *ARCHITECT:* Cornerstone Group Architects **170 TOP** *INTERIOR DESIGN:* Steven R. Gambrel, www.srgambrel.com; *ARCHITECT:* Historical Concepts, www.historicalconcepts.com **170 BOTTOM** *INTERIOR DESIGN:* Ann Bertelsen and Mary Jo Bowling **171 TOP** *INTERIOR DESIGN:* Susan Sargent **171 BOTTOM** *INTERIOR DESIGN:* Julie Hart and Associates, www.juliehartandassociates.com **173 TOP** *INTERIOR DESIGN:* Lovelace Interiors, www.lovelaceinteriors.com; *ARCHITECT:* Cooper Johnson Smith, www.cjsarch.com **173 BOTTOM** *ARCHITECT:* J. Allen Sayles, www.jasarch.net **174** *INTERIOR DESIGN:* Susan Sargent **175** *INTERIOR DESIGN:* Sasha Emerson Design Studio **176 BOTTOM** *INTERIOR DESIGN:* Tobeler Design, www.tobelerdesign.com **177 TOP** *KITCHEN DESIGN:* Cathy Macfee **177 BOTTOM** *INTERIOR DESIGN:* Kit Parmentier and Allison Rose **178 TOP** *DESIGN:* Mary Jo Bowling **178 BOTTOM** *INTERIOR DESIGN:* Tres McKinney Design, www.tresmckinneydesign.com **179 TOP** *DESIGN:* Kevin Price, J.A.S. Design-Build, www.jasdesignbuild.com **179 BOTTOM** *INTERIOR DESIGN:* Nancy Bostwick, Nancy's Maison et Jardin Antiques **180 BOTTOM** *KITCHEN DESIGN:* Nancy and Ed Hillner, Kitchen Classics **181 TOP** *ARCHITECT:* SHKS Architects, www.shksarchitects.com **181 BOTTOM** *INTERIOR DESIGN:* Steven R. Gambrel, www.srgambrel.com; *ARCHITECT:* Historical Concepts, www.historicalconcepts.com **182 TOP** *INTERIOR DESIGN:* Beach House Style, www.mybeachhousestyle.com **182 BOTTOM** *INTERIOR DESIGN:* Daphne Pulsifer and Andrea Perry, femme fatale, www.femmefatale.com **183 TOP** *INTERIOR DESIGN:* Eugenia Erskine Jesberg, EJ Interior Design, www.ejinteriordesign.com **185 TOP** *INTERIOR DESIGN:* Susan Sargent **185 BOTTOM** *DESIGN:* Emma Star Jensen **186 BOTTOM** *DECORATIVE PAINT:* Debra Disman, The Artifactory **187 TOP** *DESIGN:* Emma Star Jensen **187 BOTTOM** *INTERIOR DESIGN:* Joan Osburn, Osburn Design, www.osburndesign.com **188 BOTTOM** *INTERIOR DESIGN:* Susan Sargent **189 TOP** *ARCHITECT:* Steven Goldstein **189 BOTTOM, 191 TOP** *INTERIOR DESIGN:* Susan Sargent **191 BOTTOM** *DESIGN:* Bess Wiersema and Megan Matthews, Studio 3 Design, www.studio-three.com **192 BOTTOM** *INTERIOR DESIGN:* Mary McWilliams **193 TOP** *INTERIOR DESIGN:* Kendall Wilkinson, www.kendallwilkinsondesign.com **194 BOTTOM** *INTERIOR DESIGN:* Gigi Rogers Designs, www.gigirogersdesigns.com **195 BOTTOM** *INTERIOR DESIGN:* Bethe Cohen Design Associates, www.bethecohen.com **196 BOTTOM** *ARCHITECT:* Lindy Small Architecture **197 TOP** *DESIGN:* Mary Jo Bowling **198 TOP** *ARCHITECT:* Michelle Kaufmann Designs, www.michellekaufmanndesigns.com **198 BOTTOM** *INTERIOR DESIGN:* Laura Britt Design, www.laurabrittdesign.com; *ARCHITECT:* BBG Architects, www.bbgarchitects.com **199 TOP** *INTERIOR DESIGN:* Joan Osburn, Osburn Design, www.osburndesign.com **201 TOP** *INTERIOR DESIGN:* Lovelace Interiors, www.lovelaceinteriors.com; *ARCHITECT:* Cooper Johnson Smith, www.cjsarch.com **201 BOTTOM** *INTERIOR DESIGN:* McDonald & Moore, www.mcdonaldmoore.com; *ARCHITECT:* Dahlin Group Architecture/Planning, www.dahlingroup.com **202 TOP** *INTERIOR DESIGN:* L. Kershner Design, www.lkershnerdesign.com **203 TOP** *INTERIOR DESIGN:* Joel Hendler and Christopher Pollack, Hendler Design, www.hendler.com **203 BOTTOM** *INTERIOR DESIGN:* Jeff Shuller **212–213** *ARCHITECT:* Jeffrey Alan Marks Inc., www.jam-design.com **216** *ARCHITECT:* Smith & Vansant Architects, www.smithandvansant.com **217 TOP** *ARCHITECT:* Nestor Matthews, Matthews Studio, www.matthewsstudio.com **217 BOTTOM** *INTERIOR DESIGN:* Colienne Brennan, Brenco Design; *ARCHITECT:* Urban Development Group of Denver, adapted by Pacific Peninsula Architecture, www.pacificpeninsula.com

practical design

218 TOP LEFT *INTERIOR DESIGN:* Marc Reusser and Debra Bergstrom, Reusser Bergstrom Associates, www.rbadesign.net **218 TOP CENTER** *ARCHITECT:* Gordon Olschlager **218 BOTTOM** *INTERIOR DESIGN:* Phillip Sides Interior Design; *ARCHITECT:* Arc Design Atlanta, Inc. **220** *ARCHITECT/INTERIOR DESIGN:* Bill Ingram Architect, www.billingramarchitect.com **221 TOP** *ARCHITECT:* Richard Osborn, Osborn Design Group, www.osborndesigngroup.com, and Kent Chilcott, Kent Chilcott Planning and Design; *INTERIOR ARCHITECT:* Mary Dooley, MAD Architecture, www.madarc.com **221 BOTTOM** *INTERIOR DESIGN:* Camille Fanucci, Interior Design Concepts, www.fanucciinteriordesign.com, and Patricia Whitt Designs **222** *INTERIOR DESIGN:* David H. Mitchell Design, www.davidmitchellinteriordesign.com; *ARCHITECT:* Harrison Design Associates, www.harrisondesignassociates.com **223 BOTTOM** *INTERIOR DESIGN:* Molly McGowan Interiors **224** *FABRICS:* Pindler & Pindler Inc., www.pindler.com

226–227 *INTERIOR DESIGN:* Vanessa De Vargas, www.turquoise-la.com 228 *INTERIOR DESIGN:* JoAnn Van Atta; *BUILDER:* De Mattei Construction, Inc. 229 *INTERIOR DESIGN:* Susan Sargent 230 *INTERIOR DESIGN:* Lorrie Merck, Sunrise Home, www.sunrisehome.com 231 *DESIGN:* Kevin Price, J.A.S. Design-Build, www.jasdesign build.com 232 *INTERIOR DESIGN:* Tres McKinney Design, www.tresmckinneydesign.com 235 **LEFT** *INTERIOR DESIGN:* Jennifer Hershon and JoAnn Hartley, Hershon Hartley Design, Inc., www.hershonhartley.com 235 **RIGHT** *INTERIOR DESIGN:* David Ramey, David Ramey Interior Design, www.davidrameyinteriordesign.com 236 *INTERIOR DESIGN:* L. Kershner Design, www.lkershnerdesign.com 237 *INTERIOR DESIGN:* Sherry Snodgrass 239 **BOTTOM** *INTERIOR DESIGN:* Mary Evelyn McKee Interiors; *ARCHITECT:* Henry Sprott Long & Associates 240 *INTERIOR DESIGN:* Charles de Lisle, www.dpsinteriors.com; *ARCHITECT:* Heidi Richardson, Richardson Architects, www.richardsonarchitects.com 241 **TOP** *INTERIOR DESIGN:* CGA Interiors; *ARCHITECT:* Cornerstone Group Architects 241 **BOTTOM** *INTERIOR DESIGN:* Annie Speck Interior Designs, www.anniespeck.com; *ARCHITECT:* Eric Trabert & Associates, www.etadesign.com 242 **TOP** *INTERIOR DESIGN:* David Dalton 242 **BOTTOM** *INTERIOR DESIGN:* Marc Reusser and Debra Bergstrom, Reusser Bergstrom Associates, www.rbadesign.net 243, 244 **LEFT** *INTERIOR DESIGN:* Lovelace Interiors, www.lovelaceinteriors.com; *ARCHITECT:* Folck West + Savage 244 **RIGHT** *INTERIOR DESIGN:* Laura Britt Design, www.laurabrittdesign.com; *ARCHITECT:* BBG Architects, www.bbg architects.com 245 **TOP RIGHT** *INTERIOR DESIGN:* Catherine Bailey and Robin Petravic 245 **BOTTOM** *INTERIOR DESIGN:* Annie Speck Interior Designs, www.anniespeck.com; *ARCHITECT:* Eric Trabert & Associates, www.eta design.com 246 *INTERIOR DESIGN:* David H. Mitchell Design, www.davidmitchellinteriordesign.com; *ARCHITECT:* Harrison Design Associates, www.harrisondesignassociates.com 247 **TOP** *INTERIOR DESIGN/DECORATIVE PAINT:* Peggy Del Rosario, www.peggydelrosario.com 247 **BOTTOM** *INTERIOR DESIGN:* Phillip Sides Interior Design; *ARCHITECT:* Arc Design Atlanta, Inc. 248, 249 **BOTTOM** *INTERIOR DESIGN:* McDonald & Moore, www.mcdonald moore.com; *ARCHITECT:* Dahlin Group Architecture/Planning, www.dahlingroup.com 250 *ARCHITECT:* Steven Goldstein 251 *INTERIOR DESIGN:* Phillip Sides Interior Design; *ARCHITECT:* Harrison Design Associates, www.harrisondesignassociates.com 252 *INTERIOR DESIGN:* Kimberly Lamer Interiors 254 **TOP** *INTERIOR DESIGN:* Agins Interiors 254 **BOTTOM** *ARCHITECT:* Gordon Olschlager 255 **TOP** *INTERIOR DESIGN:* Cathy Kincaid Interiors, www.cathykincaid.com; *ARCHITECT:* Fusch-Serold & Partners, www.fuschserold.com 255 **BOTTOM** *INTERIOR DESIGN:* Phillip Sides Interior Design; *ARCHITECT:* Arc Design Atlanta, Inc. 256 *INTERIOR DESIGN:* Francesca Harris, FHIG, www.fhig.net 257 **TOP** *INTERIOR DESIGN:* Nancy Bostwick, Nancy's Maison et Jardin Antiques 257 **BOTTOM** *INTERIOR DESIGN:* Nancy Gilbert 259 *INTERIOR DESIGN:* Lamperti Contracting & Design Inc., www.lampertikitchens.com 260 **TOP** *INTERIOR DESIGN:* Tobeler Design, www.tobelerdesign.com 260 **BOTTOM** *INTERIOR DESIGN:* Eugenia Erskine Jesberg, EJ Interior Design, www.ejinteriordesign.com; *FLORAL DESIGN:* Gayle Nicoletti, Bloomin' Gayle's 261 **LEFT** *INTERIOR DESIGN:* Sarah Kaplan, Great Jones Home; *FLORAL DESIGN:* Nisha Kelen, Fleurish 261 **RIGHT** *INTERIOR DESIGN:* Cathy Kincaid Interiors, www.cathykincaid.com; *ARCHITECT:* Fusch-Serold & Partners, www.fuschserold.com 262 *INTERIOR DESIGN:* Mary E. Solomon Interiors; *ARCHITECT:* Looney Ricks Kiss Architects, www.lrk.com 263 *INTERIOR DESIGN:* T.S. Hudson Interiors; *ARCHITECT:* George Graves

elements of a room

264 **TOP LEFT** *INTERIOR DESIGN:* D. Kimberly Smith, Deer Creek Design 264 **TOP CENTER** *DESIGN:* Lamperti Contracting & Design Inc., www.lampertikitchens.com 264 **TOP RIGHT** *INTERIOR DESIGN:* JoAnn Van Atta; *CABINETS:* Midland Cabinet Company 264 **BOTTOM** *INTERIOR DESIGN:* Shane Reilly, www.decorati.com 266 *INTERIOR DESIGN:* Tres McKinney Design, www.tresmckinneydesign.com; *DECORATIVE PAINT:* Peggy Del Rosario, www.peggydelrosario.com 267 **TOP** *INTERIOR DESIGN:* J. Edwards Interiors; *ARCHITECT:* Frusterio & Associates, Inc. 268 *INTERIOR DESIGN:* Mary Evelyn McKee Interiors; *ARCHITECT:* Henry Sprott Long & Associates 269 **LEFT** *ARCHITECT:* Philip Volkmann, Barry & Volkmann Architects, www.bvarchitects.com 269 **TOP RIGHT** *INTERIOR DESIGN:* Lovelace Interiors, www.lovelaceinteriors.com; *ARCHITECT:* Folck West + Savage 270 **BOTH** *DECORATIVE PAINT:* Shauna Oeberst Gallagher, www.artisticlivingstudio.com 271 **LEFT** *INTERIOR DESIGN:* Melissa Griggs Interior Design 272 **TOP** *INTERIOR DESIGN:* Joan Osburn, Osburn Design, www.osburndesign.com; *DECORATIVE PAINT:* Iris Potter 272 **CENTER** *DECORATIVE PAINT:* Shauna Oeberst Gallagher, www.artisticlivingstudio.com 272 **BOTTOM** *DECORATIVE PAINT:* Robert O'Conner Designs 273 **TOP** *DECORATIVE PAINT:* Joanna Seitz, Marcia Litwin, Melinda Kuzman, Color-washed canvas by Donald Southern and Cliff Schorr 273 **BOTTOM** *DECORATIVE PAINT:* Shauna Oeberst Gallagher, www.artisticlivingstudio.com 274 **BOTTOM** *INTERIOR DESIGN:* Kit Parmentier and Allison Rose 275 **TOP** *INTERIOR DESIGN:* Debra S. Weiss 275 **SECOND FROM TOP** *INTERIOR DESIGN:* Heidi M. Emmett 275 **SECOND FROM BOTTOM** *INTERIOR DESIGN:* Tobeler Design, www.tobelerdesign.com 275 **BOTTOM** *ARCHITECT:* Nancy Hayden 276–277 *INTERIOR DESIGN:* Tres McKinney Design, www.tresmckinneydesign.com 278 *INTERIOR DESIGN:* D. Kimberly Smith, Deer Creek Design 279 *PORCELAIN TILE:* Sierra Tile & Stone, www.sierratileandstone.com; *CORK, LINOLEUM, FRIEZE CARPET, SHEET VINYL, AND BIRCH LAMINATE:* Young's Carpet One, www.youngscarpetone.com 280 **TOP** *INTERIOR DESIGN:* Sandra Bird Interiors, www.sandrabird.com

280 BOTTOM *INTERIOR DESIGN:* D. Kimberly Smith, Deer Creek Design **281 SECOND FROM BOTTOM** *KITCHEN DESIGN:* Karen Austin, Creative Kitchens & Baths **281 BOTTOM** *ARCHITECT:* Lindy Small Architecture, www.lindy smallarchitecture.com **282 BOTH** *INTERIOR DESIGN:* D. Kimberly Smith, Deer Creek Design **283 TOP** *CARPET:* Young's Carpet One, www.youngscarpetone.com **283 SECOND FROM BOTTOM** *ARCHITECT:* Ana Williamson, www.awarchitect.com; *INTERIOR DESIGN:* Surrina Plemans, By Design Interiors **283 BOTTOM** *ARCHITECT:* Morimoto Matano Kang Architects, www.mmkarch.com **284 TOP** *ARCHITECT:* David S. Gast & Associates, Architects, www.dsga.com **285 SECOND FROM TOP** *INTERIOR DESIGN:* Debra S. Weiss **285 SECOND FROM BOTTOM** *LAMINATE FLOORING:* Formica **285 BOTTOM** *INTERIOR DESIGN:* Arabesque **286 TOP** *INTERIOR DESIGN:* D. Kimberly Smith, Deer Creek Design **287 SECOND FROM TOP** *INTERIOR DESIGN:* D. Kimberly Smith, Deer Creek Design, and Melinda D. Douros **287 SECOND FROM BOTTOM** *INTERIOR DESIGN:* Jeanese Rowell Design, www.jrdesign.com **287 BOTTOM** *CONCRETE FLOORING:* Colormaker Floors **288** *INTERIOR DESIGN:* JoAnn Van Atta; *CABINETS:* Midland Cabinet Company **289 TOP** *INTERIOR DESIGN:* Kathryn A. Rogers, Sogno Design Group, www.sognodesign group.com **289 BOTTOM** *KITCHEN DESIGN:* Carole White; *ARCHITECT:* David S. Gast & Associates, Architects, www.dsga.com **290 LEFT** *INTERIOR DESIGN:* Sandra Bird Interiors, www.sandrabird.com **290 TOP RIGHT** *INTERIOR DESIGN:* Mary Evelyn McKee Interiors; *ARCHITECT:* Henry Sprott Long & Associates **290 BOTTOM RIGHT** *CABINETS:* Woodgrain Woodworks **291 TOP** *INTERIOR DESIGN:* Pamela Pennington Studios, www.pamelapennington studios.com **291 CENTER LEFT** *KITCHEN DESIGN:* Karen Austin, Creative Kitchens & Baths **291 CENTER RIGHT** *ARCHITECT:* Peter Brock, Architect, www.peter-brock.com; *CABINETS:* Peter Witte **291 BOTTOM LEFT** *DESIGN:* Craig Reece, Indian Rock Design/Build, www.indianrockdesign.com **291 BOTTOM RIGHT** *INTERIOR DESIGN:* Debbie Schwartz, The Village Collection, Inc. **292** *ARCHITECT:* Philip Volkmann, Barry & Volkmann Architects, www.bv architects.com **293** *DESIGN:* Lamperti Contracting & Design Inc., www.lampertikitchens.com **294 CENTER** *INTERIOR DESIGN:* D. Kimberly Smith, Deer Creek Design **294 BOTTOM** *INTERIOR DESIGN:* Marcy Voyevod Design, www.marcyvoyevod.com **295 TOP** *INTERIOR DESIGN:* Sandra Bird Interiors, www.sandrabird.com **295 SECOND FROM TOP** *INTERIOR DESIGN:* De Witt Design Studios, www.dewittvision.com; *ARCHITECT:* Siegel & Strain Architects, www.siegelstrain.com **295 SECOND FROM BOTTOM** *ARCHITECT:* SHKS Architects, www.shksarchitects.com **295 BOTTOM** *INTERIOR DESIGN:* McDonald & Moore, www.mcdonaldmoore.com; *ARCHITECT:* Dahlin Group Architecture/Planning, www.dahlingroup.com **296** *INTERIOR DESIGN:* Annie Speck Interior Designs, www.annie speck.com; *ARCHITECT:* Eric Trabert & Associates, www.etadesign.com **297** *INTERIOR DESIGN:* JoAnn Van Atta; *BUILDER:* De Mattei Construction Inc. **298 LEFT** *INTERIOR DESIGN:* JoAnn Van Atta **298 RIGHT** *DESIGN:* Kevin McPhee **300 TOP TWO** *INTERIOR DESIGN:* JoAnn Van Atta **300 BOTTOM** *INTERIOR DESIGN:* Joan Osburn, Osburn Design, www.osburndesign.com **301 TOP** *ARCHITECT:* Mark Maresca **301 CENTER LEFT** *ARCHITECT:* J. Stephen Peterson & Associates **301 CENTER RIGHT** *INTERIOR DESIGN:* JoAnn Van Atta **301 BOTTOM RIGHT** *INTERIOR DESIGN:* Phillip Sides Interior Design; *ARCHITECT:* Harrison Design Associates, www.harrisondesignassociates.com **302–303** *INTERIOR DESIGN:* Bethe Cohen Design Associates, www.bethecohen.com; *LIGHTING DESIGN:* Angie Ferone **304** *INTERIOR DESIGN:* Tina Martinez **305 TOP** *INTERIOR DESIGN:* Tres McKinney Design, www.tres mckinneydesign.com **305 BOTTOM** *INTERIOR DESIGN:* Carol Corcoran, ONE Interiors, www.oneinteriors.com; *ARCHITECT:* Mark Donohue, Visible Research Office, www.visibleresearch.com **306 LEFT** *INTERIOR DESIGN:* Vanessa De Vargas, www.turquoise-la.com **306 RIGHT** *INTERIOR DESIGN:* Emily Taylor Interiors **307 TOP** *CURTAINS:* Smith + Noble, www.smithandnoble.com **307 SECOND FROM TOP** *INTERIOR DESIGN:* Kathryne Designs, www.kathrynedesigns.com **307 BOTTOM** *INTERIOR DESIGN:* Steiner + Schelfe Design, LLC; *ARCHITECT:* Allison Ramsey **308 TOP** *INTERIOR DESIGN:* Lovelace Interiors, www.lovelaceinteriors.com; *ARCHITECT:* Folck West + Savage **308 BOTTOM LEFT** *SHADE:* Smith + Noble, www.smithandnoble.com **308 BOTTOM RIGHT** *DESIGN:* Lamperti Contracting & Design Inc., www.lampertikitchens.com **309 TOP** *INTERIOR DESIGN:* Deborah M. Robertson, Designs by Deborah, dbdmail@sbcglobal.net **309 BOTTOM THREE** *WINDOW COVERINGS:* Smith + Noble, www.smith andnoble.com **310 TOP** *BLINDS:* Levolor, www.levolor.com **310 BOTTOM** *INTERIOR DESIGN:* Colienne Brennan, Brenco Design **311 TOP** *BLINDS:* Bali, www.baliblinds.com **311 CENTER RIGHT** *INTERIOR DESIGN:* Pacific Bay Homes **311 BOTTOM** *DESIGN:* Japan Woodworking and Design **312 TOP** *INTERIOR DESIGN:* Monty Collins Interior Design, www.montycollins.com **313 TOP** *WINDOW TREATMENT:* Geri Ruka **313 CENTER** *WINDOW TREATMENT:* Smith + Noble, www.smithandnoble.com **313 BOTTOM** *INTERIOR DESIGN:* Janice L. McCabe, McCabe & Sommers Interiors **315 TOP** *INTERIOR DESIGN:* Joan Osburn, Osburn Design, www.osburndesign.com **315 THIRD FROM TOP** *INTERIOR DESIGN/DECORATIVE PAINT:* Peggy Del Rosario, www.peggydelrosario.com **316** *INTERIOR DESIGN:* Nancy Gilbert **317** *INTERIOR DESIGN:* Gigi Rogers Designs, www.gigirogersdesigns.com **318** *INTERIOR DESIGN:* Pamela Green Interiors, www.pamelagreeninteriors.com **319 LEFT** *INTERIOR DESIGN:* Phillip Sides Interior Design; *ARCHITECT:* Harrison Design Associates, www.harrisondesignassociates.com **319 RIGHT** *INTERIOR DESIGN:* Geoffrey De Sousa, De Sousa Hughes, www.desousahughes.com **320** *INTERIOR DESIGN:* Roberta Brown Root **321 TOP** *INTERIOR DESIGN:* Tish Key Interior Design, www.tishkey.com **321 BOTTOM** *INTERIOR DESIGN:* Tres McKinney Design, www.tresmckinneydesign.com **322 TOP** *INTERIOR DESIGN:* Joel Hendler and Christopher Pollack, Hendler Design, www.hendler.com **323 TOP** *INTERIOR DESIGN:* Gigi Rogers Designs, www.gigirogersdesigns.com

323 **SECOND FROM TOP** *INTERIOR DESIGN:* Camille Fanucci, Interior Design Concepts, www.fanucciinterior design.com 324 **SECOND FROM TOP** *INTERIOR DESIGN:* Sarah Kaplan, Great Jones Home, www.greatjones home.com 324 **SECOND FROM BOTTOM** *INTERIOR DESIGN:* JoAnn Van Atta 324 **BOTTOM** *FABRIC:* Donghia 325 **TOP** *INTERIOR DESIGN:* D. Kimberly Smith, Deer Creek Design 326 *INTERIOR DESIGN:* Shane Reilly, www. decorati.com 327 *INTERIOR DESIGN:* Tres McKinney Design, www.tresmckinneydesign.com 328 **BOTH** *INTERIOR DESIGN:* Tres McKinney Design, www.tresmckinneydesign.com 329 *INTERIOR DESIGN:* David H. Mitchell Design, www.davidmitchellinteriordesign.com; *ARCHITECT:* Harrison Design Associates, www.harrisondesign associates.com 330 *SOFA:* Flegel's Fine Furniture, www.flegels.com 331 **TOP** *SOFA:* Calico Corners, www.calico corners.com 331 **SECOND FROM TOP** *INTERIOR DESIGN:* Angela Free, Angela Free Interior Design, www.angela freedesign.com 331 **CENTER, SECOND FROM BOTTOM** *DESIGN:* De Sousa Hughes, www.desousahughes.com 331 **BOTTOM** *SOFA:* Flegel's Fine Furniture, www.flegels.com 332 **TOP LEFT** *INTERIOR DESIGN:* Tucker & Marks, Inc., www.tuckerandmarks.com 332 **BOTTOM LEFT** *INTERIOR DESIGN:* Kathleen Navarra, Navarra Design Inc., www.navarradesign.com 332 **BOTTOM RIGHT** *DINING CHAIR:* Flegel's Fine Furniture, www.flegels.com 333 **TOP** *INTERIOR DESIGN:* Shirley Jensen, Forget-Me-Nots Designs 333 **CENTER RIGHT** *INTERIOR DESIGN:* Jean Horn Interiors, www.jeanhorninteriors.com 333 **BOTTOM** *OTTOMAN:* Flegel's Fine Furniture, www.flegels.com 334 **LEFT** *INTERIOR DESIGN:* Charles de Lisle, www.dpsinteriors.com; *ARCHITECT:* Heidi Richardson, Richardson Architects, www. richardsonarchitects.com 334 **RIGHT** *ARCHITECT:* Cary Bernstein Architect, www.cbstudio.com 335 **TOP LEFT** *INTERIOR DESIGN:* Tres McKinney Design, www.tresmckinneydesign.com 336 **TOP** *ARCHITECT:* J. Allen Sayles, www.jasarch.net 336 **BOTTOM** *COFFEE TABLE:* Flegel's Fine Furniture, www.flegels.com 337 **TOP** *INTERIOR DESIGN:* David H. Mitchell Design, www.davidmitchellinteriordesign.com; *ARCHITECT:* Harrison Design Associates, www.harrisondesignassociates.com 337 **CENTER** *INTERIOR DESIGN:* Sue Kalm 337 **BOTTOM**, 338 **TOP** *INTERIOR DESIGN:* Lovelace Interiors, www.lovelaceinteriors.com; *ARCHITECT:* Folck West + Savage 338 **CENTER LEFT** *INTERIOR DESIGN:* T.S. Hudson Interiors; *ARCHITECT:* George Graves 338 **BOTTOM** *FURNITURE DESIGN:* Paul Scardina, Paolo Design Group, www.paolodesigngroup.com 339 **TOP** *INTERIOR DESIGN:* Phillip Sides Interior Design; *ARCHITECT:* Harrison Design Associates, www.harrisondesignassociates.com 339 **CENTER** *INTERIOR DESIGN:* Cathy Kincaid Interiors, www.cathykincaid.com 340 **TOP** *CABINETS:* Tom Hampson 340 **BOTTOM** *INTERIOR DESIGN:* G. Kelly Interiors; *ARCHITECT:* Looney Ricks Kiss Architects, www.lrk.com 341 **TOP** *INTERIOR DESIGN:* Linda Woodrum; *ARCHITECT:* Summerour and Associates Architects, www.summerour.net 341 **CENTER** *INTERIOR DESIGN:* Brooks Interior Design; *ARCHITECT:* Looney Ricks Kiss Architects, www.lrk.com 341 **BOTTOM** *ARCHITECT:* Fox Design Group Architects, www.foxdesigngroup.com; *INTERIOR DESIGN:* Navarra Design Inc. www.navarradesign.com 342 *INTERIOR DESIGN:* Pamela Pennington Studios, www.pamelapennington studios.com 343 **TOP** *INTERIOR DESIGN:* Suzanne Warrick 343 **BOTTOM LEFT** *INTERIOR DESIGN:* Tres McKinney Design, www.tresmckinneydesign.com

techniques and projects

344 **BOTTOM** *DESIGN:* Lisa and Brete Williams, From Shabby to Chic Interior Re-Design, www.fromshabby tochic.com 348 *DECORATIVE PAINT:* Shauna Oeberst Gallagher, www.artisticlivingstudio.com 350 *DECORATIVE PAINT:* Heidi M. Emmett, From Shabby to Chic Interior Re-Design, www.fromshabby tochic.com 352 *DECORATIVE PAINT:* Debra S. Weiss 354, 356 *DECORATIVE PAINT:* Shauna Oeberst Gallagher, www.artisticlivingstudio.com 359 *DESIGN:* Heidi M. Emmett, From Shabby to Chic Interior Re-Design, www.fromshabbytochic.com, and Debra S. Weiss 366 *DESIGN:* Melinda D. Douros and D. Kimberly Smith, Deer Creek Design 368 *DESIGN:* Debra S. Weiss 372 *TECHNIQUE:* Rich Ramey 374 *TECHNIQUE:* JoAnne Liebeler 377 *DESIGN:* Debra S. Weiss 380 *DESIGN:* Heidi M. Emmett, From Shabby to Chic Interior Re-Design, www.fromshabbytochic.com 384 *TECHNIQUE:* JoAnne Liebeler 388, 389, 394 *DESIGN:* Heidi M. Emmett, From Shabby to Chic Interior Re-Design, www.from shabbytochic.com 398 *DESIGN:* Christine E. Barnes 400 *DESIGN:* Kathryn Robison 402 *DESIGN:* Christine E. Barnes 405 *DESIGN:* Jess Chamberlain 406 *DESIGN:* Sheila Schmitz 408 *DESIGN:* Melinda D. Douros 412, 415 *DESIGN:* Lisa and Brete Williams, From Shabby to Chic Interior Re-Design, www.fromshabbytochic.com 418 *DESIGN:* Heidi M. Emmett, From Shabby to Chic Interior Re-Design, www.fromshabbytochic.com

photography

Jean Allsopp: 6, 60 both, 73, 152–153 all, 173 top, 201 top, 267 top, 269 top, 307 bottom, 308 top, 337 bottom, 338 top, 341 top; **Jean Allsopp and Rex Perry:** 12–13 all; **Jean Allsopp and Harry Taylor:** 72, 243, 244 bottom; **Ralph Anderson:** 77 top, 129 bottom; **Michel Arnaud/Beateworks/Corbis:** 239 top; **Graham Atkins-Hughes/RedCover.com:** 193 bottom; **Bali:** 311 top; **James Balston/RedCover.com:** 311 center left; **Richard Barnes:** 10–11 all; **Edmund Barr:** 191 bottom; **Laurie Black:** 338 bottom two; **Antoine Bootz and Jeff McNamara:** 339 center; **Rob D. Brodman:** 23, 299 top, 405 all, 406–407; **Caroline Bureau, Robert Chartier, Michel Thibault:** 346–347 all, 364–365 all, 392–393 all; **Jayson Carpenter:** 270 both, 272 center, 273 bottom, 348–351 all, 354–358 all; **Van Chaplin:** 262, 301 top; **Jennifer Cheung/Botanica/Jupiterimages.com:** 197 bottom; **Colormaker Floors:** 287 bottom; **Christopher Covey/Beateworks/Corbis:** 287 top; **Pieter Estersohn/Beateworks/Corbis:** 160–161 all, 180 top; **Cheryl Fenton:** 96 top, 304, 306 right; **Scott Fitzgerrell:** 371 bottom; **Formica Corporation:** 285 second from bottom; **James Scott Geras:** 203 bottom; **Tria Giovan:** 7, 24, 25, 36 top, 39 top, 74 both, 78 both, 97, 98 both, 121 right, 129 top, 170 top, 181 bottom, 184 bottom, 198 bottom, 218 bottom, 220, 222, 244 top, 246, 247 bottom, 251, 255 bottom, 301 bottom right, 319 left, 329, 337 top, 339 top; **Laurey W. Glenn:** 117 top, 275 bottom, 341 center; **Thayer Allyson Gowdy:** 29 top, 340 bottom; **John Granen:** 20, 22 right, 41 bottom, 42, 43, 162 bottom, 179 top, 181 top, 231, 295 second from bottom; **Ken Gutmaker:** 189 top, 203 top, 260 bottom, 271 left, 275 second from bottom, 281 second from top, 333 top; **Jamie Hadley:** 2–3, 8–9 all, 14 top right two and bottom, 18 bottom, 19, 26–27 all, 37, 39 bottom, 41 top, 44–45 all, 48–49 all, 50 bottom, 51–53 all, 58, 59, 61 both, 64 bottom, 77 bottom, 79 top, 85–89 all, 99 both, 102–109 all, 112 bottom, 113–115 all, 122–123 all, 130 top, 131–137 all, 144–149 all, 154–159 all, 162 top left, 173 bottom, 175, 177 bottom, 179 bottom, 194 bottom, 195 bottom, 218 top right, 224 all, 228, 230, 233 all, 235 left, 236, 237, 257 both, 259, 264–265 all, 269 bottom right, 271 right, 273 center, 274 both, 275 second from top, 278–280 all, 282 both, 283 top and second from bottom, 286 both, 288, 290 left, 291 center right, 293, 294 center, 295 top, 297, 298 left, 300 top two, 301 center right and bottom left, 302–303 all, 305 right, 307 second from top, 308 bottom right, 309 top, 314 all, 315 second from top and bottom two, 316, 318, 319 right, 321 top, 322 bottom two, 323 center two, 324 top and second from bottom, 325 bottom three, 326, 330, 331 top three and bottom, 332 top and bottom right, 333 bottom, 335 top right and bottom, 336 both, 343 top, 344 top right and bottom, 400–404 all, 412–417 all, 429; **Margot Hartford:** 14 top left, 65–67 all, 84 both, 90–92 all, 165 top, 281 second from bottom, 284 top, 289 both, 290 bottom right, 291 center left and bottom two, 341 bottom; **Philip Harvey:** 130 bottom, 187 bottom, 217 both, 247 top, 272 top, 284 bottom, 310 bottom, 315 third from top; **Alex Hayden:** 62 bottom; **Richard Horn:** 333 center right; **James Frederick Housel:** 301 center left; **InsideOutPix/Jupiterimages.com:** 307 second from bottom; **Bryan Johnson:** 285 top; **Ron Jones Photography:** 202; **Rob Karosis:** 182 bottom, 216; **Muffy Kibbey:** 63 bottom, 269 left, 292, 294 bottom; **Dennis Krukowski:** 273 top; **Rob Lagerstrom and John O'Hagan:** 116; **Levolor:** 310 top; **davidduncanlivingston.com:** 54–55 all, 177 top, 199 top, 338 center right; **Charles Maraia/Getty Images:** 176 top; **Sylvia Martin:** 94, 95, 192 bottom; **E. Andrew McKinney:** 21 right, 30–32 all, 34, 35, 50 top, 56, 80–81 all, 162 top center, 164, 176 bottom, 178 bottom, 183 top, 186 bottom, 188 top, 193 top, 194 top, 218 top left, 221 bottom, 223 bottom, 225 all, 232, 235 right, 242 both, 250, 260 top, 266, 272 bottom, 275 top, 276–277 all, 283 bottom, 285 second from top and bottom, 287 center two, 299 bottom, 300 bottom, 305 left, 311 center right and bottom, 312 top, 313 bottom, 315 top, 317, 321 bottom, 322 top, 323 top and bottom, 324 bottom, 325 top, 327, 328 both, 332 top and bottom left, 333 center left, 335 top left, 337 center, 339 bottom, 340 top, 343 bottom left, 344 top left, 352–353 all, 359–363 all, 366–370 all, 371 top three, 372–373 all, 377–383 all, 388–391 all, 394–399 all, 408–411 all, 418–419 all, 430, 432; **Jeff McNamara:** 75 both, 239 bottom, 252, 254 top, 255 top, 261 right, 268, 290 top right; **Melabee M. Miller:** 313 top; **John O'Hagan:** 21 left, 165 bottom, 241 top, 283 second from top; **Marvin Rand:** 218 top center, 254 bottom; **Lisa Romerein:** 16, 17, 171 bottom, 190 top, 192 top, 212–213 all, 226–227 all, 258 top, 306 left, 424; **Eric Roth:** 162 top right, 171 top, 172, 174, 183 bottom, 184 top, 185 top, 186 top, 188 bottom, 189 bottom, 191 top, 196 top, 199 bottom, 214–215 all, 223 top, 229, 249 top, 258 bottom, 312 bottom, 343 bottom right; **Mark Samu:** 281 top, courtesy of Hearst Publications; **Christina Schmidhofer:** 126 bottom; **Brad Simmons/ Beateworks/Corbis:** 267 bottom; **Michael Skott:** 36 bottom, 261 left, 320, 324 second from top; **Smith + Noble:** 307 top, 308 bottom left, 309 center two and bottom, 313 center; **Thomas J. Story:** 1, 5, 18 top, 22 left, 28, 29 bottom, 38 left and top right, 40, 62 top, 63 top, 68–70 all, 76 left, 79 bottom, 82, 83, 100–101 all, 110–111, 112 top, 117 bottom, 118–120 all, 124, 125, 126 top, 127, 128, 138–143 all, 150–151 all, 170 bottom, 178 top, 182 top, 185 bottom, 187 top, 196 bottom, 197 top, 198 top, 201 bottom, 221 top, 240, 241 bottom, 245 both, 248, 249 bottom, 256, 281 bottom, 291 top, 295 second from top and bottom, 296, 298 right, 334 both, 342 both; **Tim Street-Porter:** 200; **Studio Ton Kinsbergen/Beateworks/Corbis:** 238; **Sue Tallon:** 331 second from bottom; **Valspar:** 190 bottom; **Scott Van Dyke/Beateworks/Corbis:** 195 top, 234; **Dominique Vorillon:** 64 top; **David Wakely:** 96 bottom; **Jessie Walker:** 180 bottom; **Deborah Whitlaw:** 46–47 all, 263, 338 center left; **Michele Lee Wilson:** 344 top center, 374–376 all, 384–387 all

index